Jewish Education in England, 1944–1988

Jewish Education in England, 1944–1988

Between Integration and Separation

DAVID S. MENDELSSON

PETER LANG

Oxford · Bern · Berlin · Bruxelles · Frankfurt am Main · New York · Wien

Bibliographic information published by Die Deutsche Nationalbibliothek
Die Deutsche Nationalbibliothek lists this publication in the Deutsche Nationalbibliografie;
detailed bibliographic data is available on the Internet at http://dnb.d-nb.de.

A catalogue record for this book is available from the British Library.

Library of Congress Cataloging-in-Publication Data:

Mendelsson, David S.
 Jewish education in England, 1944-1988 : between integration and
separation / David Mendelsson.
    p. cm.
 Includes bibliographical references and index.
 ISBN 978-3-03911-960-8 (alk. paper)
 1. Jewish day schools--England--History--20th century. 2.
Jews--Education--England--History--20th century. 3. Multicultural
education--England--History--20th century. 4. Jews--England--Identity.
I. Title.
 LC746.E5M46 2011
 371.0760942--dc23

                    2011030734

ISBN 978-3-03911-960-8

Cover image: Mr Cook's class of 1966–7, the Jewish Free School, Camden Town, London.

© Peter Lang AG, International Academic Publishers, Bern 2011
Hochfeldstrasse 32, CH-3012 Bern, Switzerland
info@peterlang.com, www.peterlang.com, www.peterlang.net

Printed in Germany

Contents

Acknowledgements

This book is based, in part, on my doctoral dissertation, submitted to the Hebrew University in 2002. My advisers were Peter Gordon and Gideon Shimoni, and I want to take this opportunity to express my gratitude for their guidance. At various stages in this research project, I benefitted from the advice of David Cesarani, Tony Kushner, Michael Marmur, Helena Miller, Alex Pomson, Marlena Schmool and Marc Silverman. My research was supported by grants from the Hebrew University of Jerusalem's Institute of Contemporary Jewry, whose Alexander M. Dushkin Fund also provided support for the publication of this book. Additional aid for publishing the book was received from Hebrew Union College. Special thanks are due David Ellenson, President of Hebrew Union College, for his interest and encouragement.

Among the archives I consulted were those of former Chief Rabbi Jakobovits and Ernest Frankel (former treasurer of the ZFET). I would like to thank the latter's sons Jonathan and Raphael Frankel for granting me this access. My research took me to numerous libraries and archives in the UK and Israel. Staff at the following institutions were particularly helpful: Central Zionist Archives; Jewish National University Library; Hebrew University's Bloomfield Library; National Archives (Public Record Office), Kew, Richmond, Surrey; Hartley Library at the University of Southampton; Greater London Records Office; Office of the Chief Rabbi, London; Mocatta Library at University College, London.

Thanks are also due Nessa Olshansky-Ashtar, who edited the manuscript, and worked tirelessly to tighten the narrative.

I thank Routledge for permission to reproduce material originally published in my 'Embracing Jewish Day School in England, 1965–1979', *History of Education: Journal of the History of Education Society* 38 (2009), 545–63, and available at <http://www.informaworld.com>.

I also thank Springer for permission to reproduce material from my 'Anglo-Jewish Education: Day Schools, Funding and Religious Education in State Schools', in H. Miller, L. Grant and A. Pomson (eds), *International Handbook of Jewish Education* (Dordrecht: Springer, 2011), 1105–24.

Last but by no means least, I would like to thank my children, Galit, Yael and Itai, for their patience and understanding as I pursued this project. My wife Dalia has been a constant source of encouragement, and it is to her that I dedicate this modest contribution to the study of Anglo-Jewry.

List of Tables

Map: The London Boroughs

The London Boroughs. From Barry Kosmin et al., *The Social Demography of Redbridge Jewry* (Board of Deputies of British Jews, London 1979). Reprinted with permission.

Preface

Overview

Exploring the evolving profile of Jewish education in England provides important clues to Anglo-Jewry's changing sense of identity, and how it chose to project itself to the wider society. As historians of education have amply demonstrated, schools provide a window onto a society's self-understanding. In the case of minorities, attitudes to state education, and parental recourse to other educational options, reflect deeply held views on the preferred relationship with the broader society, the two polar positions being 'integration' and 'separation'. In our context, separation entails social and cultural walls between the Jewish community and the broader society, with interaction limited chiefly to economic activity; integration entails rejection of such walls, merging into the broader society, and maintaining only a nominal or tenuous connection to the Jewish community. Anglo-Jewry overwhelmingly eschews the polar positions, and falls on the continuum between them. Yet the history of Anglo-Jewish education reveals movement along the continuum, first toward the integration pole, then away from it. As we will see, the latter movement does not attest to rejection of integration, but rather reflects a new conception of the broader society, and what membership in that society entails. In multicultural England, many Anglo-Jewish parents are comfortable sending their children to Jewish schools, and do not fear that this stigmatizes them as insular, separatist, 'unEnglish'.

Research into the history of Anglo-Jewish education has until recently focused on the period at the end of the nineteenth century and the beginning of the twentieth, when schools functioned primarily as agents for anglicizing the new immigrants from Eastern Europe.[1] Apart from some pioneering early studies,[2] only recently have the post-World War II decades begun to receive sustained attention. But little has been written about the entry of the Zionists into the field of day-school education, the notorious 'trust funds controversy', or the impact of the secondary school reorganization. There has been some research into Jewish day-school enrolment statistics.[3] Parental attitudes to Jewish education, however, were not surveyed until the 1960s, and even then, research was piecemeal. Articles and letters published in the Jewish press, and enrolment statistics, offered some clues as to parental thinking. Following the establishment of the Jewish Education Development Trust (JEDT) in 1969, internal studies into the provision of Jewish education were conducted;[4] the impact of Jewish education on Jewish identity also began to receive scholarly attention.[5] Specific schools were investigated: there is a history of the Jews' Free School, a short article on Jewish pupils at the Hackney Downs Grammar School,[6] and a study of the founding of the independent modern-Orthodox Immanuel School, which opened in Bushey, Hertfordshire in 1990.[7] Prior to my doctoral

---

1   L. Gartner, *The Jewish Immigrant in England 1870–1914* (London: Allen and Unwin, 1960); E. Black, *The Social Politics of Anglo-Jewry 1880–1920* (Oxford: Basil Blackwell, 1988), ch. 4.

2   See B. Steinberg, 'Anglo-Jewry and the 1944 Education Act', *Jewish Journal of Sociology* 31(1989), 81–108 and 'Jewish Education in Great Britain during World War II', *Jewish Social Studies* 29 (1967), 27–60.

3   Jacob Braude began this work by compiling records from 1952 to 1977; these statistics were published bi-annually in the *Jewish Chronicle*.

4   *Let My People Know* (London: Office of the Chief Rabbi, 1971).

5   B. Kosmin and C. Levy, *Jewish Identity in an Anglo-Jewish Community: The Findings of the 1978 Redbridge Survey* (London: Board of Deputies, 1983), S. Miller, 'The Impact of Jewish Education on the Religious Behaviour and Attitudes of British Secondary School Pupils', in J. Aviad (ed.), *Studies in Education* 3 (Jerusalem: Magnes, 1988), 161.

6   G. Black, *A History of the Jews' Free School, London, since 1732* (London: Tymsder, 1998); G. Black, 'The Jews of Hackney Downs School', in S. Massil (ed.), *The Jewish Yearbook 2001* (London: Vallentine Mitchell, 2001), 53–60.

7   S. Caplan, 'Immanuel College: The Beginnings of an Educational Project', in W. Ackerman (ed.), *Studies in Education* 7 (Jerusalem: Magnes, 1995), 54–80.

research, however, the overall history of Jewish education in England, and what it reveals about Anglo-Jewish parental priorities with respect to their children's education, had not been studied. Hence the present book fills an important lacuna.

After briefly surveying the history of Jewish schools in Britain before World War II, our journey will begin with the 1944 Education Act, a.k.a. the Butler Act after R. A. Butler (1941–5), the minister popularly credited with its passage. The Education Act affected most aspects of schooling in England and Wales. The principles it set down regarding state funding of denominational schools, the daily act of worship, and religious education, remained unchanged for forty-four years, though the interpretations given to specific clauses of the Act, especially those pertaining to the religious education syllabus and the voluntary-aided sector, evolved considerably. In 1988 another Education Act was passed. Though making no major changes with respect to religious education or denominational schools, it was just as significant as the 1944 Act, in that it reduced the power of the LEA's. The Butler Education Act and its ramifications for Jewish education will be discussed in Chapter 1. Chapter 1 also presents a panoramic picture of Anglo-Jewish society at mid-century, and in particular, its access to, and views on, education, both Jewish and secular.

Between 1944 and 1988, Jewish parental preferences vis-à-vis their children's education changed dramatically. In 1944, the vast majority of parents chose non-denominational maintained schools for their children's general education, and part-time Hebrew classes for their Jewish education. Yet by 1988, more children attended Jewish day schools than Hebrew classes, despite a drop in the Jewish population. How and why this transition occurred will be explored in Chapters 3, 4 and 5. A salient causative factor, I will argue, was the government's decision to wind down selective education, and replace grammar schools with comprehensive schools. This will be analysed in detail in Chapter 4.

In Chapter 2, we will examine the historical roots and operational consequences of the ideological differences between competing organizations involved in provision of day-school and part-time Jewish education, including the United Synagogue, the Zionist Federation and the Union of Orthodox Hebrew Congregations. A school's value system is reflected not merely in its course of studies, but also in more oblique indicators, such as prerequisites for hiring staff, admissions policies, assemblies and summer programs. In Chapters 5 and 6, we will revisit the ideological landscape of Anglo-Jewish education in the wake of the day-school revolution.

Of course, schools cannot be discussed in isolation from the communal politics of Jewish education: the ideological disputes and operational interaction between the various organizations that funded, oversaw, or delivered Jewish educational services. This theme is a constant throughout the book, and will be interwoven into every chapter. To what degree were the various groups prepared to cooperate with each other? From 1944 to 1988, attempts were made to establish a community-wide coordinating council that would negotiate with the national and local authorities so as to reduce duplication of effort within the community; none succeeded. In uncovering the reasons for this failure, we will trace the sorry saga of the 'trust funds' controversy, which pitted the London Board of Jewish Religious Education (LBJRE) against Rabbi Solomon Schonfeld's Jewish Secondary Schools Movement (JSSM). Ultimately, the controversy was resolved, allowing for reconstruction of the Jews' Free School (JFS). Another dispute that sheds light on the balance of power within the Jewish community during the 1950s revolved around the entry of the Zionists into the day-school arena. How did the United Synagogue and the Schonfeld community respond to the establishment of Zionist day schools? Did the Zionist Federation Education Trust (ZFET) attempt to adopt a secular and nationalist curriculum along the lines of that taught in Zionist-run schools in Israel? The role played by Chief Rabbis Brodie and Jakobovits, both in regard to specific controversies, and in regard to Jewish education generally, will also be explored. Were they neutral mediators, or did they actively seek to advance a specific agenda? We will track Chief Rabbi Jakobovits's efforts to establish the Jewish Educational Development Trust (JEDT), which was intended to tackle the 'Jewish continuity' crisis. This endeavour challenged other communal priorities, particularly funding for Israel. The response of key community philanthropists to Jakobovits's initiative, we will see, attested to the shifting dynamics of communal authority, and a new assessment of communal priorities.

The book's penultimate chapter will focus on the impact of multiculturalism on Jewish education. From the 1960s to the 1980s, England underwent a dramatic social, demographic and cultural transformation. Its early stages took place concurrently with the shift to comprehensive secondary schools, a development that, as we will see, precipitated the rise of the day schools. Chapter 6 will discuss the impact of this confluence on Jewish education, vis-à-vis withdrawal classes, the mainstream day schools, and the ultra-Orthodox (haredi) educational institutions.

This book does not purport to be an exhaustive study of Anglo-Jewish education. Its scope is limited to formal education provided by primary and secondary schools, and part-time Hebrew classes under the aegis of the LBJRE and the Reform and Liberal movements. London is the main focus, given Anglo-Jewry's demographic concentration there, but developments in the provinces will be invoked where relevant.

This account of the vicissitudes of Anglo-Jewish education sheds light not only on developments in the field of Jewish education, but on the mindset and self-understanding of Anglo-Jewry more generally. Although I do not compare Jewish schools in England to their counterparts in other Diaspora communities, there are both parallels and divergences. I invite others to engage in comparative study, which should prove edifying.

Anglo-Jewry and its institutions

At mid-century, Anglo-Jewry was well on its way to extricating itself from the working class and the inner city. Its socioeconomic profile was increasingly middle-class, and upward mobility within the middle class was ongoing. Its immigrant status and East End beginnings had largely receded into the past; most members of the community were second or third generation Britons. Demographically, the community was fairly homogeneous: the forebears of most were from Russia and Poland, a far smaller group originated in Germany and Holland. A new wave of immigrants arrived in the 1930s and 1940s: refugees fleeing or displaced by World War II, many of them Orthodox.

In the first half of the twentieth century, Anglo-Jewry had gone through a process of acculturation, not only adopting the manners, speech and attire of the wider society, but also internalizing many of its values. Anglo-Jewish parents sent their children to state schools, where they were very successful at achieving the results needed for entry into selective secondary schools and the universities. The communal leadership was transitioning from an old guard, made up of members of a few preeminent and pedigreed families in England for many generations – the Rothschilds, Samuels, Montefiores, Cohens, Henriques, Goldsmids and Montagus – to a new guard of self-made magnates, many children or grandchildren of immigrants. Though the community was well-integrated, antisemitic prejudice was quite prevalent, and Britain's Jews adopted a defensive and apologetic stance, seeking to mitigate bias by downplaying their particularism and blending in.

Anglo-Jewry's main centres of population were London, Manchester and Leeds. Within these centres, the Jewish populations had, since the 1930s, been moving out of the immigrant neighbourhoods and into the suburbs. This pattern was common to London and the provincial centres. In London, the Jewish population shifted eastward and northward.

Anglo-Jewry's central communal organs included the Board of Deputies, Anglo-Jewry's main representative body; the *Jewish Chronicle* (*JC*), a newspaper that had served the community since 1841 and was widely read; the Chief Rabbi; and the United Synagogue, with which most synagogues were affiliated. Throughout our period, the majority of the community belonged to nominally Orthodox congregations affiliated with the United Synagogue or the much smaller Federation of Synagogues. A small minority of the community attended synagogues affiliated with the Reform and Liberal movements; there was also a growing ultra-Orthodox (haredi) community.

The major communal institutions of relevance to the provision of Jewish education were the following:

Board of Deputies of British Jews	The representative body of British Jewry, founded in 1760.
Federation of Synagogues	Created in 1887 by Samuel Montagu to bring together synagogues established by immigrants from Eastern Europe, who found worship in the anglicized synagogues of the United Synagogue foreign and uncongenial.
Jewish Educational Development Trust (JEDT)	Organization founded by Chief Rabbi Jakobovits in 1969 to fight assimilation and intermarriage by improving Jewish education; its primary goal was expansion of the day-school movement.
Jews' Free School (JFS)	Founded in 1732 as a Talmud Torah for orphaned boys, the JFS was attended by a third of London's Jewish children in the late nineteenth century. By 1900 it had over 4,000 pupils, mainly immigrant children, whom it expressly sought to anglicize. The Rothschilds provided financial support. The building was destroyed in World War II and the school remained closed until reopening in 1958 on Camden Road as JFS Comprehensive.
Jewish Secondary Schools Movement (JSSM)	High school network founded in 1929 by Rabbi Avigdor Schonfeld to provide day-school education for his separatist community; headed by his son Solomon from the 1940s through the 1970s.
London Board of Jewish Religious Education (LBJRE)	Founded in 1946 under the aegis of the Chief Rabbi and the United Synagogue; its main mandate was coordinating provision of part-time Jewish education and withdrawal classes[8] in state schools.

---

8   Under the various Education Acts, parents were permitted to withdraw their children from religious education. In 1946, the LBJRE established alternative classes, chiefly within state schools, to provide the 'withdrawn' children with Jewish education.

Union of Orthodox Hebrew Congregations (UOHC)	Founded in 1926 by Rabbi Avigdor Schonfeld as an umbrella organization for the strictly Orthodox community.
United Synagogue (US)	Founded in 1870 when England's five Ashkenazic synagogues joined together, and sanctioned by an act of Parliament. Under the jurisdiction of the Chief Rabbi in religious and ritual matters, and governed by an elected council representing the constituent congregations.
Zionist Federation Education Trust (ZFET)	Educational arm of the Zionist Federation of Great Britain, founded in 1955 to establish and operate day schools with a Zionist outlook.

Other Jewish institutions include the following:

Agudas Yisrael (Aguda)	Ultra-Orthodox communal organization active throughout the Diaspora and in Israel; non-Zionist.
Jewish Agency	Founded in 1929 to represent, and administer the internal affairs of, the Jewish community in Mandatory Palestine.
Mizrachi/Hapoel Hamizrachi	Religious Zionist movements active throughout the Diaspora and in Israel; modern-Orthodox in orientation.
World Zionist Organization (WZO)	Zionist organization founded by Herzl in 1897 to work toward establishing a national home for the Jewish people in Palestine. Among its units were the Education and Culture in the Diaspora and Torah Education in the Diaspora departments.

Personalities

A number of the individuals and families who played a significant role in the annals of Anglo-Jewish education were very prominent in their day, and their names will, even today, be recognized by many readers. Others were philanthropists, functionaries and leaders whose names are no longer widely known. I will identify these individuals here, so that readers will be better able to follow the narrative:

Lavy Bakstansky (1904–1971)	Leading British Zionist activist, general secretary of the Zionist Federation of Great Britain (ZF) from 1931 until his death.
Chaim Bermant (1929–1998)	Novelist; journalist; social historian and critic; *Jewish Chronicle* columnist, first under the pseudonym 'Ben Azai', then under his own name ('On The Other Hand').
Selig Brodetsky (1888–1954)	President of the Board of Deputies (1940–49); Hon. President of the ZF; member of the Executive of the WZO and Jewish Agency for Palestine; President of the Hebrew University of Jerusalem (1949–51).
Rabbi Israel Brodie (1895–1979)	First Chief Rabbi (1948–65) to be born and educated in Britain.
Moshe Davis (1926–1987)	Executive Director, Office of the Chief Rabbi; director, JEDT. This Moshe Davis is not to be confused with Moshe Davis the historian.
I. Solomon Fox (1896–1971)	Chairman of ZF and a key figure in the ZFET day schools.
Ernest Frankel (1902–1990)	Vice President, ZF and Treasurer, ZFET.

Levi Gertner (1908–1976)	Head of the ZF's Education Dept.; director of the British branch of the Jewish Agency's Dept. of Education and Culture; initiator of ZFET schools.
Rev. J. K. Goldbloom (1872–1961)	Headmaster of the Redman's Road Talmud Torah, prominent educator; fervent Zionist; advocate for *Ivrit b'Ivrit* method of teaching Hebrew.
Dayan Isidore Grunfeld (1900–1975)	Member of London Beth Din (rabbinical court) and LBJRE.
Rabbi Joseph Hertz (1872–1946)	Chief Rabbi (1913–46).
Rabbi Immanuel Jakobovits(1921–1999)	Chief Rabbi (1967–91).
Elsie Janner (1905–1994)	Communal leader, magistrate, social welfare activist; chair of the Board of Deputies' Education Committee, wife of Labour MP Barnett Janner.
Salmond S. Levin (1905–1999)	Chairman of LBJRE (1954–68); chairman of Jews' College; President of the United Synagogue (1977–81); brother-in-law of historian Vivian Lipman.
Ewen Montagu (1901–1985)	Judge, naval intelligence officer, President of the United Synagogue (1954–62); son of Louis Samuel Montagu 2nd Baron Swaythling; nephew of Sir Robert Waley-Cohen. Described by Bermant as 'the last of the Cousinhood'.
Nathan Morris (1890–1970)	Education officer of Jewish Religious Education Board and director, Joint Emergency Committee for Jewish Religious Education (JEC); Director, Jewish Agency's Dept. of Education and Culture.
Rabbi Kopul Rosen (1913–1962)	Founded Carmel College, a Jewish boarding school modelled on the English 'public' boarding school, in 1948.

Nathan Rubin (1922–1996)	Worked at the London County Council (LCC) before becoming Secretary of the LBJRE; Day Schools Adviser (1950–68); Secretary of United Synagogue 1968–83.
Michael Sacher (dates unavailable)	Vice Chair of Marks and Spencer; philanthropist; chair of Joint Palestine Appeal; leading donor to ZFET.
Rabbi Solomon Schonfeld (1912–1984)	Son of Rabbi Victor (Avigdor) Schonfeld; founder of Hasmonean High School and head of JSSM; Presiding Rabbi of Union of Orthodox Hebrew Congregations.
(Sir) Robert Waley-Cohen (1877–1952)	President of the United Synagogue (1942–52); Vice-President of the Board of Deputies (1936–43).

Terminology

To aid readers who may be unfamiliar with the nomenclature of British education, and other terminology used in this book, let me present some historical background and define some terms.

Between 1944 and the late 1960s, state secondary schools in Britain were organized according to a 'tripartite system', comprising three types of schools: secondary modern schools, secondary technical schools, and grammar schools. At age eleven, pupils took an examination called the '11 plus' to determine which type they would attend. The 20 per cent who passed were deemed to have academic ability, and sent to 'grammar schools'. The remainder mainly attended 'secondary modern schools', which focused on basic, practical subjects; pupils were prepared for factory jobs rather than higher education. 'Secondary technical schools' were intended for pupils deemed to have technical but not academic aptitude; they were, however, very few in number. As we will see, the tripartite system was phased out, and replaced with a non-selective 'comprehensive' system of secondary education.

A 'Local Education Authority' (LEA) is the body responsible for all state schools in a given area. 'Non-provided schools' are schools that receive no state funding. 'Voluntary schools' receive state funding for operation and maintenance of the school, but a foundation or a trust (usually a religious organization) owns the school buildings, contributes to building costs, and has significant input into the running of the school. 'Public' schools are in fact independent fee-paying private schools, many of which offer boarding facilities; outside the UK, such schools would be referred to as private schools.

The terms 'strictly Orthodox' and 'fervently' or 'ultra' Orthodox (haredi) will be used to distinguish two specific sectors within Anglo-Jewry. The former term will refer to the community affiliated with the Adath Yisroel synagogue and the JSSM; during the period covered in this book, it was led by Rabbi Solomon Schonfeld; the latter terms will refer to the more separatist Hasidic and Lithuanian communities.

Education and Anglo-Jewry

From the late 1960s on, British Jewry has increasingly embraced Jewish day schools as a preferred format for the delivery of secular education. This is so despite the fact that, beginning in the 1970s, government funding for the building and maintenance of these schools has been dramatically reduced, and the burden of financing the building has been borne almost entirely by the Jewish community. Yet when legislation that encouraged the building of such schools – the Butler Education Act – was introduced in 1944, Anglo-Jewry showed little interest.[1] This chapter will explore the pervasive feeling within the community, up to the mid-1960s, that the acceptable parameters of being Jewish in Britain did not include the 'separation' of Jewish children from their Gentile peers during the school day. To understand these issues, acquaintance with 'the Cousinhood', which established the first Jewish schools in Britain, is essential.

The 'Cousinhood' and the founding of Jewish schools

The Cousinhood was mainly composed of Jews of Dutch and German origin who had moved to England in the second half of the eighteenth century, hoping to improve their economic situation. The second and third generations sought not only financial opportunity, but also to overcome the social and political barriers to their integration into British society.

1   See B. Steinberg, 'Anglo-Jewry and the 1944 Education Act', *Jewish Journal of Sociology* 31(1989), 82; G. Alderman, *Modern British Jewry* (Oxford: Clarendon, 1992).

Cousinhood members took their responsibilities to Judaism and their co-religionists seriously, organizing a voluntary poor law, and later establishing the Jewish Board of Guardians. They fed the hungry and clothed the poor, so that Jews would not need to depend on the church; they established schools and set up endowment funds; they built and supported synagogues, reinforcing the rabbinate and defending both the faith and the faithful.[2]

These families, in particular the Rothschilds, Samuels, Montefiores, Cohens, Henriques, Goldsmids and Montagus, dominated Anglo-Jewry. Like their non-Jewish counterparts, they assumed leadership roles with a sense of obligation, expecting in return only deference and respect. At the Board of Deputies, British Jewry's closest institution to a representative council, Sir Stuart Samuel Montagu (the 3rd Baron Swaythling) presided from 1917 until 1922. He was succeeded by Cyril Henriques, another member of the Anglo-Jewish elite. Four years later Osmond d'Avigdor Goldsmid was elected. The vice-presidents of the Board of Deputies were drawn from the same circle, including, e.g., several Rothschilds.[3] In 1871, members of the Cousinhood founded the Anglo-Jewish Association, to steer communal foreign policy stances. Its first president was Jacob Waley, who was succeeded by Baron Henry de Worms (1872–86) and Sir Julian Goldsmid (1886–95). Claude Montefiore took over in 1895, and until he resigned in 1921 was the key figure in the Association's campaign against Zionism. Osmond d'Avigdor Goldsmid held the office until 1926, when Leonard Montefiore, Claude's son, became president, a position he held until 1939.[4] A similar leadership pattern existed at the United Synagogue, which though ostensibly committed to Orthodoxy, was led by many honorary officers whose lifestyles were decidedly un-Orthodox. Lionel

---

2   C. Bermant, *The Cousinhood* (London: Eyre & Spottiswoode, 1971), 1–3.

3   The one exception was Joseph Prag (1925–28), whose origins were humbler, though he had been active in communal office since the 1890s and as such was 'virtually part of the establishment', see D. Cesarani, 'The Transformation of Communal Authority in Anglo-Jewry, 1914–1940', in idem (ed.), *The Making of Modern Anglo-Jewry* (Oxford: Basil Blackwell, 1990), 122.

4   See V. D. Lipman, *A History of the Jews in Britain since 1858* (Leicester: Leicester University Press, 1990).

de Rothschild was titular president until 1942, though vice president Sir Robert Waley-Cohen was effectively in charge. Ewen Montagu, from another Cousinhood family, served as president of the United Synagogue until 1962, when the plutocracy's reign finally came to a close.[5] At the Jewish Board of Guardians, an organization originally established in 1859 to care for the Jewish poor, the Cohens were the dominant family, occupying the presidency until 1947, aside from one decade-long interregnum.[6]

The Cousinhood assumed responsibility for almost every sphere of Jewish communal affairs, including Jewish education. As with social services in general, education in England was the preserve of voluntary organizations until 1870, when the government passed legislation assuming authority in this sphere.[7] Until then, the Cousinhood established several day schools for the growing number of poor Jews, children of illiterate, impoverished immigrants, mainly from Germany.

Six associations for founding voluntary (i.e., non state-supported) Jewish schools were established during this period. The first and largest was the Jews' Free School (JFS), which grew out of an eighteenth century Talmud Torah for poor children. In 1821 the school moved to Bell Lane, Spitafields, in the heart of the East End, and by the turn of the century had an enrolment of some 4,300, making it the largest elementary school in the country.[8] The Rothschild family took a special interest in the school, generously supporting it as their own personal charity; in gratitude, the school emblem and colours were taken from the Rothschild family crest.

---

5   Bermant describes the resignation of Ewen Montagu and the election of Sir Isaac Wolfson to the presidency of the United Synagogue as a clear statement that 'the Cousinhood had retired from the Orthodox establishment', see Bermant, *Cousinhood*, 413. This retirement was, I will argue, foreshadowed in 1945 with the handing over of the trust funds to the LBJRE.

6   V. D. Lipman, *A Century of Social Service, 1859–1959: The Jewish Board of Guardians* (London: Routledge & Kegan Paul, 1959), 256. From 1868 to 1955, the position of treasurer was held by members of the Rothschild, Waley, Samuel, Cohen, d'Avigdor Goldsmid and Franklin families, all Cousinhood members.

7   It is no coincidence that after 1870, no new Jewish day schools were founded for almost sixty years, until the establishment of the JSSM.

8   Gartner, *Jewish Immigrant*, 222.

The family had a representative on the school's board of governors for an uninterrupted 150 years, and several family members served as school president.[9] To counter missionary activity in the East End, a Jews' Infants' School was established in 1841; most of its pupils then continued at the JFS.[10] In the same way the Rothschilds were benefactors of the JFS, so the Infants' School was sponsored by the Montefiore family. In its early years, Nathaniel Montefiore (1819–83) served as the school's president; he was succeeded by his son Claude, leader of Liberal Judaism in Britain and avowed anti-Zionist, who in turn handed over responsibility to his son, Leonard.[11] Claude Montefiore, in partnership with the Waley and Davidson families, was also active in sponsoring the Westminster Jews' Free School. Initially opened for boys, the school added a girls' division in 1846. In 1905, the school had 570 pupils.[12] There were similar developments in the provinces: Jewish schools were opened in Manchester (1838), Liverpool (1840), and Birmingham (1840).

In the 1860s, three additional school associations were founded in London: the Stepney Jewish Schools, considered ahead of their time for including vocational training and physical education in the curriculum; the Bayswater Jewish Schools, whose academic achievements were such as to attract even middle-class pupils; and the South London (Borough) schools. Although these schools were not directly identified with specific families, they were supported by the wealthy. In 1905, Sir Edward Stern was president and patron of the Stepney Jewish Schools, and J. Bergtheil, a member of the Cousinhood-run Anglo-Jewish Association council, held the same position at the Bayswater Schools.

When many more immigrants from Russia and Poland began streaming in during the last decades of the nineteenth century, the need for such schools increased significantly. Evidence that various organizations were endeavouring to proselytize Jews in London's East End by tempting them with free education was another factor in the opening of these schools.[13] A

9   Black, *JFS*, 56–7.
10   Black, *Social Politics*, 111; *Jewish Year Book 1905/6*, 75.
11   Bermant, *Cousinhood*, 226–7.
12   *Jewish Year Book 1905/6*, 79.
13   Black, *Social Politics*, 111.

statement from the constitution of the Westminster Jews' Free School well exemplifies the schools' objectives: 'that male children of the Jewish persuasion (whose parents are unable to afford them education) be instructed in Hebrew and English, writing, and arithmetic; that the principles of religion be carefully inculcated, and every exertion be used to make them good and useful members of society'.[14]

Yet at the same time, these schools generally sought to anglicize their pupils. The rationales for inculcation of English mores were two: 'the conviction that the majority society would not, even could not, tolerate that which made immigrant Jews different. Next was the fear that English born Jews would be lumped together with the immigrants, and that the rejection of the latter would extend to the former'.[15] Anglicization was intended to protect not only the newcomers, but the old timers as well.

The JFS, as the most established of these schools, took the lead in this crusade, spearheaded by its long-serving headmaster Moses Angel, who articulated the prevailing attitude to the newcomers: 'Their parents were the refuse population of the worst parts of Europe. Until they (the children) had been anglicized or humanized it was difficult to tell what was their moral condition. They knew neither English nor any intelligible language'.[16] In 1905, at the annual prize-giving ceremony, his successor, Louis Abrahams, encouraged parents and schoolchildren to throw off their 'foreign habits' and 'foreign prejudices', and 'become English – truly English'. He continued:

> Strengthen the efforts of the teachers to wipe away all evidences of foreign birth and foreign proclivities, so that your (children) shall be so identified with everything that is English in thought and deed, that no shadow of anti-Semitism might exist, that (your) boys and girls may grow up devoted to the flag which they are learning within these walls to love and honour, that they may take a worthy part in the growth of this great Empire, whose shelter and protection will never be denied them.[17]

---

14   *Jewish Year Book 1905/6*, 78.
15   D. Cesarani, *The Jewish Chronicle and Anglo-Jewry 1841–1991* (Cambridge: CUP, 1994), 75.
16   Quoted in Gartner, *Jewish Immigrant*, 223.
17   Quoted in Black, *Social Politics*, 110–11.

Although the Cousinhood broadly identified with these sentiments, there was some opposition to the extreme views expressed by the head-masters, which at times provoked stormy discussions at Board of Deputies meetings.

Given the extent of Jewish immigration from Eastern Europe, there were obviously insufficient places in Jewish 'voluntary' schools, also referred to as 'non provided'. Fortuitously, under the 1870 Forster Education Act and later the Balfour Education Acts of 1902 and 1903, denominational schools were given grants and subsidies, initially on the basis of academic results. More importantly, the government began building its own schools, run by local elected school boards. Referred to as 'Board' schools, they soon won the confidence of the new immigrants. Confidence-building measures included appointment of a Jewish headmaster at Old Castle Street School and observance of Jewish holidays.[18] Within a short time most Jewish children in London were enrolled in such schools, where – in immigrant neighbourhoods – they often comprised the majority of pupils.[19] There was discussion about whether it might be prudent to forego Jewish day schools in favour of the Board schools, but in any event, as the Jewish population gradually dispersed to districts with no Jewish day schools, the numbers attending these schools declined. JFS enrolment, for instance, dropped from about 3,400 in 1904 to 900 in 1939. By the 1930s, there was a sense that the schools had outlived their purpose. Mass Jewish immigration had long since ended, and the anglicization policy had succeeded. The South London (Borough) School and the Westminster schools closed when their leases expired in 1940.[20]

---

18   Black, *Social Politics*, 118–19.
19   In 1894, the total number of Jewish children enrolled in London schools was around 16,000, with slightly over half attending Jewish voluntary schools and the others Board schools. By 1905, the combined attendance had risen to over 40,000, of which slightly under a quarter attended Jewish schools. See *Jewish Year Book 1894*, 58; *1905/6*, 82.
20   See S. Levin, 'Changing Patterns of Jewish Education', in idem (ed.), *A Century of Anglo-Jewish Life 1870–1970* (London: 1970), 61.

Over the years, the national and local authorities took on some of the responsibility for maintaining the schools, a process that will be detailed below. In September 1944, following passage of the Education Act, the education authority of the London County Council (LCC) requested that Anglo-Jewry submit plans for the future of its day schools. In response, the Joint Emergency Committee for Jewish Religious Education (JEC), soon to become the London Board for Jewish Religious Education (LBJRE), established a committee made up of some of its members and representatives of the mainly defunct Jewish voluntary schools. The latter nominated Digby Solomon and Hyman Isaacs to represent the JFS, Leonard Montefiore for the Westminster Jews' Free School and the Jews' Infants' School, and Mr Kaye for the Bayswater Jewish Schools.[21] Their role was to represent the interests of the trustees, who were mostly members of the Cousinhood.

The transfer of responsibility for day-school education from the Cousinhood to the new leadership within the community, as represented by the LBJRE, involved little animosity. Although the Cousinhood fought to preserve its control over Anglo-Jewish policy on issues relating to foreign affairs and communal defence, it had lost interest in the day schools, perceiving them as having outlived their usefulness. In effect, the old elite relinquished control of its day schools and endowment funds without a fight. As we will see, they did stipulate that their resources could not fall into the hands of religious 'extremists' such as Solomon Schonfeld of the Jewish Secondary Schools Movement (JSSM), but their acceptance of leaders like Alfred Woolf, Salmond Levin, Nathan Morris, and Nathan Rubin as the central figures in Jewish education attested to their lack of interest in this sphere of communal activity. Indeed, this acquiescence can be viewed as the Cousinhood's serving notice of its withdrawal from leadership in the educational sphere.

---

21   Digby Solomon was honorary architect of the Federation of Synagogues and a trustee of the JFS; Hyman Isaacs was an honorary solicitor of the United Synagogue; Leonard Montefiore was the treasurer and former president of the Anglo-Jewish Association.

Two decades later, when Ewen Montagu retired from the presidency of the United Synagogue, he was replaced by Isaac Wolfson, the Great Universal Stores magnate, who was not only a man of new wealth, having grown up in the poverty-stricken Gorbals district of Glasgow, but also an *observant* Orthodox Jew. Poignantly encapsulating the changing of the guard is the fact that by 1954, Wolfson had become the key benefactor of the former Bayswater Schools, now renamed the Solomon Wolfson School in honour of his father. While cynics might claim that no major transformation had occurred, but rather, one wealthy elite had been replaced by another, the new regime clearly reflected a shift in the socio-demographic contours of Anglo-Jewry.[22]

Anglo-Jewry: An overview

In 1944, most British Jews traced their origins to the massive wave of immigration from Russia between 1881 and 1905. Though immigration declined dramatically following the 1905 Aliens Act, Jews continued to arrive until the outbreak of World War I. Initially, they lived in the poorer neighbourhoods of Britain's major cities, particularly London, Manchester, Leeds, Glasgow, and Liverpool. During the 1920s and 1930s, they began moving out of these ghettos to upper working-class and middle-class districts. This migration, though slow at the outset, intensified during and after the war, partly due to the blitz and evacuation, and ensuing drops in rental prices and property values. This mobility was encouraged by new housing developments, construction of which was accompanied by the extension of railway lines and other means of public transport. In London, the decline of the historic East End and the concomitant rise of Hackney and Dalston, Stam-

22   On the new elite, see Cesarani, 'Transformation', 115–40.

ford Hill and Stoke Newington, illustrated this process.[23] Many continued further northward to the more affluent suburbs of Golders Green, Hendon, and Edgware. With the development of the railway to East and West Ham, Leyton, and Ilford, there was also a pronounced move eastward.

The departure from the East End was not a uniquely Jewish phenomenon. Overcrowding, substandard housing, and the conversion of residential property into offices, warehouses and industrial sites led to a general pattern of relocation, epitomized by the borough of Stepney, whose population declined from close to 300,000 in 1911 to under 100,000 in 1948.[24] Of course, not all the London Jews left the East End: between 20,000 and 30,000 continued to reside there in the mid 1960s.[25] Provincial patterns of migration from the inner city to suburbia were similar: in Manchester Jews left Cheetham and Broughton for Prestwich and Whitefield; in Leeds, the old immigrant areas of Leylands and of Chapletown gave way to Moortown and Alwoodley.[26]

These changes also reflect the changed occupational structure of Anglo-Jewry, with a shift away from manual labour to trade, business, and the professions. The first decades of the immigrant experience in England witnessed a concentration of Jewish workers in the furniture, textile, hat, boot, jewellery, and fur industries. Between the wars, tailoring remained an important trade for Jews – probably the largest single trade – though its relative importance declined. During and after World War II, the textile industry moved toward large factories, whereas the Jewish preference was to work in, manage, or own small-scale workshops.[27] This was more pronounced in London than in textile hub cities such as Leeds and Liverpool,

---

23   See V. D. Lipman, *Social History of the Jews in England 1850–1950* (London: Watts, 1954), 168–9.

24   H. Brotz, 'The Outlines of Jewish Society in London', in M. Freedman (ed.), *A Minority in Britain* (London: Vallentine Mitchell, 1955), 141.

25   T. Kushner, 'Jew and Non-Jew in the East End of London: Towards an Anthropology of "Everyday" Relations', in G. Alderman and C. Holmes (eds), *Outsiders and Outcasts* (London: Duckworth & Co., 1993), 51.

26   E. Krausz, *Leeds Jewry* (Cambridge: W. Heffer, 1964), 22–6.

27   Lipman, *Century*, 150 n. 2.

where Jews were disproportionately involved in the garment industry (aka the shmatte trade).[28] Large numbers of Jews were also engaged in furniture manufacturing; in 1930, an estimated 6–8,000 Jews worked in the trade in East London alone.[29] But by the end of the 1950s, fewer than 1,000 remained.[30]

From the 1920s through the 1940s, Jews increasingly became owners of their own businesses. Whether retail shops, factories, or wholesalers, they were typically small-scale and fell within the aforementioned trades; there were relatively few large industrialists. In the jewellery, shoe and fur trades, Jews operated a fifth, an eighth, and two-thirds, respectively, of all firms identified in a Board of Deputies' Trades Advisory Council (TAC) survey conducted during the war years.[31]

Overall, though, until World War II Anglo-Jewry was mainly a working-class community whose members belonged to trade unions and tended to support the Labour Party. But this phenomenon was transitory: whereas during the first decade of the twentieth century there were over twenty Jewish trade unions, only one small union remained after 1945.[32] Jews did not take pride in working-class culture and instilled in their children aspirations to upward mobility. A survey of Edgware Jewry in the early 1960s showed that though the community was thoroughly working class in origin, over half having been born in London's East End, 80 per cent regarded themselves as middle class. Some Jews continued to vote for the Labour Party even after moving to middle-class neighbourhoods, but the trend was in the opposite direction.[33]

28 H. Pollins, *Economic History of the Jews in England* (London: Associated University Presses, 1982), 186–7.

29 Lipman, *Social History*, 174.

30 A. Rollin, 'Jews in the Industry', *Jewish Chronicle (JC)* (Supplement) 25 January 1957, 30.

31 N. Barou, *The Jews in Work and Trade* (London: Trades Advisory Council, 1945), 5–6.

32 J. Parkes, 'History of the Anglo-Jewish Community', in Freedman, *Minority*, 30–1.

33 See G. Alderman, *The Jewish Community in British Politics* (Oxford: Clarendon, 1983), chs. 7–8, citing Krausz's Edgware survey.

Anglo-Jewry experienced three main occupational developments in the 1930s and 1940s. Growing diversification took Jews into new fields, such as engineering, radio and (later) television servicing, and printing. Increasing numbers engaged in business-related office jobs as salespersons, clerks, and managers.[34] Second, many aspired to the professions, as reflected in disproportionately high rates of enrolment in universities, especially in medicine, dentistry, accountancy and law programmes, and teacher training colleges.[35] By 1951, Jews constituted almost 3 per cent of university students, though they made up just 1 per cent of the population.[36] This trend increased significantly after World War II, when free secondary school education became available and more scholarships were offered for university education. Another salient trend was toward increased self-employment. The TAC had estimated that 15 per cent of Jews were self-employed, more than double the national rate; later surveys suggest that this rate was far lower than it would have been but for the war.[37] A survey from the early 1950s found that 75 per cent of males in trades were self-employed, as were 50 per cent of those in the professions.[38]

Thus at the time of the proposed educational reform, Anglo-Jewry was in the midst of transitioning from the working class to the middle class. The professions, business, and trades outside the traditional shmatte, fur, and furniture sectors, were the preferred paths up the socioeconomic ladder. Though these patterns were shared by the wider society, Anglo-Jewry underwent the transition more quickly, and hence more visibly, than other groups.

In assessing Anglo-Jewish attitudes to education, the desire for upward mobility and membership in the English middle class cannot be underestimated. It manifested itself in parental eagerness to secure their children's career success even at the cost of foregoing Jewish education. In his 1944

34 See J. Gould and S. Esh (eds), *Jewish Life in Modern Britain* (London: Routledge & Kegan Paul, 1964), 30; Lipman, *Social History*, 174.
35 Lipman, *History*, 212.
36 R. Baron, 'Jewish Students – A Survey', *JC* 16 February 1951; 23 February 1951.
37 Barou, *Jews in Work*, 7.
38 H. Neustatter, 'Demographic and other statistical aspects of Anglo-Jewry', in Freedman, *Minority*, 126.

inaugural address as communal rabbi of Glasgow, Rabbi Kopul Rosen expressed disappointment with this attitude, saying that parents were chiefly concerned 'with their children's material career', whereas 'whether their child was to live the life of a Jew' was deemed of minor importance and 'left to chance'.[39]

Most Jews, unable to afford private education, saw grammar schools as the gateway to the English middle class. Indeed, the grammar schools in the eastern and northern districts of London, such as Hackney Downs and Central Foundation, had a 40 to 50 per cent Jewish enrolment.[40] Although no exact data is available for the number of Jews attending grammar schools, an estimate for Manchester in 1950 puts this figure at 25 per cent, though the national rate was only 16 per cent.[41]

Anglo-Jewish parents in the decades prior to World War II were the children or grandchildren of immigrants, and could look to their more established co-religionists as models of absorption into British society. These Jews had succeeded financially and lived in the more salubrious districts of central London. By dint of their wealth and status as 'old-timers', they headed Anglo-Jewry's communal organizations. Over time, however, serious differences emerged between the old guard and the new immigrants over issues such as religious observance, Zionism, and the fight against antisemitism. Jewish education, in contrast, was not a contentious issue. At one time, Jewish day schools, such as the JFS in London, had been viewed as instruments for 'anglicizing' the children of immigrants, but by the end of the 1930s, these schools were in serious decline.[42] Some argued that these schools were victims of their own success: having educated their pupils to integrate into British society, these pupils saw no need for separate schools for their own children.[43]

39   *JC* 25 February 1944, 1.
40   G. Alderman, *London Jewry and London Politics 1889–1986* (London: Routledge, 1989), 105.
41   Neustatter, 'Demographic', 132.
42   In London, of 13,500 children enrolled in Jewish educational institutions in 1939, only 3,030 attended Jewish voluntary schools (viz., day schools); the others attended Hebrew classes or *cheder*. See Levin, *Century*, 68, quoting the Jewish Memorial Council, report of the Central Committee (1939).
43   Steinberg, 'Anglo-Jewry', 87.

Government proposals for educational reform

Most historians of education maintain that the war was the catalyst for passage of the Education Act in 1944, arguing that this legislation should be understood in the broader context of proposals for enhancing social welfare in the UK.[44] The experiences of evacuation, conscription, rationing, and the blitz, not to mention the general sense of unity surrounding the war effort, are thought to have heightened sensitivity to the plight of the poorer classes.[45] Even the staunchly conservative *Times*, had, shortly after Dunkirk, expressed support for the establishment of a 'welfare state' that supplied the basic needs of its citizens. The blueprint for this policy was the Beveridge Report of December 1942, which outlined plans for the alleviation of poverty (social insurance and assistance), disease (a national health service), ignorance (extensive responsibility for the education of all), squalor (housing) and idleness (employment programmes).[46]

The wartime government decided to pursue educational reform rather than focusing on other areas of social reform proposed by the Beveridge Report. Relative to the daunting financial burden that implementation of the other Beveridge proposals would entail, educational reform would be relatively cheap, at least in the immediate post-war years.[47] This was no minor consideration given the debt incurred due to wartime expenditure. Moreover, in contrast to the complex nature of welfare legislation, whose navigation through Parliament was likely to be difficult, educational reform was relatively straightforward.

---

44 Some, however, argue that the wartime experience exacerbated class and regional divisions; see P. Gordon et al., *Education and Policy in England in the Twentieth Century* (London: Woburn, 1991), 37–41.

45 J. Lawson and H. Silver, *A Social History of Education in England* (London: Methuen, 1973), 416; A. Marwick, *Britain in the Century of Total War* (Harmondsworth: Penguin 1968), 268.

46 See R. Lowe, *The Welfare State in Britain since 1945*, 2nd edn (London: Macmillan, 1999).

47 See K. Jefferys, 'R. A. Butler, The Board of Education and the 1944 Education Act', *History* 69 (1984), 227.

Other historians contend that Conservative Party leaders, including Churchill, were alarmed at the growing enthusiasm for radical social change and sought ways to stem it. The mile-long queue outside His Majesty's Stationery Office, where copies of the Beveridge Report were available for purchase, attested to significant public interest, as did the 1943 'mini-election' in which Conservative Party candidates lost six by-elections. On this explanation, the Conservative leaders used the Education Act to deflect calls for more extensive reform.[48] This assessment has been partially endorsed by the editor of Butler's diaries, who claims that the Education Act 'reflected a conscious attempt to move with the trend of politics created by the war, while ensuring that reform was carefully moulded to Conservative Party ends'.[49]

Indeed, in excluding change in the so-called 'public' (i.e., private) schools, deferring raising the school-leaving age to sixteen, and making no serious attempt to introduce a single system of secondary education, the Education Act actually reinforced elitism – 'the old order in a new disguise' – rather than creating equal opportunity.[50] Despite awareness of these deficiencies in the legislation, Labour did not put up a major fight against the proposals as tabled. Nor was educational reform controversial outside Parliament. As the editor of the *Times Educational Supplement* commented in 1944, the new educational policy received 'an almost overwhelmingly cordial reception from practically every shade of professional and public opinion'.[51]

In June 1941, shortly before Butler's arrival at the Board of Education (later, the Ministry of Education), a Green Book entitled *Education after the War* – the first in a series of wartime documents by Board of Education officials proposing educational reform in England and Wales – was confidentially circulated among interested parties, including denominational leaders such as the Chief Rabbi. There was considerable opposition to the

---

48   B. Simon, 'The 1944 Education Act: A Conservative Measure?' *History of Education* 15 (1986), 41–2. Sales of the Beveridge Report are said to have reached 635,000.
49   Jefferys, 'R. A. Butler', 431.
50   Simon, '1944 Education Act', 43.
51   H. C. Dent, *Education in Transition* (London: Kegan Paul, 1944), 232.

proposal to eliminate the dual system of state and denominational schools in favour of a single state-run system, and an alternative scheme, entitled the White Memorandum, acquiesced in the continued existence of denominational schools. Two years later, following further negotiations with interested parties, particularly the Church of England, the Board formulated its White Paper on Educational Reconstruction. In December 1943, Butler presented his proposed legislation to the House of Commons.[52]

Butler had broached the idea of educational reform to the Prime Minister in the summer of 1941, following his appointment to the Board of Education. At that time, his main recommendations involved linking schooling to the needs of industry, securing an agreement over denominational schools and religious instruction, and the question of the 'public' schools. Churchill was not interested, warning Butler not to stir up trouble, but rather to focus on getting the schools to work 'as well as possible under all the difficulties of air attack, evacuation, etc'.[53] Butler was not deterred, and spent the next eighteen months holding negotiations with interested parties and outlining possible legislation. His supporters at the Board of Education helped keep his negotiating partners, especially the Anglicans, from hearing of the Prime Minister's opposition.

To grasp the significance of Butler's proposals for reform of the educational system, it is necessary to understand the evolution of schooling in England. When the government decided in 1870 to intervene in this sphere, it had to contend with existing schools run by various denominations. The Church of England controlled the largest schools, and was particularly strong in rural areas. Roman Catholic schools were mainly found in inner-city districts. Rather than replacing the existing voluntary denominational schools with a unified state school system, the 1870 Forster Act merely sought to 'fill in the gaps' by mandating that elementary education be provided to all children. This generated an inequity: parents

---

52   See D. Akenson, 'Patterns of English Educational Change: The Fisher and Butler Acts', *History of Education Quarterly* 11 (1971), 151–2.

53   Quoted in A. Howard, *Rab: The Life of R. A. Butler* (London: Jonathan Cape, 1987), 116.

in urban centres could choose between council or denominational schools, whereas in rural areas only church schools were available. This situation caused tension, especially among Dissenters, who, like their secular allies, were interested in removing education from the purview of the churches. This tension was exacerbated in 1902, when the Balfour Education Act instituted financial support for both state and denominational schools.

Most denominational schools were elementary schools, and apart from religious instruction, taught a simple curriculum of reading, writing, and arithmetic. Rising costs adversely impacted the denominations' ability to maintain their schools, and between 1902 and 1942, the number of Church of England schools declined from some 12,000 to 9,000. Given that most of the schools that survived were in rural areas, the actual percentage of children attending Church of England schools declined from 40 to 20 per cent. The Roman Catholics fared better; the number of their schools rose from 1,000 in 1902 to 1,200 in 1944.[54] Nonetheless, the facilities of both the Anglicans and the Catholics compared unfavourably to those of the state schools. The denominational buildings were older, their classrooms antiquated; amenities such as playgrounds were generally inferior. It was this factor, more than any other, that provided Butler with the necessary ammunition in his negotiations with the denominational authorities, and impelled the Archbishop of Canterbury to compromise. Butler convinced the Anglicans that their inability, due to rising costs, to provide education comparable to that offered by the state system, was an injustice to their pupils. Better to accept a compromise whereby the state would guarantee a non-denominational Christian education in council schools and partial funding for denominational schools, than be faced with ultimate collapse due to financial strain or parental withdrawal of their children.

The Catholic response to the legislation was far more hostile. Butler's strategy was to avoid a clash by presenting the legislation as tantamount to a fait accompli. Although the Catholics were not overly enthusiastic about the proposed partial funding for denominational schools, by the time of

---

54   M. Cruikshank, *Church and State in English Education: 1870 to the Present Day* (London: Macmillan, 1963), 143.

the Act's third reading in Parliament, Butler 'had succeeded in buying off his most combative Roman Catholic opponents by offering favourable government loans ... to finance the capital expenditure which would necessarily be incurred in bringing the schools up to standard'.[55]

Let us now consider the Jewish community's response to plans for educational reform. We will track this response from 1941, when proposals for reform were made public, to the November 1945 'Communal conference on educational reconstruction'. This was an exigency period for Anglo-Jewry. It was, of course, a time of war, and all Britons endured privation and suffering. But Anglo-Jewry had to contend with additional problems: fears about brethren in Nazi-occupied lands, absorption of refugees from Central Europe, and local antisemitism. Less immediate concerns included communal conflict over supporting the establishment of a Jewish state in Palestine, and over cooperation between the Orthodox majority and the emerging Liberal and Reform streams of Judaism.[56] Overall, education was not a priority on the communal agenda.[57]

The Jewish response to educational reform

In 1941, the main Jewish organization dealing with formal education was the Joint Emergency Committee for Jewish Religious Education (JEC), which had been formed in response to the upheaval of wartime evacuation. The JEC represented the three Orthodox agencies dealing with part-time Jewish education: the Jewish Religious Education Board, responsible for withdrawal classes in state primary schools, the Union of Hebrew and Religion Classes, which oversaw synagogue-based classes, and the Talmud

---

55 Howard, *Rab*, 138.
56 Cesarani, 'Transformation', 115–40.
57 See N. Morris, 'Jewish Education in Time of Total War', in *Jewish Education in Great Britain; Two Talks* (London: JEC, 1946).

Torah Trust, which held more intensive weekday after-school classes. In 1939, the attendance at the withdrawal classes numbered 2,890, the Union classes had 4,930 pupils, and the Talmud Torah Trust, 2,640.[58] A decade earlier, attendance at the religion classes was 3,800 and at Talmud Torah classes 3,406, suggesting there had been a shift of pupils from the Talmud Torahs to the less rigorous religion classes.[59]

In 1939, Marcus Epstein, chair of the JEC, and its Education Officer, Dr Nathan Morris, negotiated with other communal organizations, notably the Reform and Liberal movements, to establish a unified educational body for Anglo-Jewry. Their goal was to coordinate Jewish education and pool sparse resources not only for the duration of the war, but also thereafter. They hoped the new body would succeed in forging a unified front to represent the Jewish educational institutions when dealing with state and local educational authorities. They believed that this body had to recognize the minority non-Orthodox streams within the Jewish community, but Chief Rabbi Hertz, not surprisingly, was 'vehemently opposed' to granting such recognition, fearing that the new body might undermine Orthodoxy's dominance in the community, and his own position as its spiritual leader.[60]

Of particular concern to the Chief Rabbi was the decision of Sir Robert Waley-Cohen, the United Synagogue's vice president, to invite Norman Bentwich and Lily Montagu, of the Reform and Liberal movements respectively, to co-chair a series of educational conferences to be held in Oxford.[61] Despite his position, Waley-Cohen's religious practices were far from Orthodox: it was widely known that come Saturday morning, he was more likely to be found hunting on his country estate than at synagogue services.[62] His class affiliation, social standing, and personal sympathies made him a natural ally of the Reform and Liberal movement leaders.

58   JEC, First Report, 1941.
59   I. Fishman, 'Jewish Education in Great Britain', *Jewish Monthly*, Nov. 1945, 62.
60   Steinberg, 'Jewish Education', 46.
61   Ibid., 56.
62   See Bermant, *Cousinhood*, 368.

In the face of this threat, the Chief Rabbi increasingly inclined toward the more strictly Orthodox elements within the community. In particular, he looked to his son-in-law and confidant, Rabbi Dr Solomon Schonfeld, for support.[63] They decided to forestall inroads by the Reform and Liberal elements by establishing a rival body, the National Council of Jewish Religious Education. In announcing the formation of this body, Hertz declared:

> It is my duty, as Chief Rabbi, to open the eyes of the Jews of Great Britain to the deadly peril threatening our traditional Jewish life, to rescue our educational machinery from the hands of men who are inimical to 'traditional Judaism' and its fundamental institutions.[64]

He was even more forthright in a private letter to the vice president of the United Synagogue:

> Nothing but the National Council for Jewish Religious Education can put an end to the miserable comedy enacted by the self-appointed educational dictator and his followers. The Council will rescue us from the religious nihilism of Sir Robert and awaken a new Jewish consciousness and conscience in Anglo-Jewry.[65]

As a result of these machinations, Nathan Morris distanced himself from the project. Selig Brodetsky, president of the Board of Deputies and the Zionist Federation (ZF), persuaded Waley-Cohen, Epstein, Montagu and Bentwich that they could not be insensitive to Anglo-Jewry's Orthodox tradition. The attempt to create a body that integrated the non-Orthodox streams having failed, in September 1941, Chief Rabbi Hertz was appointed honorary president of the JEC, and accorded the right to

63 A. Newman, *The United Synagogue* (London: Routledge & Kegan Paul, 1977), 156–7. Schonfeld, leader of the small and very strictly Orthodox Union of Hebrew Orthodox Congregations, did not belong to the Anglo-Jewish establishment. Schonfeld's religious outlook was in line with Samson Raphael Hirsch's '*Torah im Derech Eretz*' philosophy, and appealed mainly to recent immigrants from Central Europe.
64 *JC* 9 May 1941, 5.
65 Chief Rabbi to vice president of United Synagogue 4 May 1941. ACC 2805/6/1/45.

examine its syllabuses and the religious certification of all teachers.[66] These rights would be safeguarded by later Chief Rabbis. Yet the bitter experience of the struggles was not forgotten. Moreover, the conflict between these individuals and organizations adversely impacted the community's ability to formulate a clear response to the impending government educational reform proposals.

From the perspective of the Jewish communal leadership, the key clauses of the reform proposals pertained to religious education within the state schools; state support for denominational schools was deemed of little interest. As to the former, following government negotiations with the Anglican and Roman Catholic leadership, it was decided that religious education for at least two study periods per week would be mandatory for all children attending state schools, and in addition, that the school day would begin with communal worship.[67] According to clause 26 of the Butler Education Act, an 'Agreed Syllabus' for religious instruction would be formulated following consultations between the LEAs, the Church of England, other religious denominations, and teachers' associations. In keeping with the 1870 Education Act, it was understood that religious instruction in state schools would be non-denominational. Although the 1944 Act did not specify which religion or religions were to be studied, the Agreed Syllabus conferences assumed that apart from the few schools with mainly Jewish enrolment, Christianity of a non-denominational form would be the obvious basis for the religious education of schoolchildren. This was, it must be recalled, before multiculturalism, when it made sense to speak of Britain as a 'Christian society'.[68] Sensitive to the fact that the religious education syllabus would not be acceptable to all parents, the

---

66 Chief Rabbi and JEC: Terms of Agreement 1 September 1941. ACC 2805/6/1/46.
· 67 Replying to questions on the Education Bill posed by David Weitzman, Labour MP for Hackney North and Stoke Newington, Butler explained that the inclusion of statutory religious education in the council school syllabus was the concession that persuaded the Anglicans to bring their schools within the general system. PRO ED 136 692.
68 G. Parsons (ed.), *The Growth of Religious Diversity: Britain from 1945* (London: Routledge, 1993 and 1994), 1:25.

government had already granted parents the right to withdraw primary school children from worship and religious instruction, and have them receive alternative instruction. Clause 25 now extended these rights to secondary school pupils, if a suitable teacher could be found.

Before we consider the Jewish response to the implications of the 1944 Education Act, it should be noted that the Anglo-Jewish educational leadership paid little attention to the Act's significance for denominational schools. There were seven such schools in London and a similar number in the provinces, all supported by donations and some state funding. These schools had been in serious decline since the 1930s, and apart from those associated with the JSSM, their continued existence was uncertain. According to the reform proposals, denominational schools would be obliged to meet new and more stringent building and maintenance standards. Following negotiations with the denominational authorities, the government offered two options for reducing the financial burden that would fall on denominational schools. These schools could opt for 'controlled' status, in which case all their financial obligations, as well as the right to appoint and dismiss teachers, would be borne by the Local Education Authority (LEA), and all religious instruction, aside from two periods per week, would be in keeping with an 'Agreed Syllabus'. The Anglicans chose this option. The second option, preferred by the Roman Catholics, was to accept 'voluntary aided' status. In this case the governors of such schools were responsible for half the cost of maintenance and repairs to the school buildings. In return, the LEA would shoulder all other financial responsibilities, including the staff salaries. Religious instruction and the hiring of teaching staff would remain the schools' purview. Although voluntary-aided status was seen by many as a generous option, the Jewish community, unlike its Roman Catholic counterpart, did not take advantage of these provisions. Instead, Anglo-Jewry devoted most of its energy to questions pertaining to withdrawal classes in the council schools, such as which communal agency would be responsible for this project.

Withdrawal classes

The community's focus on denominational educational within the state school system makes sense, given that most Anglo-Jewish children attended state schools, not Jewish day schools. In London, of 13,500 children enrolled in Jewish educational institutions in 1939, only 3,030 attended day schools.[69] The war reduced the number of children in day schools even further, as a consequence of evacuation, the bombing of certain Jewish day schools, and the ongoing mobility of the Jewish population. By 1945, only one in sixteen Jewish children received their Jewish education at a day school.[70] When Nathan Morris responded to the White Paper on Educational Reconstruction in December 1943, he estimated that about 20,000 children would be affected by the proposed reforms, only a fifth of whom would be day-school pupils.[71] In fact, this prediction was grossly exaggerated, and it took almost twenty years before this figure (4,000) was reached.[72]

The communal response to the government's proposals on religious education in state schools was generally positive. Morris was the most enthusiastic champion of the legislation, travelling the length and breadth of the country to extol its benefits. His enthusiasm was based on the following reasoning. The new legislation extended the right of withdrawal to secondary schools, and thus children aged 11–15 would now be eligible to be withdrawn. If Jewish parents took advantage of their statutory rights to withdraw their children from religious instruction, then in one fell swoop an (estimated) additional 5,000 children would, via withdrawal classes, fall within the orbit of the Jewish educational agencies.[73] This was

---

69   JEC, First Report, 1941, 15.
70   *JC* 30 November 1945, 6.
71   JEC Report, 'Jewish Education Today and Tomorrow, 1943', London, 1944, 59.
72   I. Fishman and H. Levy, 'Jewish Education in Great Britain', in Gould and Esh (eds), *Jewish Life*, 69.
73   Morris made this argument in an address to the United Synagogue Council in January 1944 on the virtues of the Education Act, see *JC* 7 January 1944, 1, 5. And see JEC Report, 'Jewish Education Today', 54–6.

heartening to educators, who bemoaned the accepted attitude that Jewish education could end at Bar/Bat-Mitzvah age. Moreover, this instruction was to take place during 'normal, healthy hours of the day', in contrast to supplementary Jewish education, offered in the late afternoon or evening when children were tired out from their regular school day.[74]

Morris was assuming that Jewish parents would take full advantage of the withdrawal class provision, and that if necessary, Anglo-Jewry would make the funds, staff and resources available to facilitate this instruction. In his negotiations with the Board of Education, the Chief Rabbi had requested that the funding of the withdrawal classes – where sufficient children were enrolled – be borne by the Treasury. This proposal 'bemused' the Board's senior civil servants, as it clearly contravened the Cowper-Temple clause of the 1870 Education Act, which proscribed the teaching of denominational catechisms in state schools. Butler explained this to the Chief Rabbi, adding that funding of withdrawal classes could not be confined to Jewish children.[75] Instead, responsibility was to fall upon the community. Nathan Morris estimated that £15,000 per annum would be required to support the necessary infrastructure.[76]

The Chief Rabbi took an interest in the details of the withdrawal classes. One recommendation was that the number of lessons be increased from two to three per week. Of particular concern to the Chief Rabbi was that the teachers of these classes be Jewish, as he felt that 'non-Jews are unable to teach this subject without a bias which, in some cases, would give the instruction a tendentious character'. Now the Chief Rabbi was well aware (and agreed) that, 'no questions can be asked about the religious belief or observance of the teachers', but was anxious to circumvent this stipulation.[77] The idea of a correspondence course supervised by a Jewish director of studies seemed to him an acceptable alternative. The children would receive and submit work on a weekly basis, and periodic

74   JEC Report, 'Jewish Education, 1944 and After', London, 1944, 10.
75   Note on the Chief Rabbi's Proposals for Religious Education, 3 August 1942, and EO/52/108 2 September 1942. PRO ED 136 240; *JC* 15 January 1943, 6.
76   JEC Report, 'Jewish Education Today', 54; see also *JC* 10 December 1943, 6.
77   Chief Rabbi to R. A. Butler 25 September 1942. PRO ED 136 240.

examinations would be invigilated by visiting teachers to the school. All the personnel to be employed would be approved by the Board of Education and the Chief Rabbi.[78]

While the idea of a correspondence course met with little opposition from the Board of Education, the proposal that there be Jewish directors of studies, paid from public funds, was clearly unacceptable. Similarly, the idea that outside teachers would enter the council schools to monitor denominational education was deemed in breach of the Cowper-Temple clause of the 1870 Act. Butler rejected the Chief Rabbi's proposal.[79] The attempt by Hertz and Schonfeld to challenge the parameters of the Cowper-Temple clause in the hope of securing more intensive Jewish education in state schools failed.[80]

Morris's figure of 5,000 new pupils for withdrawal classes did not take into account the fact that many parents were uninterested in the classes. Jewish parents were, as coming chapters will make clear, generally indifferent to the quality of their children's religious education, and equally indifferent to the possibility that they might find (non-withdrawal) religion classes enticing. The following anecdote is typical. The *Jewish Chronicle* published a letter from a parent describing her experience upon requesting withdrawal classes for her child. Though the school was in a Jewish district, the principal informed her that the parents of other children had 'never made such a request'. This letter provoked no response from the Jewish public or its educational authorities.[81] Logistical problems, such as the difficulty of serving small classes or schools in isolated areas, also adversely impacted participation. Recruiting qualified teachers and coordinating their travel from one learning centre to another was problematic.

78 'Suggestions for Correspondence Instruction in the Agreed Syllabus for Jewish Children where no Jewish Member of Staff is Available' [no date, presumably early 1943]. PRO ED 136 430.

79 R. A. Butler to Chief Rabbi 27 September 1943. PRO ED 136 430.

80 Interview Note, Chief Rabbi, Dr Schonfeld 15 September 1942. PRO ED 136 240; S. Schonfeld, *Jewish Religious Education* (London: 1943), 7–10.

81 *JC* 1 January 1943, 18.

Eight years after passage of the Act, and six years after the founding of the London Board for Jewish Religious Education (LBJRE), the body established to deal with withdrawal classes, the number of children participating in these lessons fell far short of the predicted 5,000. In 1952, 3,171 children attended the LBJRE withdrawal classes in primary and secondary schools, and by 1954, the number had declined to 2,836.[82] The paucity of pupils was due principally to the failure of parents to demand that their children be excused from the regular religion lessons and instead participate in withdrawal classes. Parents were uncomfortable about invoking their rights for fear of isolating their children. A Board of Deputies survey revealed that 'most parents prefer not to make their children conspicuous'; others did not oppose their children being taught the Old Testament by Christians. Nathan Morris had been overly optimistic.[83]

To predict the size of classes and overcome logistical difficulties, the Chief Rabbi had requested of the government that each pupil's denominational affiliation be recorded at the beginning of the school year. This proposal was rejected on the grounds that imposing that duty on the LEAs was 'impracticable'. The Board of Education informed the Chief Rabbi that the onus was on the parents to assert their rights.[84] Clearly, keeping a register of pupils' religious affiliations would contravene the principle of non-denominational schooling. More generally, the prevailing ethos was that such questions were matters of private conscience and not germane to the public realm. This was also the JEC's view: it had expressed reservations about the Chief Rabbi's request, especially the fear that a list of names and addresses might 'fall into the wrong hands'.

82   LBJRE, Fifth Report, 1955, 6.
83   *JC* 24 July 1953, 12 (editorial).
84   Chief Rabbi to R. A. Butler 13 December 1943; Butler to Chief Rabbi, 17 December 1943. PRO ED 136 430.

Day schools

The government's proposals for denominational schools provided an opportunity to restructure the community's day schools, several of which had
been in decline even before the war. The communal authorities explained
this decline by invoking Jewish mobility, a declining birth rate, and school
buildings near busy intersections. They were well aware, however, that most
members of the community were not in favour of separate Jewish schools.[85]
In assessing the ramifications of the new legislation vis-à-vis day schools,
they took this attitude into account, realizing that though the Chief Rabbi,
Nathan Morris, and the *Jewish Chronicle* lost no opportunity to extol the
virtues of such schools, they held no appeal for the wider Jewish community. The communal leaders' policy, therefore, was to consolidate the old
schools and protect the possibility of re-establishing those that had failed,
but not to press for additional day schools.

This is evident in a report issued by the JEC's Voluntary Schools
Committee, whose members represented the trustees and managers of
the London Jewish day schools. The text begins by surveying the demise
or decline of various schools, then assesses their 'source of supply'. The
authors are uneasy about advocating the building of new schools, partly
due to parental attitudes, and partly due to the realization that a considerable capital outlay would be required from a community not known
for its willingness to spend on education. The fact that the government
promised to match these funds did not allay fears that new schools might
be adversely affected by ongoing communal mobility. Nevertheless, the
report recommended that all existing primary day schools be sustained,
and a large centrally located secondary school be built in London. It further

---

85   JEC Report, 'Jewish Education 1945', 57. In a letter to the *JC*, Rev. I. Slotki, head of
      the Manchester Talmud Torah, wrote that 'parents would not send their children
      to a Jewish school where a municipal one is nearer'. He further noted that the state
      schools 'were always crowded' whereas the nearby Jewish day schools 'were half
      empty'. *JC* 10 November 1944, 12.

recommended that the managers and governors of the day schools make future decisions under a central authority that would succeed the JEC.[86]

Discussion of the days schools question was further stimulated by the announcement that the London County Council (LCC) and the JEC were giving serious consideration to re-establishing the Jews' Free School, which had been destroyed in the blitz. Morris announced these deliberations at a meeting of rabbis held under the auspices of the JEC. He asked those present for their views on the feasibility of the project, acknowledging the financial difficulties associated with it, and parental objections to separate schooling. If the practical difficulties could be overcome, he asserted, the school 'might kindle in the heart of Jewish youth a new respect for Jewish educational values, a respect which would extend to the community as a whole. ... and might create a focal point of the religious and cultural life of British Jewry'. Two participants in the conference, the Reverends Levine and Livingstone, both of whom were governors of local council schools, took a different view.[87] They argued that the history of Jewish day schools in England did not show that the community's religious outlook, piety, or Jewish knowledge had been enhanced by these schools. Nor had the schools produced many communal leaders.[88] The *Jewish Chronicle* participated in the debate via its editorial column, arguing against opponents of the day-school system.

At another meeting, the Chief Rabbi and Nathan Morris adduced additional arguments for day-school education. They extolled the pedagogic advantages of the denominational school relative to afterschool or weekend Hebrew classes: more study hours, congenial atmosphere, regular daytime hours, alert children, and motivated teachers. Conscious of the fact that most parents were primarily concerned with the secular academic level

---

86 JEC Report, ibid., 60–1.
87 Reverend Livingstone was rabbi of the (Orthodox) Golders Green synagogue, honorary secretary and treasurer of the Union of Anglo-Jewish Preachers, governor of Hendon County (Grammar) School and a member of the LBJRE. Reverend Levine was rabbi of the (Orthodox) New West End synagogue and a former lecturer in homiletics at Jews' College.
88 *JC* 27 October 1944, 14.

of these schools, Morris pledged that the planned new day school 'would have to meet and even surpass the standards of the state schools'. Moreover, it would be open to all Jewish children, and not depend on financial contributions from parents.[89]

Jewish Chronicle readers responded to these developments by indicating that their focus was not the standard of Jewish education provided, but rather, concern that these schools perpetuated 'separation' and did not prepare pupils for careers and more generally, for 'real' life, that is, participation in the broader society.

> In this increasingly competitive world it is absolutely essential for our children to receive training and an education, which will help them to understand and be able to mix freely with their non-Jewish neighbours. ... We are not being fair to our children's future if we segregate them into a specifically Jewish secondary school.[90]

Communal activists took these criticisms seriously and sought to counter them. They argued that a Jewish school would reinforce its pupils' confidence by providing a sound basis for their identity. It was in the state school, they claimed, that Jewish children were exposed to demoralizing taunts and attacks.[91]

Many Anglo-Jews opposed day schools on the grounds that they encouraged 'exclusivity', buying into the allegation that instead of pursuing integration with their Gentile neighbours, Anglo-Jews sought to isolate themselves. This has been shown to be the prevailing non-Jewish perception of Jews at the time:

> The population as a whole appears to have regarded Judaism, as at best an anachronism, at worst barbaric. Judaism was perceived as an excuse for exclusivity, which in turn was responsible for antisemitism. What was needed, according to a Mass Observation survey, was for Jewish behaviour to 'correspond more to the life and manners of Gentiles'.[92]

---

89 *JC* 10 November 1944, 14.
90 Alex Robinson, Letter to the Editor, *JC* 15 December 1944, 15.
91 See, e.g., Dayan Grunfeld, *JC* 10 November 1944, 14.
92 T. Kushner, *The Persistence of Prejudice: Antisemitism in British Society during the Second World War* (Manchester: Manchester University Press, 1989), 197.

Indeed, during the second reading of the Education Act, the Conservative Member of Parliament for Wrekin, Mr A. Colegate, had commented, à propos denominational education, 'if you want to start an anti-Semitic movement, start segregating the Jews.'[93]

To understand Anglo-Jewish diffidence and unwillingness to seize the opportunity provided by the Butler Education Act, it is important to realize that most of the community had internalized the view that they ought to assimilate into British society, and if they did not, then they bore some culpability for the persistence of prejudice against them. Important communal bodies, in particular the Board of Deputies, accepted this notion, and reminded Jews of their role in keeping antisemitism at bay. To give but one example, upon arrival in Britain, Jewish refugees received a pamphlet from the Board entitled 'Helpful Information and Guidance for Every Refugee', informing the newcomers that it was in their best interest to keep a low profile and adapt their habits to the local norms.[94] Such comportment, the pamphlet implies, would make it easier to counter accusations that Jews are 'foreigners'. Similarly, following antisemitic allegations of Jewish black market activity, the Board of Deputies mobilized its Trades Advisory Council (TAC) to apply sanctions to members of the community suspected of being involved in such unethical practices.

The TAC put out a series of apologetic publications that sought to counter anti-Jewish sentiment. It issued a booklet of responses to accusations routinely levelled against Jews: what have Jews contributed to bettering workers' social and economic status? Do Jews control the press? Why are so many Jews engaged in trade? etc. The apologetic answers reflect the defensiveness of the communal mindset: 'many Jewish firms have a high reputation for the manner in which they treat their workers, and the

93   Hansard, HC (series 5), vol. 396, Education Bill, 2nd Reading, 22 January 1944, 483.

94   'Helpful Information and Guidance for Every Refugee' (German Jewish Aid Committee in conjunction with the Board of Deputies, London, 1939), cited in A. Sherman, *Island Refuge* (London: Elek, 1973), 219.

majority of these firms are staffed very largely by non-Jews.'[95] Such apologetics suggest that Anglo-Jews were insecure as to their status in Britain.[96] Moreover, both the re-emergence of the British Union of Fascists, and the struggle against the British Mandate in Palestine, heightened Anglo-Jewish concerns about antisemitism. Sending children to state rather than denominational schools was perceived as an important way of counteracting this hostile public opinion.

Further light can be shed on Anglo-Jewry's response to the Education Act by contrasting it with the response of the Catholic community. Unlike the Anglicans, who chose controlled status for their schools, the Catholics fought vigorously to preserve their separate school system.[97] These disparate responses are readily comprehensible if we consider that while the Anglican schools faced declining enrolment, 70 per cent of Catholic children attended Catholic schools.[98] The Catholic hierarchy campaigned avidly to ensure its schools' autonomy. In a pastoral letter by the Roman Catholic Bishop of Hexham and Newcastle, an uncompromising position was articulated: 'I therefore lay down this Catholic principle. We shall stand by it and we shall not surrender – we shall have our Catholic schools where our Catholic children shall be educated in a Catholic atmosphere by Catholic teachers approved by a Catholic authority. We cannot, and will not, surrender our schools.'[99]

The Jewish leadership, by contrast, demonstrated no such assertiveness, and indeed, assertiveness was neither the style nor the substance of Anglo-Jewry. Had the Chief Rabbi or a lay leader made similarly bold state-

95 'Questions and Answers: Facts and Figures of Jewish Economic Life and History', pamphlet issued by TAC, London, 1945, 18–19.

96 A Mass Observation Poll conducted between July and December 1946 found that over a third of those polled viewed Jews unfavourably, whereas only a fifth viewed them favourably, see MOA FR: 2463, 'Mass Observation Panel on the Jews', July–December 1946, 1. See also Kushner, *Persistence*, 195.

97 Parsons, *Growth*, 2:168.

98 J. Murphy, *Church, State, and Schools in Britain, 1800–1970* (London: Routledge & Kegan Paul, 1971), 116–17.

99 Cited in Steinberg, 'Anglo-Jewry', 86.

ments, they would undoubtedly have been censured by the community. Anglo-Jewish leaders preferred to emphasize that they appreciated the government's policies. When Butler was invited to address the Board of Deputies in January 1944, its President, Selig Brodetsky, heralded him as having 'made religious education an essential part of both elementary and secondary education, with that complete liberty of thought and mutual toleration, which are characteristic of British life. We Jews consider his educational proposals to be a spur and stimulus to us, as to every denomination in the country'.[100] The Chief Rabbi's response to the White Paper on Educational Reconstruction was similar in tone. In a private letter to Butler, he enthused that 'it is indeed a landmark in English education, and is permeated by a spirit of goodwill and deep understanding of the multiform problems which history has created in this sphere'.[101]

Yet Anglo-Jewry's low profile did not adversely affect its educational interests, because successes won by the Catholics were automatically extended to the other denominations. For instance, in negotiations with the Board of Education, the Catholic leadership secured an agreement whereby schools could be 'transferred' to new sites. Such relocations were necessary if the existing premises could not be altered to meet the new and more stringent building regulations, or because of a shift in population, slum clearance project, or action by a state agency.[102] In such cases the government and denominational authority would share the costs of establishing the relocated school. The Catholic authorities saw this provision as a victory for their educational enterprise, but its adoption also enabled the Jewish community to likewise build new facilities for almost all the schools that had existed before the war.

We see, then, that whereas Anglo-Jewry was nervous about its position within Britain, believing that separate Jewish education would be perceived as breaching a social contract whereby the Jews were permitted their individual equality so long as they did not flaunt their community's

---

100 Address of President of Board of Deputies, 10 January 1944. ACC 3121/E02/032.
101 Chief Rabbi to R. A. Butler 12 September 1943. PRO ED 136 430.
102 Dent, *Education*, 233.

differences, and tolerance was dependent on minimizing particularistic tendencies, the Catholic community was confident of its place in British society. It 'deliberately sought to be ... a distinctive sub-culture with clearly, even aggressively demarcated boundaries between itself and the surrounding non-Catholic culture. ... the differences were not merely noted by others but were proudly owned by Catholics themselves'.[103]

Conference on educational reconstruction

A communal educational conference was called for in January 1943 to coordinate a response to the proposed educational reform legislation.[104] The Chief Rabbi and the JEC were charged with formulating this response, but due to the ongoing controversy over the role of the Reform and Liberal streams in the proposed community-wide educational effort, they issued no public statement either when the Butler proposals were put forward, or when the Education Act passed. The communal conference was postponed until November 1945. By then, the community was in no position to have any impact on the legislation, which had already received Royal Assent. When the conference was finally held, the Reform and Liberal communities were not even invited, and the focus was on how the Orthodox community – principally, the United Synagogue – should adjust to peacetime and reconstruct its educational system.

Prior to the conference, three committees were established for this purpose: one to examine the organization and administration of Jewish education; the second to examine funding for Jewish education; and the third to prepare a curriculum.

The first committee proposed the establishment of two administrative bodies. The Central Council for Jewish Religious Education in Great Britain and Eire would 'co-ordinate, promote and assist religious educational

---

103   Parsons, *Growth*, 1:32.
104   *JC* 15 January 1943, 6.

activities throughout the community'. The London Board of Jewish Religious Education (LBJRE) would be responsible, in the London area, for supplementary education in Jewish facilities and withdrawal classes in state schools. The conference endorsed these proposals, expressing hope that the strictly Orthodox, Schonfeld-led Union of Orthodox Hebrew Congregations might join the new organizations.[105] The rhetoric to the latter effect was likely intended to placate the Chief Rabbi, who sought to inculcate a more vigorous Orthodoxy. This goal remained beyond the Chief Rabbi's grasp, much to the satisfaction of most lay leaders of the United Synagogue. However, the smaller Federation of Synagogues and the Spanish and Portuguese communities did join, attesting to the dominance of centrist Orthodoxy, British style.

As to funding, in the past, Jewish education had been funded haphazardly, depending primarily on the generosity of philanthropists and charities. Over time, leading figures such as Brodetsky and Waley-Cohen had called for a system of communal taxation to support Jewish supplementary education. The *Jewish Chronicle* had declared:

> To its eternal shame, British Jewry has for years shrunk from adequate expenditure on Jewish religious education, while. ... no demands by a multitude of philanthropic institutions have been too great. ... But when it has come to saving the complete destruction of Jewish religious faith in Britain by providing proper Jewish education, it has been a very different story. ... Jewish education has been not the supreme, all important, and best-loved Jewish cause it should be, but the Cinderella amid the ashes in the communal economy.[106]

A gathering of communal educationists had agreed to this as early as 1942, and the United Synagogue had determined that a 33 per cent 'voluntary' tax was to be added to membership fees for this purpose.[107] But only after the communal conference was the machinery to execute this agreement put in place.

---

105 Communal Conference on the Reconstruction of Jewish Education in Great Britain: Report of Proceedings, London, 1946, 4–10. ACC 2805/6/1/38.
106 *JC* 23 April 1943, 8.
107 Minutes, JEC 7 May 1945. ACC 2805/65 E1197; and see Newman, *United Synagogue*, 191.

The curriculum commission was composed of the Chief Rabbi and Nathan Morris. The Chief Rabbi's failing health prevented him from intensive involvement in the work or even attending the conference. It was Morris who prepared and presented the proposed curricula, covering Jewish education at every level, from nursery school through teacher training. The discussion that followed was one of the rare occasions when a communal forum examined the substance, if not the goals, of its educational programs. True, there had been a weekend seminar on the curriculum question sponsored by the JEC's youth department, and an interesting dialogue in the pages of the JEC's journal, but a public debate was rare indeed.[108]

Analysis of the debate sheds much light on the parameters of the Anglo-Jewish self-understanding. Morris's proposed syllabuses were traditional, concentrating on the Pentateuch (*Chumash*), Haftorahs (sections from the Prophets), *Siddur* (prayer-book) and Jewish law. Morris recommended that spoken Hebrew and Hebrew literature be taught to the senior classes. Morris's innovations were modest – the ZF had proposed a greater focus on modern Hebrew and developments in Palestine – but nonetheless aroused opposition from conference delegates, particularly those who feared religion would be supplanted by national/ethnic identity. Dayan Grunfeld, the Chief Rabbi's deputy, expressed opposition to the Hebrew literature component, preferring to focus solely on the traditional subjects, particularly the laws governing religious obligations. Dr M. Friedlander, a delegate from Glasgow, appealed to the Zionist delegates to 're-introduce Judaism into our lives'. Other views were expressed: some delegates campaigned for a more explicitly-Zionist syllabus, and, in the absence of Reform and Liberal representation, Nettie Adler argued for a syllabus rooted in Judaic ethics.[109] Not surprisingly, however, when put

---

108   See *JC* 21 January 1944, 6, and 'Communal Conference', n 105 above, 32. The debate, entitled 'What Shall We Teach?', featured statements by, among others, Brodetsky, Waley-Cohen, and Dayan Abramsky; it appeared in JEC report, 'Jewish Education Today', 64–79.

109   Nettie Adler, daughter of the former Chief Rabbi, had represented central Hackney on the LCC (1910–25), and served as a Justice of the Peace, a member of the governing body of Hackney Downs School, chair of Dalston County Secondary School, chair of the Anglo-Jewish Association.

to a vote, the proposed syllabus was adopted nem. con., indicating that Anglo-Jewry's self-understanding, as formalized in the educational context, remained firmly rooted in religion.

Almost a year earlier, at a gathering of Anglo-Jewry's young leadership, a different self-understanding had been championed. At the weekend 'Educational Reconstruction' seminar organized by the JEC's youth department, most participants voiced criticism of Anglo-Jewish education's religious focus, deeming it dated, and favouring a more Zionist orientation, which was touted as more meaningful and relevant to pupils' lives, and less abstract. On the other hand, some claimed that 'the Zionists' had commandeered the conference proceedings.[110] Such accusations reflected communal resentment of ongoing Zionist efforts to take over Jewish organizations.[111] In their defence, Joyce Kadish, of the Federation of Zionist Youth, declared:

> The eager participation of Zionist youth showed their very deep concern and interest in Jewish education. ... Mr Schonfeld cannot grasp that we young Zionists have an active form of Judaism, a Judaism that is not only our religion, but our life, and our Zionism is synonymous with our Judaism.[112]

Yet the reference to Schonfeld is an irony. For his strictly Orthodox community, which was growing as a result of immigration from Central Europe, the perfunctory instruction in the precepts and texts of Jewish religion favoured by most of Anglo-Jewry as the appropriate form of religious education was by no means adequate. They insisted on day-school education for their children, maintaining their own school system. The 1944 debate over the desirable curriculum for Anglo-Jewish education foreshadows the conflicts that would, in the coming years, beset the community's core educational institutions, such as the United Synagogue and LBJRE. These staunchly traditional and somewhat apologetic bodies were subjected to pressure from the religious left (the Reform and Liberal movements), the religious right (the strictly and ultra Orthodox sectors), and the Zionists.

---

110 *JC* 21 January 1944, 6, 15.
111 See G. Shimoni, 'Selig Brodetsky and the Ascendancy of Zionism in Anglo-Jewry', *Jewish Journal of Sociology* 22 (1980), 125–61.
112 *JC* 28 January 1944, 14.

To fully understand the dynamics of Anglo-Jewish education, it does not suffice to understand the terrain from the perspective of the education providers, and it is also necessary to see it from the parental perspective. This in turn calls for an understanding of post-war Jewish socioeconomic mobility.

Jewish socioeconomic mobility

Anglo-Jews were rapidly moving into the British middle class, though a working class element remained, especially in the London borough of Hackney. There was significant migration from London's inner districts to suburbia, a pattern that was replicated in the provinces.[113]

In 1965, the United Synagogue established a committee to examine the changing geographic distribution of its membership and study the policy and planning implications. The committee's findings detailed what was by then common knowledge: Jews were migrating from the three major centres of London Jewry (1) the North and North East: Hackney, Stoke Newington, Dalston, and South Tottenham; (2) the North West: Brondesbury, Dollis Hill, Cricklewood and Willesden; and (3) the East: East and West Ham – to five new centres of Jewish population. These were (1) North West London: Hendon, Finchley and Hampstead Garden Suburb; (2) Edgware, Stanmore and Mill Hill; (3) Kenton and Wembley; (4) Cockfosters, North Finchley and Brent; (5) Ilford and Wanstead.[114] The data depicted a dramatic decline in synagogue membership in the 'old' areas. For example, between 1960 and 1967, there was a 20 per cent decline in Dalston; a 24 per cent decline at the Brondesbury Synagogue, Willesden; and a 30 per cent decline in Stoke Newington. A comparison of the 1955 enrolment figures

---

113   E. Krausz, 'The Economic and Social Structure of Anglo-Jewry', in Gould and Esh, *Jewish Life*, 31–3; Pollins, *Economic History*, 210.
114   Minutes, 'Movement of Jewish Population' Standing Committee meeting 13 January 1966; First Report of Standing Committee. ACC 2712/1/136.

for LBJRE classes with those for 1962 further attests to these trends. The centres in the East End (Commercial Road, Brick Lane and Redman's Road) and North London (Clapton, Stamford Hill and Stoke Newington) recorded lower numbers than did the newer centres such as Cockfosters, Edgware, Hampstead Garden Suburb, Wembley, and Ilford.[115]

The movement to the suburbs had been achieved primarily through changes in Anglo-Jewry's occupational structure. In a 1962–3 study of Edgware Jewry, Krausz found that Jews were mainly in the professional, managerial, skilled, and self-employed sectors. Krausz found that two-thirds of his sample were 'working on their own account', whereas in the general population, the percentage was 7.4. The survey also documented a 'tremendous increase' in the percentage of Jews working in the professions.[116] These findings were corroborated by later surveys, and studies carried out by the Board of Deputies Research Unit confirmed that these trends had not been temporary, or limited to London.[117]

Krausz suggested that the academic ambitions of Jewish parents for their children 'must be regarded as an important factor' in the upward mobility of the community when compared with its non-Jewish neighbours. The great majority of the parents he surveyed stated that they hoped their children would secure a university or college education. And more than a third of their children aged fifteen and over were either attending institutes of further education or preparing to do so, once again, a figure considerably higher than the figure for the population in general.[118]

115 List of Comparative Rolls of Education Classes 1955 and 1960, as supplied to 'Movement of the Jewish Population' Standing Committee. ACC 2712/15/2425C. 1962 figures from LBJRE Annual Report, 1962.

116 E. Krausz, 'A Sociological Field Study of Jewish Suburban Life in Edgware 1962–63 with special reference to Minority Identification', PhD thesis, University of London, 1965, 93, 103.

117 Cesarani, *Jewish Chronicle*, 213; B. Kosmin et al., *Steel City Jews* (London: Board of Deputies, 1976); B. Kosmin and N. Grizzard, *Jews in an Inner London Borough* (London: Board of Deputies, 1975); B. Kosmin et al., *The Social Demography of Redbridge Jewry* (London: Board of Deputies, 1979).

118 See E. Krausz, 'The Edgware Survey: Occupation and Social Class', *Jewish Journal of Sociology* 11 (1969), 86–8; S. J. Prais and M. Schmool, 'The Social Class Structure of Anglo-Jewry 1961', *Jewish Journal of Sociology* 17 (1975), 11.

The Edgware survey attests to the middle-class nature of Anglo-Jewry. For example, 95 per cent of Jews were homeowners, well above both the national and local averages of 65 per cent.[119] Jews also had higher rates of major appliance and automobile ownership.[120] Though increasing affluence was evident in British society as a whole, Jewish consumption was well above the national average.

The *Jewish Chronicle* recognized the increasingly middle-class character of its readership, and adapted its content accordingly. In July–August of 1964, it ran a series of articles on the new Jewish communities of Golders Green, Hendon, Edgware, Kenton, Harrow, Kingsbury, Ilford and Hampstead Garden Suburb, dubbing the latter 'the New Jerusalem'. The Suburb, as its inhabitants affectionately called it, projected an image of a serene and wealthy society where good schools, garden fetes, and golf clubs were key features of the ambience. In his portrayal of the new community, the reporter noted that some Jewish families 'had gone there to escape the ghetto, to enjoy England as Englishmen enjoy her, but hardly were their lawns laid and their bushes planted than they looked over their hedges and behold, the ghetto had followed them'. The New Jerusalem was not only an affluent community, whose denizens owned large houses, even mansions, with two cars in the garage and domestic help, but also a moderately Orthodox community, by association if not by practice. 'On Shabbat morning it is like Jerusalem, with streets alive with people returning from *shool*, and clustered in small groups at every corner ... the traffic continues for a few hours as people move from Kiddush to Kiddush ... [followed by] uninterrupted sleep in the afternoon'.[121] Yet affluence did not necessarily bring acceptance. In 1960, for instance, the *Jewish Chronicle* investigated allegations of discrimination against Jews in suburban golf clubs, concluding 'beyond any doubt' that this discrimination was 'widespread'.[122]

119   E. Krausz, 'The Edgware Survey; Demographic Results', *Jewish Journal of Sociology* 10 (1968), 86.

120   *JC* 6 and 13 March 1959; A. Marwick, *British Society Since 1945* (London: Penguin, 1996), 117–18.

121   *JC* 31 July 1964, 9.

122   *JC* 8 April 1960, 7.

Another manifestation of Anglo-Jewry's middle-class status was the shift in allegiance from the Labour Party to the Conservatives. In the 1950s, Jewish voters were found in increasing numbers in many of the outer London constituencies created by the 1944 and 1948 Redistribution Acts, which became either safe Conservative seats or seats in which the Conservatives had an even chance of winning.[123] On the basis of class origin – the key determinant of British voting behaviour at this time – these Jews would have been expected to support Labour, but upward social mobility had weakened that connection. In Hendon South, for example, where Bernard Homa, an important Jewish communal leader, was the Labour party candidate in the 1951 and 1955 elections, the Conservatives nonetheless won both times. Similarly, a 1964 survey of 130 Jewish electors in Finchley found that two-fifths voted Conservative, two-fifths Liberal, and just one-fifth Labour: the newly middle-class Jews were shifting their allegiance.[124]

There were some in the community who disdained the new affluence as vulgar materialism. The most outspoken 'angry young men' of Anglo-Jewry were the novelist and football journalist Brian Glanville, playwrights Peter Shaffer and Arnold Wesker, the poet Danny Abse, and writers Wolf Mankowitz and Bernard Kops. Glanville's novel, *The Bankrupts*, was critical of the nouveau-riche mentality and alleged spiritual emptiness of suburban Anglo-Jewry.[125] In a series of interviews in the *Jewish Chronicle*, these intellectuals expressed no fondness for Anglo-Jewry. Mankowitz maintained that despite living in Hampstead, he knew 'almost nothing about what's going on in the community. Its concept of religion is not mine, its social life is of no interest to me', and Shaffer remarked, 'I'm sick and tired of Yidishkeit; it's, to me, the most boring thing in the world'.[126]

123 Alderman, *Jewish Community*, 137–9.
124 Ibid.
125 B. Glanville, *The Bankrupts* (London: Secker and Warburg, 1958).
126 *JC* 19 December 1958, 19; *JC* 26 December 1958, 13.

As Krausz and others have observed, Jewish parental ambitions were significant factors in Anglo-Jewry's rapid entry into the middle class.[127] Much energy was expended in getting children into grammar schools so as to facilitate subsequent scholastic achievement that would propel them into the professional and managerial classes. But grammar school was not the only upward path: many Jews who attended technical and secondary modern schools also prospered. These children, some of whom left school at the statutory school-leaving age and had no further formal education, succeeded in business; a few, such as Jack (John) Cohen (Tesco) and Isaac Wolfson (Great Universal Stores), who were later knighted by the Queen, became household names as giants in industry or real estate. But most Jewish parents preferred a grammar school education for their children.

Parental preference for grammar schools

Entrance to grammar schools was based on a highly competitive series of tests, which children sat during their last year at primary school. Commonly known as the 11 plus, the multi-part examination encompassed tests, teachers' assessments, and interviews. The tests usually covered verbal and mathematical reasoning, English, essay writing, and special skills. Once tabulated, the results placed pupils in the various secondary schools of the Local Education Authority (LEA), depending on availability. Given the competitive nature of the exams, most parents believed that a grammar school place was the reward for successful completion of the 11 plus. Although the number of grammar school places varied from one LEA to another – in Bootle about 12 percent of thirteen-year-old pupils attended grammar schools in 1967, whereas in Merthyr Tydfil the corresponding figure was about 40 percent – the overall average was around 20 per cent of high school pupils.[128]

---

127   See, e.g., S. Waterman and B. Kosmin, *British Jewry in the Eighties* (London: Board of Deputies, 1986), 44.
128   R. Davis, *The Grammar School* (Harmondsworth: Penguin, 1967), 11–12.

Grammar school pupils were encouraged to do well scholastically, stay in school past the school-leaving age, and go on to university, ideally to Oxford or Cambridge. Most pursued 'O' and 'A' level examinations. The grammar school curriculum focused on the humanities and sciences. Almost all grammar schools taught Latin, being committed to the classics. The grammar schools offered an array of extra-curricular activities, which typically included a debating society, a music society, an art club, a history and geography society, a chess club, and so on; these were usually organized by the pupils themselves. Sports were also an important activity, and often took place after school hours; the school teams frequently had matches on Saturdays. Pupils who took advantage of what these schools had to offer generally secured university entrance and employment in middle-class occupations.

Despite the meritocratic appearance of the 11 plus examinations, entry into grammar schools was skewed in favour of middle-class children, who had a far greater chance of success, and secured grammar school places in larger numbers, than children from working-class backgrounds.[129] Yet working-class children did enter the grammar schools, facilitating their upward social mobility. Often, those who gained entry to a grammar school and thrived there were from the upper strata of the working class, and had highly supportive parents. One study found that such pupils came

> from small families and lived in favourable, socially mixed districts. Furthermore
> ... either one or both the parents were strongly supporting the child. Many of these
> parents were both aspiring yet deferential – and it is perhaps not surprising to find
> these children to be educationally ambitious and also highly accommodating to the
> new worlds they meet. ... Most accepted the new school with its different values and
> became some of its most hard working ... members. In turn they became prefects
> and leaders.[130]

129 E.g., a 1952 survey in Middlesborough and South-West Hertfordshire showed that
     although manual workers made up, respectively, 85 and 65 per cent of the population,
     their children secured fewer than half of the grammar school places, see P. Gordon,
     Selection for Secondary Education (London: Routledge, 1980), 227.
130 B. Jackson and D. Marsden, *Education and the Working Class* (London: Routledge
     & Kegan Paul, 1962), 171.

Though this is a description of working-class youths from the industrial town of Huddersfield, it is equally apt of many Jewish children in the northern suburbs of London, many of whom were from the upper working class. These children were encouraged by their parents to achieve academic success. Communal institutions congratulated scholarly achievements: the *Jewish Chronicle*, for example, ran a regular column announcing the entrance of Jewish pupils into universities and successes at Law Society examinations. While East End Jewish families had generally been large, small families – another trait of working-class families whose children completed grammar school – were more typical after World War II, reflecting willingness, even eagerness, to adapt to the values of the wider environment.[131]

If working-class Jewish parents sought out grammar schools for their children as a path to professional occupations and the middle class, those who had already made their way into the middle class saw these schools as a means of furthering social mobility. Having achieved financial security, these parents looked to the 'public' and direct-grant schools as a means of advancing their children's opportunities. The latter were fee-paying grammar schools controlled by an independent body. They received partial funding from the state in return for which at least a quarter of the school places were reserved for children sponsored by the LEA, whose places were free. These schools' excellent academic results made them popular among Jewish parents, especially in North West London, and the Jewish intake was disproportionately high. Particularly popular were, for girls, Henrietta Barnett, South Hampstead, and Camden, and for the boys, Latymer.

Some parents became obsessive about their children's 11 plus success, paying considerable sums for private tutoring, and perceiving failure as a family disaster. In 1958, an article by the *Jewish Chronicle*'s 'women's page' correspondent drew attention to this phenomenon. 'Why do so many parents work up to what amounts to an anxiety neurosis about their children? ... Either they seek out some pukka educational establishment famed for its church tradition and register little Charles there soon after his *Brit Milah*, or they push young Chaim into kindergarten at the age of three to make him a sure winner in the eleven plus race'. Judging from the

---

131   S. J. Prais and M. Schmool, 'The Size and Structure of the Anglo-Jewish Population 1960–1965', *Jewish Journal of Sociology* 10 (1968), 5–34.

letters received in response, her plea that parents desist from pushing their children won little support.[132] She returned to the same theme later that year, suggesting that for many parents, getting their children into private or direct-grant schools had become 'a kind of fetish', and that parents felt an added sense of glory if their children secured places in private schools with a quota system.[133]

Formal statistics on the number of Jewish pupils attending grammar schools are unavailable. Such inquiries were unacceptable both to the school authorities, and to the Jewish organizations, which feared a register of this sort might be misused. However, data can be gleaned from the lists of children registered in LBJRE withdrawal classes and the Kosher Meals Service run by the LBJRE and the United Synagogue, from articles in the press, and from those who taught at, attended, or sent their children to grammar schools during this period. Thus, though the exact numbers are unavailable, a reliable picture can be drawn.

Between 1955 and 1962, the LBJRE ran withdrawal classes for eleven London secondary schools: five secondary modern, one comprehensive, and five grammar schools. Given the demographic concentration of London Jewry at this time, it is not surprising that these classes were located in the city's northern and eastern districts. The LBJRE was slow to respond to migration, and only after registration declined in one locale were classes opened in another. Thus, despite increasing numbers of Jewish pupils, there were no classes at the Hendon County School or Christ's College Grammar School.[134] It should be noted that in some cases, Jewish staff members were relied on to organize withdrawal activities in these schools, without the LBJRE's formal involvement. Table 1 shows enrolment figures for LBJRE withdrawal classes.

132   M. Drubnow, 'Jewish Parents and the Eleven Plus', *JC* 24 January 1958, 21.

133   'Parents and Higher Education', *JC* 24 October 1958, 25. Several years later, another contributor to the 'women's page' addressed this issue, complaining that Jewish children were made to feel that they had 'failed themselves and brought shame on their families if they did not reach grammar school standard', see 'Grammar or Secondary?' *JC* 6 November 1964, 35.

134   Report of Ways and Means Special Committee of LBJRE, 1966, 8–9. ACC 2712/15/2428C.

Table 1 Enrolment in withdrawal classes at London secondary schools, 1955–62

	1955	1960	1962
Grammar Schools			
Central Foundation	243	270	255
Hackney Downs	288	265	247
Paddington and Maida Vale	64	108	105
St Marylebone's	93	176	194
Skinners	218	240	215
TOTAL	*886*	*1059*	*1016*
Secondary Modern Schools			
Dalston County	103	95	114
Dempsey Street	118	115	58
Robert Montefiore	135	180	287
South Hackney	101	75	64
Upton House	188	176	119
TOTAL	*645*	*641*	*642*
Comprehensive Schools			
John Howard	170	180	186
ALL	*1691*	*1880*	*1844*

Source: LBJRE Annual Reports for 1955, 1960, 1962.

It is clear from these numbers that the percentage of Jewish children attending grammar schools was far higher than the national average of 20 per cent.[135] Moreover, at some schools, for example, the Central Foundation and Hackney Downs grammar schools, Jewish pupils accounted for some

135　E.g., the Davenant Foundation Grammar School and Raines (Stepney) Grammar school had many Jewish pupils but no withdrawal classes; a 1961 article noted that 'about half the boys' at the Davenant school were Jewish, see *JC* 17 November 1961, 12.

50 per cent of the intake, as they had from the end of the 1930s.[136] These schools had impressive academic results, and many of their graduates went on to university. Among the Jewish pupils who attended Hackney Downs were the playwright Harold Pinter, the historian Geoffrey Alderman, and Sir Cyril Domb, professor of physics at Bar-Ilan University.

In suburban areas, the pattern was similar: Jewish children won a disproportionately high percentage of grammar school places. In a 1956 interview, the headmaster of Hendon County Grammar School asserted that at his school Jewish pupils made up about 40 per cent of the intake.[137] The figure was similar at Christ's College Grammar School, in neighbouring Finchley. In 1961, the Quintin Grammar School, which served St John's Wood and Swiss Cottage, was said to have between 120 and 150 Jewish pupils; at the Copthall Grammar School for Girls, in the borough of Barnet, it was estimated the same year that a third of those enrolled, some 180 pupils, were Jewish.[138] By contrast, the number of Jewish children enrolled at secondary modern schools, which absorbed two-thirds of school pupils nationally, was well below the national average. Alder County Secondary Modern School in East Finchley rarely attracted more than ten Jewish boys, and the same was true of St David's in nearby Hendon. The Kyniston School, scheduled under the 1965 comprehensive reorganization plan to be amalgamated with the aforementioned Quintin Grammar, had a total of between 40 and 50 Jewish boys.[139]

One factor that contributed to the decline in the number of Jews attending secondary modern schools was the re-opening of the Jews' Free School (JFS) in 1958. Increasingly, parents whose children failed to secure a

---

136 See Black, 'Hackney Downs', 55; G. Alderman, *The History of Hackney Downs School* (London: Clove Club, 1972), 79. The *Jewish Chronicle* estimated that Jewish boys made up 40 per cent of the roll at Central Foundation in 1955, see *JC 14* November 1955, 11.

137 Headmaster Potts interviewed by Elsie Janner, chair of the Board of Deputies' Education Committee, September 1956. ACC 3121/E04/0345.

138 Files of the Kosher Meals Service 15 May 1961 and 27 October 1961. ACC 2805/6/1/116.

139 Ibid.

place at the grammar schools chose to enrol them at the JFS.[140] In justify-
ing their preference for sending their children to grammar schools rather
than Jewish day schools, parents generally invoked the principle that Jewish
children should be integrated with non-Jews, and did not admit that their
primary consideration, in choosing a school for their children, was the
desire for upward social mobility. As the alacrity with which they enrolled
their children at the JFS attests, however, the professed desire to encourage
interaction with a cross-section of British society was mainly rhetoric.

As would be expected, rabbis bitterly bemoaned their congregants'
disinterest in day-school education. Rabbi Kopul Rosen, for instance,
complained to the Marylebone Jewish Society that the usual attitude to
Jewish education in England 'resulted in the type of Jewish person that
can best be described as a non-Christian of Jewish parentage. He does
not know why he is Jewish. Fundamentally, he resists his Jewishness'.[141]
Nevertheless, most Anglo-Jews continued to prefer state grammar and
direct-grant schools.

Further evidence of these attitudes can be gleaned from the response
to a 1958 proposal that the community establish a Jewish grammar school
along the lines of the JFS. The idea was that in addition to providing the
best secular education possible, the school would answer the needs of Jewish
parents who sought for their children 'a sound knowledge of Jewish subjects' imparted 'in an atmosphere likely to promote and nourish a healthy
Judaism'. Parents were completely uninterested. The idea resurfaced two
years later, supported by Ben Azai, a *Jewish Chronicle* columnist (Chaim
Bermant), but again, nothing came of the proposal.[142] Ensuring that their
children received a good Jewish education was simply not a priority for

---

140   According to the *Jewish Chronicle*, the JFS received 900 applications for the 360 places
available in September 1959, see *JC* 29 August 1959, 11. Of the inaugural first form,
only one child of 126 met the grammar school standard, see JFS Headmaster's Report
to Board of Governors 4 November 1959. ACC 2805/114. In Manchester, the King
David Secondary School was popularly perceived as a school for those who failed the
11 plus, see S. Gur (Head of Jewish Studies) to Chief Rabbi 16 May 1972. CR C3 3.
141   *JC* 10 April 1959, 5.
142   Dr Moore, Letter to the Editor, 'Need for Jewish Grammar School', *JC* 31 October
1958, 33; Ben-Azai, Letter to the Editor, 'Need for Grammar Schools', 25 November
1960, 32.

Jewish parents, who saw no need to experiment with Jewish grammar schools when the state grammar schools produced satisfactory academic results, facilitating integration into the middle class. They remained loyal to the state schools, and – where finances permitted – the 'public' schools.

Jewish day-school growth

Despite the mainstream consensus that non-denominational education was preferable, there was some expansion of Jewish day-school education during this period (see Table 2).

Table 2 Jewish day-school enrolment in and outside London, 1958–65

	London	Provinces	Total	Primary*	Secondary
Jan 1958	3890	2133	6023	4611	1412
May 1959	4400	2654	7054	5069	1985
April 1961	4770	3052	7822	5404	2418
April 1963	5325	3571	8896	6315	2581
May 1965	5840	4142	9982	7324	2658

*Includes kindergarten.
Source: Adapted from J. Braude, 'Biennial Survey', *JC* 6 August 1965, 12.

In London, this growth occurred for various reasons. First, the growing strictly and fervently Orthodox communities required additional primary schools. Second, the ZF increased its educational activities, opening new primary schools and seeking to establish secondary schools. Third, a modern-Orthodox community that was migrating to the newer suburbs took the initiative to found the Kerem and Yavneh primary schools. Lastly, the LBJRE re-opened the JFS for secondary-age pupils. Table 3 summarizes these developments, which saw the total number of children enrolled at Jewish day schools rise by some 35 per cent or 1,400 places.

Although the number of Jewish secondary schools in London grew from six in 1958 to nine in 1965, this statistic is misleading, as of the four schools opened during this time (one had closed), three had only one class. Two of these were under the auspices of Lubavitch, the other was a JSSM school. In essence, the growth in secondary school places reflects the re-opening of the JFS in Camden Town. Apart from this historic development, the major expansion was in the primary school sphere, where the number of schools rose from thirteen in 1958 to twenty-two in 1965.

Table 3 Enrolment in London-area Jewish primary and secondary day schools, 1958–65

	1958	1965	Affiliation	Comments
*Primary Schools**				
Avigdor N16	273	203	JSSM	
Barclay House, NW11		98	ZFET	
Clapton Jewish, E5		411	ZFET	
Edgware Hasmonean	29	75	JSSM	
Hasmonean Primary, NW11	254	250	JSSM	
Herzlia School, E5	51			Closed
Hillel House, NW10	106	99	ZFET	
Kerem, N2	83	66	Independent	
Bnois Jerusholaim		63	Independent	
Lubavitch House (Boys)		80		
Lubavitch House (Girls)		96		
Qeter Hatorah		51		
Menorah, NW11	221	263	Independent	Associated with JSSM
NW London Jewish, NW6	215	276	YA	State-aided from 1960
North London Talmud Torah		70		
Pardes House, NW3	45	61	YH	
Rosh Pinah, Edgware	81	184	ZFET	

	1958	1965	Affiliation	Comments
Solomon Wolfson, W11	307	265		State-aided
Stepney Jewish, E1	323	264		State-aided
Talmud Torah		81		
Walthamstow and Leyton		52		
Yavneh		29	YA	
Yesodey Hatorah (Boys)	347	131	YH	
Yesodey Hatorah (Girls)		204	YH	
Total primary enrolment	*2,335*	*3,372*		
Secondary Schools				
Amhurst Park, Secondary		36		
Avigdor Secondary Grammar N16	172		JSSM	Lost state-aided status in 1960
Hasmonean Grammar (Boys) NW4	330	415	JSSM	State-aided from 1957
Hasmonean Grammar (Girls) NW4	250	220	JSSM	
Jews' Free School		506	LBJRE	State-aided; associated with ZFET from 1962
Lubavitch House (Boys)		23		
Lubavitch House (Girls)		14		
NW London Grammar NW6	35			
Yavneh Grammar		88	YA	
Yesodey Hatorah (Boys) N16	265	104	YH	
Yesodey Hatorah (Girls)		121	YH	
Total secondary enrolment	*1,052*	*1,527*		
Total enrolment	*3,387*	*4,899*		

*Includes kindergarten
YA Yavneh Association (religious Zionist); YH Yesodey Hatorah
Source: J. Braude, 'Numbers at Jewish Day Schools', *JC* 24 January 1958, 17 and
'Biennial Survey', *JC* 6 August 1965, 12.

Note the dramatic rise in haredi (ultra-Orthodox) schools. Haredi communities hardly existed in London before the arrival of a substantial haredi population from Hungary following the failed revolution in 1956. The haredi sects saw secular education as incompatible with perpetuation of their way of life, and thus objected to the state school system, preferring to train their children in traditional Torah-intensive institutions.

But how are we to explain the growing interest in Jewish primary school education among the non-haredi population, given that communal leaders and scholars detected no evidence of a religious or cultural revival, and on the contrary, characterized the community as dominated by disinterest in Jewish life?[143] An explanation of this seeming paradox can, however, be found. Parents seem to have been concerned about the increasing numbers of new immigrants who were attending state schools. Commonwealth immigration to Britain had increased significantly in the 1950s. By the late 1950s some 20,000 immigrants were entering annually; the number rose to 58,100 in 1960 and doubled to 115,150 in 1961.[144] Most of the new arrivals came from the West Indies, India, and Pakistan. As had been the case with most earlier waves of immigrants, including the Jews, the new immigrants settled in the poorer neighbourhoods of the major cities, especially London, Birmingham, Leicester, and Bradford.

In neighbourhoods such as Clapton in North London, changing demographics were a key factor motivating Jewish parents to send their children to the local ZF school. Bermant noted that 'there is a sizeable coloured population in the area, and this tends to encourage families to take their children out of the state schools and into the private ones.'[145] Indeed, the phenomenon was general and not limited to Jewish parents: new immigrants and their children were widely perceived as having a detrimental effect on the educational standards of the state schools.[146] In October 1963,

---

143   See Norman Cohen, 'Trends in Anglo-Jewish Religious Life', in Gould and Esh, *Jewish Life*, 41–66, and Esh's comments, 88–9.

144   S. Patterson, *Immigration and Race Relations* (London: OUP, 199), 3.

145   C. Bermant, *Troubled Eden* (London: Vallentine Mitchell, 1969), 133.

146   A 1966 survey found that almost a third of those polled complained that immigrants were creating difficulties for the schools, see R. Schaefer, 'The Dynamics of British Racial Prejudice', *Patterns of Prejudice* 8 (1974), 3.

for instance, parents in London's Southall district demanded that schools be segregated, but this was opposed by the Minister of Education, who instead laid down 'the general principle of dispersal, with a maximum quota of one third per school'.[147]

The Jews, forgetting their none-too-distant immigrant roots, shared these sentiments, growing increasingly uneasy about the local secondary modern schools, fearing poorer academic achievements due to their immigrant intake. As confidence in the local council schools declined, and the academic reputation of the ZF schools improved, parents grew more interested in the ZF schools. At an Anglo-Jewish Association meeting under the auspices of the Federation of Women Zionists, where the issue of immigration was discussed, one panellist argued that many parents chose the ZF schools 'for snobbish reasons', refusing to send their children to local primary or secondary modern schools.[148] This opinion was also expressed in *Living Judaism*, the journal of Reform Judaism, in an interview with the headmistress of the Clapton Jewish Primary School. It was suggested that the reason for the school's popularity – the school had seen a striking rise in the number of pupils, from 51 in 1958, when it opened, to 403 in 1965 – was that many parents 'do not want their children to mix with the largely coloured population in local schools'.[149] Parents were not deterred by the fact that the ZF schools charged fees.

The Clapton school's success was not unique, but part of a trend: when such schools were established in working-class neighbourhoods, they had a greater chance of attracting pupils than in the middle-class districts, where Jews continued to attend the local primary schools, e.g. the Hampstead Garden Suburb (NW11) and Wessex Gardens (NW11) schools, in large numbers. The working-class neighbourhoods, from which Jews were migrating, were a fertile environment, albeit only temporarily, for the

---

147 Patterson, *Immigration*, 35.

148 *JC* 2 February 1962, 9; 9 February 1962, 36. Though the chairman of the ZFET, Dr I. Fox, responded to many of the panellists' concerns about the ZF schools, he did not address the question of snobbery, invoking instead the dramatic shift in the community's attitude to Zionism, which had gone from being 'beyond the pale' to being an accepted expression of Jewish identity.

149 'The editor interviews Mrs Stiftel-Lipman', *Living Judaism*, Winter 1968/69, 85.

expansion of day-school education. In the long run these schools would face depleted Jewish populations, but until the mid-1960s, the influx of immigrants, the increasingly bourgeois mentality of the Jewish population, and the academic successes of the Jewish day schools led to a departure of Jewish children from the local state primary schools.

The ZF's success in Clapton was repeated more modestly in the lower-middle-class district of Edgware, where the Rosh Pinah School doubled its enrolment during the same period. The Selig Brodetsky School in Leeds, for which the Zionists assumed responsibility in 1956, saw a dramatic rise in pupil enrolment, from under 50 pupils to over 200.

The struggle for 'state-aided' status

Of the new Jewish day schools opened in London between 1958 and 1965, only the JFS had been established as state-aided, thereby enjoying substantial government funding. The other schools were supported by private philanthropy, and thus constantly engaged in efforts to recruit wealthy sponsors. Given their limited means, it was incumbent on the schools to charge fees, which naturally affected their ability to attract pupils. Parental willingness to pay fees varied. Obviously, those who sought curricular independence from the state school system – the Lubavitch, Yesodey Hatorah, and other haredi groups – accepted that this rendered their schools ineligible for funds from the national exchequer. The other school movements, from right-wing modern Orthodoxy to the ZF schools, would have been delighted to secure state funding and thus lighten the burden of building and operating expenses. Moreover, state support was perceived as ensuring satisfactory educational standards.

The denominational authorities, in particular the Anglican and Roman Catholic churches, had been lobbying the Conservative governments of Anthony Eden and Harold Macmillan to increase grants to aided schools. In the 1959 Education Act, the Minister of Education acceded to these requests, raising the building and maintenance subsidy from 50 to 75 per cent. This was an important victory for the denominations and a great help in alleviating their schools' chronic financial distress. It motivated schools that had not achieved aided status to redouble their efforts to meet the necessary building requirements and academic standards.

Between 1957 and 1965, after intensive efforts at improving their facilities, and significant capital outlay, several Jewish schools were awarded state-aided status. In 1960, eight years after it had submitted an application for official recognition as a voluntary state-aided school, the North West London Jewish Primary School was granted this status. Run by the Yavneh Association, which was committed to both an 'unequivocal Orthodox Judaism' and 'a standard of secular education comparable to the general school system',[150] it became the first Jewish primary school in London since the 1944 Education Act to win this status. Its sponsors had invested over £75,000 in improving the school's premises, much of these funds having been obtained from the Jewish Material Claims Conference reparations fund.[151] In 1957, Schonfeld's flagship, the Hasmonean Grammar School for Boys had, after extended negotiations, been granted voluntary-aided status.[152] Here too, the reparations fund had provided funding for the necessary renovations. The London Jewish Educational Foundation, which had been established, as we will see in the next chapter, to re-open the JFS and distribute monies from the old trust funds, also made a major contribution to the school, a historical irony. The JSSM-affiliated Avigdor Primary School won state-aided status in 1963, also after major improvements.

Despite these advances, the various Jewish organizations were frequently disappointed by what they perceived as the strictness with which the law concerning the granting of state-aided status was applied. Section

---

150 'Constitution of North West London Day School' [undated]. MS 183 395/1. The North West London day schools were originally very close to the JSSM, but following serious financial difficulties, moved closer to the religious Zionist movement, joining the Yavneh Association.

151 *JC* 6 April 1956, 10; 26 September 1958, 11; 16 January 1959, 1. M. Ebert, Ministry of Education to N. Rubin (informing him of the decision to begin public funding of the school immediately) 21 January 1960. ACC 2805/114.

152 MS 183 757/1.

76 of the 1944 Education Act stipulated that 'as far as is compatible with the provision of efficient instruction and training and the avoidance of unreasonable public expenditure, pupils are to be educated in accordance with the wishes of their parents'. Denominational groups naturally focused on the end of this clause, reminding the authorities that they were legally bound to provide denominational schooling for those parents who requested it. For their part, the authorities invoked the beginning of the clause, which obliged them to avoid unnecessary expenditure. The local education authorities (LEAs) demanded of denominational organizations that they prove not only that the proposed school met a genuine denominational demand, but also that there was an overall shortage of school places. As early as 1953, in reply to a letter from Rabbi Schonfeld complaining of these 'harsh' criteria as they applied to his Hasmonean Grammar School for Boys, the Minister of Education wrote:

> If and when additional grammar school places are needed in a district where there is a substantial Jewish population, there is no reason why the JSSM should not urge the Authority to consider a Jewish grammar school instead of another County Grammar School. The response to such a proposal would be influenced by the evidence provided of the support for the proposal among the Jewish community in the area which the school would serve. ... The brute facts of the situation, however, and of the country's present economic position, leave me with no alternative.[153]

In other words, given the economic situation and the lack of a need for extra grammar school places, extending state-aided status to Schonfeld's school was unwarranted, despite the denominational demand.

If the opening of a state-aided denominational school depended on the overall need for school places, this was beyond the control of the Jewish authorities. Granted, an increase in the birth rate would generate a shortage in school places, creating an opening for a new aided Jewish day school, and indeed, in the mid-1950s, as a result of the post-war baby-boom, the Manchester and Liverpool city councils both decided, as part of their school building programmes, to include construction of a Jewish day school.

153   Florence Horsburgh, Ministry of Education to Rabbi Schonfeld 7 January 1953. ACC 2805/6/1/38.

However, when the birth rate declined, requests for the expansion of state-aided schools were generally rejected. Between 1963 and 1975, only three Jewish day schools received state-aided status in London, and only after the community had built the schools with its own funds.[154]

Once achieved, state-aided status was not retained indefinitely. Criteria were established to ensure that the school's standards were maintained, and from time to time a visitation was made by Her Majesty's Inspectors. Subsequently, a report would be published and distributed to the school concerned and the national and local authorities. A negative report could result in annulment of state-aided status. Schools that defined themselves as grammar schools were obliged to ensure that their pupil intake was from the upper range of the mandated ability scale and that the teaching standard enabled these pupils to fulfil their potential. Moreover, to guarantee efficient administration, a school's governing body had to include five LEA appointees, the remaining seven being appointed by the denominational agency. Accountability was further encouraged by the fact that the salaries of the headmaster and teachers of secular subjects were paid by the LEA.

The Crystal affair

In 1954, a series of unfortunate developments that culminated in the Avigdor Grammar School's losing state-aided status was set in motion.[155] After protracted personal differences between Rabbi Schonfeld, chairman of the school's governors, and Mr J. D. Crystal, the headmaster, and the levelling of accusations against the latter – he was accused of humiliating pupils, inflicting corporal punishment on them, and embarrassing teachers in front

---

154   These were the Ilford Jewish (LBJRE, 1964), Menorah (JSSM, 1970) and Rosh Pinah (ZFET, 1968) primary schools.

155   Unless otherwise specified, correspondence and archival material pertaining to the Crystal affair is from ACC 2805/112.

of pupils – the governors decided to terminate Crystal's employment. The LCC, supported by the Ministry of Education, instructed the governors to reverse their decision, as Mr Crystal had been vindicated by the High Court; the governors refused to do so. Indeed, a subsequent appeal by the JSSM was also defeated. Following Rabbi Schonfeld's request that the Chief Rabbi intervene on his behalf, a meeting with the headmaster was arranged at the end of December 1955. Chief Rabbi Brodie suggested that the best course of action, under the circumstances, was for Crystal to resign, but the headmaster insisted on unconditional reinstatement. The Chief Rabbi then advised the JSSM to either return the school to independent status or restore Crystal to his position. Rabbi Schonfeld was warned that if he chose to ignore this advice and continue his public campaign against the headmaster, the Chief Rabbi would resign his position as Honorary President of the JSSM. Schonfeld, appreciating the damage that would be done to his school movement by this action, obliged the Chief Rabbi and reinstated the headmaster. However, the damage to his relations with the national and local authorities had already been done.

A senior civil servant had already notified Rabbi Schonfeld that, given what had transpired, the Minister of Education would have to ascertain that the school was well run. Shortly thereafter the school received a visitation from inspectors, who confirmed parental complaints about the school's poor academic level.[156] The inspectors' report listed serious deficiencies, alleging that the school was not maintaining a grammar school standard as to either its pupil intake or its teaching level. Very few children continued their studies beyond the age of seventeen; indeed, the inspectors discovered that the sixth form, 'hardly exists'. The report expressed serious concern about the low rate of pupil retention: of 65 pupils who began the 1954 academic year, only 45 remained two years later. Teacher turnover was also a problem. Other criticisms included insufficient availability of text-

---

156   The parents' chief complaint concerned academic standards, which they believed were upheld by the JSSM headmaster, but challenged by the principal, who insisted on giving precedence to Jewish studies; see 'Letter to the Editor from Avigdor School Parent's Group', *JC* 4 March 1955, 29.

books, the tiny room for art class, the limited number of hours allocated to French, history, and science, and the school's 'extremely' poor showing on 'O' level examinations. The report concluded by stating that the school 'was at a disquietingly low ebb'.[157]

Further inspections in 1957 and 1958 demonstrated no change in the school's academic performance, and the LCC's Education Committee determined that 'the school has failed educationally and the Council is no longer justified in continuing to maintain it from public funds'.[158] Despite proposals from Schonfeld that the facility be transformed into a girls' school, and an appeal for public sympathy through the press, the school lost its state-aided status in September 1960. In response to a question put to him in the House of Commons, the Minister of Education commented that it was 'harmful for the cause of denominational schools to continue the expenditure of public money on one which has proved a failure'.[159]

The sorry state of the Avigdor Grammar School brought to light by the Crystal affair was not simply the outcome of a personal dispute or poor administrative skills. Rather, it reflected the fact that observant families in the area now had additional options. For those parents who believed that the JSSM ratio of 75 per cent general to 25 per cent religious studies was inadequate, the independent Yesodey Hatorah Grammar School, where Jewish studies comprised 50 per cent of the curriculum, was an attractive alternative. On the other hand, for parents who preferred a more substantial general studies curriculum – and judging from the parental complaints, there seem to have been quite a few – the newly-opened Woodberry Down Comprehensive School offered another option. The JFS, which reopened as a state-aided school in September 1958, also presented a more appealing educational option than the dispute-ridden Avigdor school. In 1960, the year it lost its aided status, Avigdor Grammar School closed, and its premises were taken over by the Avigdor School's junior division.

157 Ministry of Education Report by Her Majesty's Inspectors (HMI) on Avigdor Secondary School 19, 20, 21 November 1956. MS 183 72/4.
158 ACC 2805/112.
159 Questions and Answers, House of Commons, 24 May 1960.

The Crystal affair constituted abuse of state-aided status. The relationship between state educational authorities and denominational schools that gain state-aided status is transparent by design. Unlike an independent school whose governing authority is answerable mainly to fee-paying parents, a state-supported school must answer to the national and local authorities. It cannot take autonomous decisions on the hiring and firing of the headmaster, or ride roughshod over specifications for teaching standards and pupil intake. The curriculum must meet requirements that limit denominational studies to a maximum of one or two periods per day. Should the denominational authority fail to ensure that the school meets the requirements attendant on state-aided status, its status will be reviewed.

The role of the headmaster in this new configuration is particularly complex. On the one hand, the headmaster receives a salary from the LEA and is expected to meet its specifications, yet on the other, he is answerable to a board of governors dominated by the sponsoring denomination. Indeed, Mr Crystal was not the only headmaster of a Jewish state-aided school to experience a conflict of this sort.[160] These tensions surfaced more frequently in Orthodox schools, where pressure for more intensive Judaic studies created greater potential for conflict with the authorities.

Denominational state-aided schools were constantly on their guard lest they fail to satisfy parental expectations. In the case of Jewish day schools, parental commitment to facilitating their children's academic success, as measured by exam results, was high. Most schools invested considerable energy in publicizing their academic achievements in the Jewish press or through school brochures and magazines. Failure to achieve the expected standards led to protests from parents' associations, but the ultimate sanction was withdrawal of the children and their enrolment in another school.

While the national and local educational authorities were dissatisfied with Schonfeld's treatment of Crystal, and indeed his administration of

---

160   In 1961, the LBJRE's Nathan Rubin wrote to the Chief Rabbi expressing concern that at the North West London primary school, 'another case as experienced in a certain school in London over the loyalties of the headmaster is about to emerge'. Rubin to Chief Rabbi 14 September 1961. ACC 2805/114.

the JSSM, it would be inaccurate to claim that they acted vindictively.[161] Despite everything, the JSSM managed during and after the Crystal affair to extend the number of its aided schools. In the very midst of the crisis, the Middlesex County Council awarded the Hasmonean Grammar School for Boys state-aided status, and three years after the cessation of government funding for the Avigdor Grammar School, its junior division was granted state support. In both cases negotiations between the parties were arduous, with the state demanding a series of guarantees to ensure effective administration and improvements to the school premises, and Schonfeld resisting and failing to respond.[162] For example, the Ministry took the unusual step of asking the Chief Rabbi to nominate three of the Hasmonean Grammar School's denominational governors, to weaken Schonfeld's control. Though the Chief Rabbi refused, he did secure a promise from Rabbi Schonfeld that the school administration would consult with all of the governors more than it had in the past.[163] Schonfeld resented the demands of the educational authorities, but by his mishandling of the Avigdor Grammar School, he brought their pressure upon himself.

---

161 In a letter to the Chief Rabbi, Rabbi Schonfeld complained that the Ministry of Education was out to 'get him' because of the Crystal affair. He promised that the JSSM would 'fight with all our might against such interference'. Schonfeld to Chief Rabbi 22 May 1956.

162 In a letter to the Ministry of Education, the Deputy Chief Education Officer of the Middlesex County Council wrote that 'we have experienced great difficulty over this project. ... On the occasions when meetings have been arranged to discuss building work ... Dr Schonfeld uses these meetings to argue and state what he will and will not do. In these circumstances recently we have preferred to send him information regarding our requirements in letter form'. 25 March 1957. MS 183 757/1. A sense of exasperation pervades the correspondence. Particularly striking are the complaints that Dr Schonfeld does not respond to requests from the MCC to provide information, drawings and other material to help advance the project.

163 R. N. Heaton (Ministry of Education) to Chief Rabbi 1 May 1956; M. Wallach (Office of the Chief Rabbi) to R. N. Heaton 13 July 1956 (both MS 183 248/1). The correspondence concerning the granting of state-aided status to the Hasmonean Grammar School was exceptionally detailed, and this clearly reflects Ministry wariness about the JSSM in light of the Crystal affair. On the promises secured by the Chief Rabbi concerning the future administration of JSSM state-aided schools, see Chief Rabbi to Minister of Education 28 September 1959.

Schonfeld's behaviour during the course of the Crystal affair was severely criticized by the Chief Rabbi and the *Jewish Chronicle*. Early on, the Chief Rabbi had warned that even if Schonfeld won his case in the courts, it would be a 'pyrrhic victory', since

> You will have created a chain of hostility stretching from the Ministry downwards which would seriously affect the future relationship of the Education authority not only to your schools but to all other Jewish day schools, apart from the repercussions on the community as a whole. I am definite, therefore, that the continuance of your present attitude is fraught with great dangers.[164]

Schonfeld's decision, in mid-1959, to publicize his position in *The Times* led to further criticism from the Chief Rabbi, who believed that while the matter was under consideration by the authorities, Schonfeld would have been better advised to await their decision. The *Jewish Chronicle* shared the Chief Rabbi's concern and attacked Schonfeld's stance as 'irresponsible'. Though deeming the decision to rescind the Avigdor Grammar School's state-aided status 'regrettable', the newspaper saw it as a direct consequence of the school governors' 'reckless policies'.[165]

Clearly, the Chief Rabbi believed that Rabbi Schonfeld's conduct would reflect badly on other Jewish organizations. Yet at no point in the saga had the authorities threatened that as a result of Schonfeld's misconduct, Jewish day schools would be in jeopardy. Indeed, the Minister of Education explicitly assured the Chief Rabbi of his continued support for Jewish denominational education.[166] The Chief Rabbi's apprehensiveness is indicative of the pervasive communal mindset of the era: despite Anglo-Jewry's economic, political, and cultural integration, many remained nervous as to their status in Britain.

---

164 Chief Rabbi to Rabbi Schonfeld 11 January 1956.
165 *JC* 17 July 1959, 12.
166 Sir David Eccles to Chief Rabbi 24 May 1960.

Conclusion

At the time of the 1944 Education Act, Anglo-Jewry was struggling to extricate itself from the working class districts of the inner cities, and saw education as its ticket to the middle class. Parents hoped that their children would pass the 11 plus exam and secure a place at a local grammar school, the surest route to scholastic achievement and university entrance. Jewish children attended these selective schools in numbers well above the national average. For those who failed to secure grammar school places, Jewish day schools provided a possible alternative to the secondary modern schools, which were overwhelmingly working class in composition, and offered pupils virtually no chance of proceeding to university.

Most parents ascribed far greater importance to general education than to Jewish education, as attested not only by the small percentage of Jewish children who attended day schools, but also by the ongoing complaints of religious and sometimes even lay leaders about the apathy of Jewish parents. Even when withdrawal classes were introduced, parents failed to take advantage of the opportunity. Many did not want their children to be conspicuous and were averse to having them withdraw from religion classes or collective worship.

In the 1940s and 1950s, Jewish education was almost always supplied privately by neighbourhood synagogues. The model for these classes was the Anglican Sunday School, although Hebrew classes were somewhat more ambitious, generally attempting to compel mid-week attendance as well. Emulation of the Anglicans was based on the assumption that integration into Britain involved minimizing public religious and ethnic differences. The British ethos expected minorities, including the Jews, to adjust to local comportment and values, the implication being that failure to do so might provoke antagonism, and in the case of the Jews, antisemitism. Jews typically internalized these sentiments, and communal defence organizations tended to censure and 're-educate' members of the community whose conduct was deemed to reinforce stereotypes or to be overly conspicuous. This apologetic tendency to downplay particularity so as to avoid eliciting antisemitism was exacerbated by a very real rise in antisemitism as evidenced by the post-war re-emergence of the British Union of Fascists, the spillover of violence in Palestine to some of Britain's provincial cities, and polls indicating that Jews were widely considered 'foreigners'. Under these conditions, most Jewish parents felt it was not advisable to send their children to separate schools.

The strictly and fervently Orthodox were an exception, as they were less interested in social integration into English society, and preferred to maintain high walls around their communities. They founded a number of independent schools, most of them small. But the financial burden of running independent schools induced several, mainly those affiliated with Schonfeld's movement, to apply for state aid. Accepting state aid, by requiring the schools to maintain specific standards and rendering them subject to inspection, compromised their educational autonomy. But on the other hand, aided status not only provided the schools with much needed financial relief, but also served to reassure parents that their children would receive a satisfactory education.

The community's response to the educational reform proposals must be viewed in this context. The communal leadership was aware of parental opposition to Jewish day schools, hence the Chief Rabbi and the JEC concentrated their efforts on aspects of the legislation relating to withdrawal classes in state schools, and did not seek to take advantage of the opportunity to expand the number of voluntary-aided schools.

Another key development vis-à-vis the Anglo-Jewish education system at this time was the waning of the Cousinhood's control over this sphere of communal affairs, and the rise of the Chief Rabbi. As honorary president of the JEC, the Chief Rabbi's status on matters of Jewish education was not dissimilar from that of the Archbishop of Canterbury, who the state authorities saw as the principal address for issues pertaining to Anglican educational concerns. Having successfully thwarted an attempt to include the progressive wings of Judaism in a proposed community-wide organization that would deal with education during the wartime emergency, Chief Rabbi Hertz was not only able to set the syllabus for Hebrew classes, but also the standards for teachers. Not surprisingly, he was more concerned about their religious observance than their pedagogic skills and training.

CHAPTER 2

Ideologies and Jewish Day Schools

This chapter will explore the divergent religious and pedagogic orientations of the various organizations that provided day-school and part-time Jewish education, and the degree to which these disparate ideologies precluded cooperation between the groups.

The Jewish Secondary Schools Movement

Though most of Anglo-Jewry was unfavourably disposed toward Jewish day schools, some strictly Orthodox Jews saw in them the most appropriate instrument for educating future generations in their responsibilities as both Jews and British citizens. In 1953, there were seven primary and five secondary Jewish day schools operating in the London area. Of these, only three were not strictly Orthodox: two large state-aided primary schools (Stepney Jewish and the Solomon Wolfson), and the earliest Zionist day school in Britain, Hillel House School, also a primary school. The remainder were mostly affiliated with the Jewish Secondary School Movement (JSSM).

The JSSM was founded by Rabbi Solomon Schonfeld (1912–84), who had inherited the responsibility for these schools and the Adath Yisroel synagogue in Stoke Newington from his father, Rabbi Victor (Avigdor) Schonfeld, who immigrated from Hungary in 1909. The Adath Yisroel synagogue was established to counter the 'milk and water Orthodoxy' of Chief Rabbis Nathan Marcus Adler (held office 1845–90) and his son Hermann Adler (1891–1911), both of whom were seen as lenient on key religious matters such as *shechita* (ritual slaughter).[1] The Adath Yisroel evolved into a separate community with its own arrangements for solemnizing marriages, effecting divorces, burials, kashruth, and education (initially just supplementary schools, but ultimately a network of secondary day schools, the JSSM).[2]

Solomon Schonfeld was born in London and educated at Highbury County Grammar School. Upon graduation, he worked as an articled solicitor. But when his father died at 49, Schonfeld changed his plans, and instead of practising law returned to the yeshiva in Tirnau, Slovakia, where he had previously spent a year studying. From there, he continued to the Slobodka Yeshiva, where he received rabbinic ordination from eminent Lithuanian rabbis. Before returning to London, he completed doctoral studies at the universities of Vienna and Koeningsberg.

By 1952, Schonfeld was a familiar figure in the Anglo-Jewish community, not only as leader of the Adath Yisroel separatist synagogue, its affiliated synagogue organization, the Union of Orthodox Hebrew Congregations (UOHC), and its JSSM, but also because of his courageous work in bringing refugees to England from Europe both before and after World War II. During the emigration crisis in the late 1930s, when Jews sought to leave Austria and Germany, the Agudas Yisrael organization, which was anti-Zionist, alleged that the communal agencies favoured those whose ultimate destination was Palestine, either from Zionist motives or to prevent exacerbation of 'Britain's "Jewish problem"'.[3] In response to this alleged discrimination, Agudas Yisrael endeavoured to facilitate its members' emigration. Schonfeld was the key activist in Britain. Unlike the established Anglo-Jewish community, which followed formal procedures in applying to the governmental authorities, Schonfeld did whatever he thought necessary, often disregarding protocol. Some claim that hundreds, maybe thousands, were rescued through Schonfeld's activities. One of the

1   Bermant, *Troubled Eden*, 220.
2   Alderman, *Modern*, 146.
3   D. Kranzler and G. Hirschler (eds), *Solomon Schonfeld: His Page in History* (New York: Judaica Press, 1982), 23; the volume's overall presentation of Schonfeld's work is rather hagiographic.

fortunate refugees was Immanuel Jakobovits, who became Chief Rabbi.[4] After the war, Schonfeld resumed his efforts and brought several hundred Holocaust survivors to England, helping to reinforce the Orthodox populations in Stamford Hill and Golders Green.

Schonfeld was deeply influenced by Samson Raphael Hirsch (1808–1888), the founder of neo-Orthodoxy in Germany. Hirsch coined the maxim '*Torah im Derekh Eretz*', the idea that the Jew is to strictly observe Jewish law (*halakha*) while participating fully in civic life. Hirsch's vision of modern Jewish existence was committed to the acquisition of secular knowledge alongside intensive Jewish studies, to enable integration into the economic and civil spheres of society. After Hirsch's death, when the Zionist movement gained steam, his followers made clear that on the Hirschian outlook, religious observance is the primary element in Judaism.

Schonfeld perceived the British national ethos as appreciative of tradition:

> An 'orthodox' outlook upon life has been the hallmark of the English people, of British history and of Commonwealth development in many spheres. In literature, education, church, art and formality there has been a persistent effort to continue in the line already adopted by the people of the Isles. However plebeian, yet not to break with aristocracy; however enterprising, yet still to retain the old methods and principles of dealings; however English, yet to study and learn from the ancient Bible; however modern, yet to feel oneself at one with the framework of old forms in the fields of mental and spiritual activities – that is the true English attitude.[5]

Arguing that the British admiration for tradition reinforced the values to which his movement subscribed, Schonfeld was confident that Britain was a fertile environment for the development of Hirschian Orthodoxy. Yet his thesis that respect for tradition fostered commitment to religious observance was by no means borne out by the religious practice of most

---

4   Jakobovits acknowledged this debt to Schonfeld on a number of occasions, e.g., 'If I am alive today, it is entirely due to the efforts of that man, and the same can be said for countless others'. C. Bermant, *Lord Jakobovits* (London: Weidenfeld and Nicolson, 1990), 19.

5   Schonfeld, *Jewish Religious*, 5.

Britons, for whom membership in the Church of England was expressed chiefly through baptism, marriage, and burial, but not daily life. In this sense, the United Synagogue, and not Schonfeld's group, mirrored the British attitude to religion. Though at this time, some 70 per cent of the Jewish community belonged to United Synagogue congregations, attendance at services was irregular, and ritual observance, even of core precepts such as kashruth, was generally lax. Even the officers of the United Synagogue were far from punctilious in their observance. When a rabbinical court for the whole of London was being planned, it was proposed that the management committee should be composed solely of Sabbath observers. Sir Robert Waley-Cohen, the former president of the United Synagogue, found the clause completely unacceptable, since it would disqualify him and all his colleagues.[6] It was precisely this sort of behaviour that fuelled Schonfeld's critique of mainstream British Orthodoxy.[7]

Needless to say, he wanted nothing to do with the Reform and Liberal elements of Anglo-Jewry. Appealing, as he often did, to the 'shared values' of strict Orthodoxy and British culture, Schonfeld invoked the English propensity to 'play according to the rules of the game', expressed in the idiom 'it's not cricket'. Just as no football player would presume to be so liberal as to use hands and call it football, so Jews must behave according to the rules, and if they dispensed with central religious tenets such as Sabbath-observance, or denied the divinity of the Torah, then they could hardly call it Judaism.[8]

Schonfeld saw the Jewish day school, particularly at the secondary level, as the ideal environment to instil loyalty to the values of intensive Judaism. His hope was that such schools would produce lay and religious leaders desirous of preserving and disseminating strictly Orthodox Judaism.

6   Norman Cohen, 'Trends', 44.
7   E.g., he explained the necessity of a separate synagogue association (the UOHC) as follows: 'A community where *Mechallelai Shabbat* [Sabbath desecrators] and *Ochelai Treifot* [those who eat unkosher meat] can and do preside and "sit in synagogue boxes" is hardly conducive to the preservation of intensive, live Judaism in the present, or future generation'. *JC* 20 August 1954, 11.
8   Schonfeld, *Jewish Religious*, 30.

Though he had much respect for the *cheder*, Schonfeld recognized that this educational framework did not appeal to modern parents, nor could it prepare its pupils for the life in the broader society. He reproached parents who, fearful of Gentile derision and rejection, erected barriers and withdrew from the surrounding society. He attacked this self-induced segregation as a vestige of the ghetto mentality, and called for balancing the past with 'new found freedom'.[9]

On the other hand, Schonfeld attacked those Jews who, having embraced the wider society, avoided being reminded of their past. He saw them as either 'expecting trouble' or 'humbly grateful for fair play'. In their enthusiasm to integrate into new surroundings, such Jews were opposed to anything that was purely Jewish, whether a hospital, club or organization. In particular, he remonstrated, they shunned Jewish day schools, which not only called to mind the past, but would separate their children in the future. Schonfeld argued that whereas in state schools Jewish children were excluded from general prayer assemblies and religious instruction, and absented themselves on Jewish holidays and winter Fridays, in the Jewish day school, being Jewish was natural and a cause for pride. Having experienced and learned to cherish his Judaism within the safe and nurturing atmosphere of the Jewish day school, the child could then venture beyond the ghetto and 'weather the storm'.[10]

As we have seen, most Anglo-Jews saw separate schooling as an unnecessary wall, and Schonfeld's prescription for integration into the surrounding society by way of separate Jewish day schools was popular only in his own strictly Orthodox community. Schonfeld sought to clearly delineate between the Jewish and general spheres of life. Interaction in the spheres of employment and civic duty was to be encouraged, but Schonfeld was frank about his conviction that social interactions with Gentiles should be pleasant but perfunctory. Separate schools were not merely an expression of the desire for intensive Jewish studies, but reflected an unwillingness to foster social integration.

9   Ibid., 144.
10   Ibid., 145–8.

When Schonfeld assumed his father's responsibilities in 1933, the JSSM had a single school, the Avigdor School, whose enrolment reached 300 in 1938.[11] The school was situated in Stamford Hill. By the time of its wartime evacuation to Shefford, Bedfordshire, an increasing percentage of the students were refugees from Nazi Germany.[12] By the mid-1940s, many more places were required, and two single-gender secondary schools, known as the Hasmonean Grammar Schools, were opened in NW London, in line with the migrations of the strictly Orthodox population.[13] By 1950, 180 pupils attended the boys' school, and just over 100 the girls'; three primary schools (Avigdor Primary in North London, Hasmonean Primary in Hendon, and the Menorah school in Golders Green) had also been established.[14] From very modest beginnings, Schonfeld's educational network had become the dominant Anglo-Jewish day-school provider.

The JSSM curriculum reflected the Hirschian synthesis to which Schonfeld subscribed. Knowing that pupils were more alert in the mornings, he mandated that Jewish subjects be taught at that time. These studies were traditional, concentrating on Bible, Mishna, prayers, Jewish observances, laws and customs, festivals and songs. Modern Hebrew and Jewish history were accorded relatively little time. Rather than focusing on the historical experiences of the Jewish people, the Jewish history course emphasized the great rabbinic authorities. Non-Orthodox figures such as Herzl and the philanthropists Barons Edmund de Rothschild and Maurice de Hirsch were mentioned only in passing.

Schonfeld was committed to a high standard of secular education, both because he recognized the inherent value of such studies, and because he knew that parents were particularly concerned about achievements in

11   *Jewish Year Book 1939*, 132.
12   See J. Grunfeld, *Shefford: The Story of a Jewish School Community in Evacuation 1939–45* (London: Soncino, 1980).
13   When Chief Rabbi Hertz opened the first of these, in Golders Green, Schonfeld announced that he hoped it would be 'a first class modern school ... a Jewish Eton, Harrow or St Paul's'. *JC* 13 April 1945, 6.
14   'The Schools Movement', *Jewish Review* 14 April 1950. Schonfeld had originally intended to leave primary education to other bodies, but when none stepped in to fill this role, he had extended the mandate of his JSSM.

this sphere. He frequently reassured them of the academic standing of his schools, but his speeches and articles indicate that he gained greater satisfaction from the success of his students in mastering Jewish texts.

While the substance of the JSSM curriculum reflected firm commitment to intensive religious engagement, in terms of procedure, Schonfeld eagerly adopted British norms. He was partial to the prefect system, interhouse sports competitions, sports days, prizes, uniforms, academic gowns, and speech days. All these traditions reflected admiration of the English 'public school' atmosphere, where discipline, deference to authority, and what he deemed a 'healthy sense of competition' were ever-present.[15] In particular, he was keen on the English commitment to sports: 'We believe in games, because it is essential for the Jews to learn what Englishmen rightly regard as one of the most important factors in life– how to be a good loser'.[16] Schonfeld's affection for British culture and values was also evident in a 1943 list of recommended reading, which included Joseph Conrad, Oscar Wilde, George Eliot, Dickens, Shakespeare and Thomas More.[17] Schonfeld's schools, we can conclude, genuinely sought to translate the '*Torah im Derekh Eretz*' ideology into an educational philosophy that could be applied in day schools.

Yet the schools' financial situation was precarious, and many who would have liked to enrol their children were undoubtedly deterred by the need to pay fees. Gaining state-aided status, which entitled a school to a 50 per cent grant toward its building and maintenance costs, was thus viewed as desirable. Although for the 'fervently' Orthodox sector, the autonomy of their schools was the paramount consideration, the 'strictly' Orthodox parents who sent their children to the JSSM accepted that in return for the elimination of school fees, these institutions – their premises, board of governors, staff, teaching methods and syllabus – would be monitored by the local and national authorities. Matters relating to the headmaster and other staff would no longer be the sole preserve of the principal and his trustees. As we saw in Chapter 1, this accountability to the education

---

15   Kranzler and Hirschler, *Solomon Schonfeld*, 101.
16   S. Schonfeld, *Message to Jewry* (London: JSSM, 1959), 190.
17   Schonfeld, *Jewish Religious*, 100.

authorities was by no means just a formality, and for some parents, such governmental scrutiny was an inducement to enrolling their children.

Schonfeld's avowed goal was to attain state-aided status for his schools. The Ministry of Education had stringent criteria for determining which denominational schools received aided status. Invariably, these criteria entailed improvements to the school buildings, necessitating a significant capital outlay. Schonfeld was constantly engaged in fundraising. When he learned that negotiations were underway to pool the substantial endowment funds of various defunct Jewish schools in order to rebuild the Jews' Free School, he decided to challenge this plan, hoping to secure the funds needed to make the mandated improvements and secure the future of his schools by gaining state-aided status. Given that his schools were the only Jewish day schools that had survived the war intact, Schonfeld and his associates felt they were entitled to the funds.

The trust funds controversy

In 1945, the trustees of the mainly defunct voluntary schools agreed that the LBJRE would be the accredited agency for negotiating the creation of a new foundation that would dispose of their funds (which, as we saw, had been donated by wealthy patrons in the preceding half century) for the benefit of Jewish education in London. Their decision was conditioned on the LBJRE's acceptance that its first priority would be the rebuilding of the Jews' Free School. The trustees stipulated that a democratically-elected body in sympathy with the broad aims for which the JFS was founded was to be established to dispose of the remaining funds. Given the prospect that pending claims, for war damages and freeholds on the old sites, would soon be settled, funding would be available to build modern schools comparable to those of the London County Council (LCC).[18]

18   Black, *JFS*, 190–1. Unless otherwise specified, correspondence and archival material
      pertaining to the trust funds controversy is from ACC 2805/66.

The Voluntary Schools Committee, a joint committee of the LBJRE and the trustees, made several proposals. First, it recommended establishing a primary school in the Hackney/Stoke Newington area, which had a large and young Jewish population. However, the committee cautioned against immediate action, preferring, given Jewish migratory trends in the capital, that a more detailed study be undertaken. The second proposal endorsed an LCC recommendation to establish a large secondary school in central London, rather than several smaller establishments.[19] The hope was that some 1,000 pupils would attend the mixed-ability school, raising the number of Jewish children in day schools to one in ten. It was also recommended that old premises, such as the Westminster JFS and Jews' Infants' schools, be sold, and that the Jewish school building in Bayswater be transferred to the LCC in the hope that the school might be reopened elsewhere in the future.

Nathan Morris presented these proposals at the 1945 communal conference on educational reconstruction, which we discussed in Chapter 1. It will be recalled that the focus of the conference was withdrawal classes in the state schools. The future of Jewish day schools was deemed a minor issue and received limited attention, in line with the general disdain in which day-school education was held. Nonetheless, the recommendations were accepted as part of the overall reorganization of Jewish education in Britain.[20]

In accordance with the requirements of the relevant government departments, before the plans could be implemented, any objections to them from the public had to be addressed. As we will see, objections were indeed raised: given that the sums involved were considerable, the monies, though earmarked for rebuilding the JFS, were coveted by various educational organizations. The question of who was entitled to the voluntary school trusts became the focus of a communal controversy that raged unabated until 1954, tying up the funds, delaying the building of new schools, and forcing the LBJRE to engage in protracted negotiations with the Ministry of Education.

19   Minutes, Meeting of the JEC 6 September 1944. ACC 2805/65 E1197.
20   'Communal Conference', cited in Chapter 1 above, n 105, 24–5.

A key contender for the funds was the JSSM, which argued that as the frontrunner in Jewish education in Britain, and the only organization that had maintained a day-school system throughout the war, it was entitled to at least a share of the monies. As we have seen, by 1952 the JSSM operated five schools, one of which had been awarded state-aided status and three of which were recognized by the Ministry of Education, a designation indicating that they were comparable to state schools with respect to premises, staffing, and equipment. Rabbi Schonfeld had over twenty-five years of experience in day-school education, and claimed that former Chief Rabbi Hertz had deferred to him as the communal expert on educational matters.[21] The LBJRE recognized that, being newly forged, it could not claim comparable experience, but insisted that it was nonetheless Anglo-Jewry's central communal educational agency. It adduced two arguments for this claim. First, it noted that the LBJRE was the educational network in which the trustees of the old voluntary schools had placed their confidence. Second, it asserted that the LBJRE, having been formed from the JEC, which had been tantamount to the educational arm of the United Synagogue and allied Orthodox groups, was mainstream Orthodox, whereas the JSSM was separatist. Indeed, while the LBJRE, though in theory a community-wide organization, was functionally Orthodox in orientation, it was much closer to the religious outlook of the old trustees than was the JSSM. And whereas the LBJRE was prepared to submit to democratic control and public supervision, Schonfeld's willingness to defer to the majority was questionable.

From the outset, Schonfeld took an assertive stance in the debate. In a letter to the *Jewish Chronicle* regarding the proposed central secondary school, he insisted that only Orthodox teachers be employed, and that maximal teaching hours be allocated to religious instruction.[22] However, the debate was premature. The Voluntary Schools Committee was still negotiat-

---

21   See Schonfeld's 8 July 1952 letter to the Chief Rabbi, where he states, 'For twenty years the Chief Rabbinate, the Deputies and the Community have granted me one sphere – Jewish day schools'.

22   *JC* 3 November 1944, 5.

ing plans for the reorganization of the schools, and their re-establishment in areas where the Jewish population was dense. In 1946, the Committee and the JFS managers concluded that it would be advisable to move the secondary school to North London, but little progress was made. Meanwhile, the LCC recommended closing the old JFS in Stepney, and despite fears about the school's continuity, the committee agreed to sell the site and set aside the proceeds for rebuilding the school in the future. The Ministry of Education had promised that when a suitable location was found, the LCC would regard the application favourably.

In 1950, Chief Rabbi Brodie brought Nathan Rubin from County Hall, the headquarters of the LCC, where he had been a civil servant, to work for him as Secretary to the LBJRE, and specifically, to disentangle the voluntary schools issue. Upon writing to the Ministry of Education to apply for state-aided status for six defunct day schools the LBJRE wished to reestablish, he discovered the deadlock over finances and the communal disagreement over plans for the future.[23] Rubin also discovered that Schonfeld had, in 1947, submitted his own plans for the development of Jewish day schools in London, in which he proposed to use the trust fund monies for JSSM schools; Schonfeld reiterated this proposal at the end of 1950.

Aware that in order for the trust funds to be transferred to the LBJRE, notice to this effect would have to be published in a national newspaper, so that objections could be voiced, Schonfeld realized he could threaten to block the development plans unless a settlement favourable to his interests could be reached. He proceeded to propose his own scheme for the disposal of the trust funds, 'The Jewish Day Schools Trust', and sent a draft constitution to the Chief Rabbi, intimating that he might also submit it to the Ministry of Education.[24] Schonfeld enlisted not only his own JSSM schools in support of the proposed Trust, but also independent right-wing Orthodox establishments such as the North West London Jewish Day Schools and the Yesodey Hatorah schools. The objects of his Trust were 'the

---

23   Steinberg, 'Anglo-Jewry', 100; and see JSSM London School Plan. MS 183 248/5.
24   Schonfeld to Chief Rabbi 15 October 1950; 25 July 1951, 30 July 1951.

furtherance of the activities and financial support of all Orthodox Jewish Schools in Greater London who are affiliated to the Trust, both primary and secondary, that provide general and Jewish religious education.[25] Schonfeld called on the Chief Rabbi to co-ordinate the financing and future plans for Jewish education in London with both the LBJRE and the JSSM. Although Chief Rabbi Brodie sought to appear as a neutral arbiter in the dispute, it was clear that he sided with the LBJRE. He not only co-ordinated policy with its chairman, Alfred Woolf, but was particularly close to Nathan Rubin, the LBJRE Secretary he himself had appointed.

Complying with the express wishes of the trustees of the old voluntary schools, Woolf wrote to Schonfeld that he was not opposed to cooperation between their organizations, nor to a sharing of funds, provided Schonfeld accepted public and democratic control of their distribution. From the correspondence, it is evident that Schonfeld was furious at the suggestion that he did not administer school funds appropriately, retorting that this would be an intrusion into the internal affairs of his organization. Yet clearly, Schonfeld was not a good financial manager. Some years later, when a receiver-manager was appointed for the JSSM, it was discovered that the movement's debts were five times higher than the £35,000 Schonfeld admitted to.[26]

Rubin pressed ahead with his quiet negotiations with the LCC over development plans. Recalling that during his days at County Hall, the Catholic diocese in the Camden Town area had rejected a site for school development, he investigated the possibility of its use by the LBJRE. The land was still available, and its allocation was approved by the Chief Rabbi and the LCC.[27] Although Camden Town had no sizable Jewish population, it was close to major Jewish centres and easily accessible by bus and underground. However, not everyone concurred that the site was appropriate.

25   Constitution for Jewish Day Schools Trust 1951. MS 183/248/5.
26   Black, *JFS*, 195–6.
27   T. Brown (Education Officer of LCC) to N. Rubin (LBJRE) 18 October 1951; [notes re] meeting held 4 December 1951 at County Hall [LCC headquarters].

In October 1951, Chief Rabbi Brodie, popularly considered a concili-ator, decided to establish a commission into the trust fund and develop-ment plan controversy. He appointed Vivian Lipman, the Anglo-Jewish historian, and Salmond Levin, both of whom were members of the LBJRE, to conduct the study. The commission's task was to outline a plan for the future development of Jewish day schools in London, combining as autono-mous units within a single system both the existing day schools and any new voluntary schools that could be supported by the trust funds of the former non-provided schools.[28] Its findings were to be put before a com-munal conference of interested parties.

In their report, Lipman and Levin argued that a comprehensive plan for the development of Jewish day schools would avoid unnecessary dupli-cation and the waste of valuable communal resources. Moreover, it would enable the co-ordination of building projects, so that primary schools, which were small and served specific neighbourhoods, would feed larger and centrally located secondary schools. They determined that Jewish primary schools were feasible in areas of one square mile where the Jewish popula-tion numbered at least 2,000 and preferably 5,000. Although they found that eleven districts met these criteria, they recommended opening new primary schools in just four locations: Belsize Park, Maida Vale, Edgware and Hackney. They proposed that the LBJRE administer the first two of these, and the JSSM the latter two.

The report gave considerable attention to the question as to where a new secondary modern day school should be situated. Its authors believed that a school of this type should serve a wider catchment area than the primary schools, but nonetheless be situated in a Jewish area – a disap-proving allusion to the proposed Camden Town site. They felt it would be too risky to situate the community's main secondary school in an area without feeder schools.

The report instead recommended utilizing existing sites and build-ings. It therefore proposed that a small secondary modern day school be

---

28   V. Lipman and S. Levin, Memorandum: Towards an Integrated System of Jewish Day Schools, 1 November 1951.

established in the Hackney/Dalston area, and that existing schools in North West London be expanded with a view to acquiring state-aided status. This proposal was far from what Rubin had had in mind; his sole consolation was that the report recommended that the LBJRE administer the new school. Lipman and Levin proposed a two-tier framework to oversee distribution of the trust funds and implementation of the day-school development plan. The first level would be a committee of five trustees, one of whom would be the Chief Rabbi, another, a party acceptable to the JSSM, and the remainder, nominated by the LBJRE. This obviously gave the LBJRE an advantage, although the proposed second tier, a 'Voluntary Schools Council', gave equal representation to the LBJRE and the JSSM.[29]

Though the authors were members of the LBJRE, their recommendations seem to be a genuine attempt at an impartial resolution to the communal conflict. However, Lipman and Levin had overlooked two crucial points: the old trustees and Nathan Rubin were committed to rebuilding the JFS on the Camden Town site, and sceptical about the JSSM's willingness to accept democratic control. The senior leaders of the LBJRE were thus highly apprehensive about the report, fearing that if its recommendations were adopted, the old trustees would rescind their promise to transfer the funds to the LBJRE. Woolf shared his concerns with Michael Wallach, the Chief Rabbi's secretary:

> The important thing is for the [proposed] scheme, which is being prepared by the authorities, not to be opposed, so that the money in question may be successfully passed over to the London Board. If there is any opposition to the scheme then I know from the present trustees that there is every likelihood that no portion of the orthodox section of Anglo-Jewry would receive it, and that would be disastrous.[30]

Woolf knew that most of the former trustees sympathized with the small but growing Reform and Liberal communities, which opposed day-school education, favouring non-denominational schooling. Indeed, as we saw, even the membership of the United Synagogue was largely averse to denominational education at this time. The senior leadership of the LBJRE qui-

29   Ibid., 6.
30   A. Woolf to Wallach 19 December 1951.

etly dropped the Lipman-Levin report, and there seems to have been no discussion of its findings at any LBJRE meeting.[31]

In his history of the *JFS*, Black argued that Schonfeld 'wanted the bulk of the money, and sought overall control of the situation.'[32] In an article published in the Orthodox periodical *Jewish Review*, Schonfeld wrote bitterly of the day-school funds that had lain idle for several years. He estimated the sum in question to be around £250,000, and claimed that the state would have provided a matching capital grant. He complained that the LBJRE was obstinate in adhering to the 'obsolete and impracticable scheme of a comprehensive school to be situated in Camden Town'. Only moderate-sized schools in densely populated Jewish areas could work, he argued.[33] Schonfeld called a meeting of his alliance, where various resolutions critical of the LBJRE were adopted.[34] He was eager to run a campaign to convince Anglo-Jewry and the Ministry of Education that 'the heritage of the old schools had passed over to the excellent and widespread schools that were functioning so successfully' – namely, the JSSM and allied fervently Orthodox schools.

Conscious of these developments, and mindful that the option on the Camden Town land might expire, Rubin pleaded with the Chief Rabbi to do everything possible to quell the opposition to the trust scheme. Brodie turned to Schonfeld and in the strongest possible terms requested of him not to impede the negotiations with the authorities over disposition of the trust funds. In a bid to end the deadlock and placate Schonfeld, the Voluntary Schools Committee adopted two amendments to their trust scheme. The first enabled officials from the JSSM and its allies to become board members of the new trust fund. The second widened the geographic range of the new trust's activity to include the Middlesex County Council, where some JSSM schools were located.[35]

---

31 Interestingly, in his article 'Changing Patterns of Jewish Education', Levin makes no reference to the report.

32 Black, *JFS*, 196.

33 *Jewish Review*, 30 November 1951.

34 Minutes, Meeting of Representatives of Jewish Day Schools 9 December 1951. MS 183 248/5.

35 Minutes, Meeting of Voluntary Schools Committee, January 1952.

Schonfeld responded positively to these overtures, accepting an invitation to participate in informal talks with the LBJRE that the Chief Rabbi hoped would pave the way for a communal conference that would end the dispute. The *Jewish Chronicle* summarized the point of contention as follows:

> This then is the problem. There is a body of Jewish day schools with no funds; on the other hand there is the London Board with the prospect of considerable funds but owning no schools, and with no day-school experience. There seems real justification for a *shidduch* [arranged match] in which each party has much to give the other.[36]

It had been hoped that the Chief Rabbi would be present at the negotiations, but he had a long-standing commitment to make a pastoral tour of Australia and New Zealand. Before departing, the Chief Rabbi had implored the community leaders to resolve their differences and had nominated Frank Samuel, senior United Synagogue vice president, to convene meetings for this purpose. Samuel met with Schonfeld in February and March for what were described as 'pre-preliminary meetings'. The atmosphere improved, and a sub-committee of the LBJRE and the JSSM was established to pursue negotiations, under the chairmanship of Alfred Woolf, on the basis of the Lipman-Levin plan.[37] Although, upon viewing the outline of the proposed scheme for the disposition of the trust funds that had been negotiated between the Ministry of Education and the LBJRE, the JSSM representatives raised various objections, the sides reached an in-principle accord on the establishment of a Council of Jewish Day Schools.[38]

Shortly before the Chief Rabbi returned from abroad, the Ministry of Education published the proposed trust fund scheme, that is, the arrangements for disposition of the trust fund monies through a new trust fund, officially called the London Jewish Educational Foundation. The proposal

---

36   *JC* 11 January 1952, 13 (editorial).

37   Frank Samuel to Dr Schonfeld 6 February 1952. MS 183 307/2.

38   Minutes, Meeting 7 April 1952 between LBJRE, JSSM and North West London Jewish Day Schools.

coupled the monies remaining in the old trust funds with the LBJRE's personnel and organizational framework, for the purpose of building the new JFS and developing Jewish education in London. Its governing body was to have twelve members: the Chief Rabbi as an ex officio appointment, seven representatives from the LBJRE, and four governors from the old trust funds: Sir Henry D'Avigdor Goldsmid,[39] Digby Lewis, Frank Samuel, and Leonard Montefiore.

No sooner had notices of the new Foundation been published, in June 1952, than Schonfeld's organization expressed opposition to it.[40] Schonfeld accused the Chief Rabbi of 'double dealing'. How was it possible, he protested, that at the same time negotiations were in progress over future development plans, the Chief Rabbi would submit a trust fund scheme without consulting the leader of the JSSM?[41] Despite this, Schonfeld wrote to the Chief Rabbi in July pledging that regardless of his opposition to the proposed arrangement, he recognized that the Ministry might take matters into its own hands, hence once the Chief Rabbi took a final decision, Schonfeld would withdraw his opposition.

> I am writing to confirm what I unreservedly stated to you last Friday concerning the dispute between our Movement and the London Board. Once you in person arrive at your final decision concerning the future of the Jewish Day School trust funds, and you in person convey your decision to the Ministry of Education, we shall not officially object, no matter how disagreeable your decision may be to us.[42]

One might have assumed that this would put an end to the matter. The Chief Rabbi certainly thought so, and announced to the LBJRE that he had received a written promise from the JSSM that it would abide by his decision. Yet only a week later, Schonfeld retracted his promise, stat-

---

39   Sir Henry was Conservative MP for Walsall South, a banker and bullion broker, and 'in keeping with the family tradition, a member of the Reform synagogue'. Alderman, *Jewish Community*, 134.

40   The proposal was also published in the *JC* 12 September 1952, 9.

41   Schonfeld to Ministry of Education 10 June 1952; to Chief Rabbi 18 June 1952. See also *JC* 20 June 1952, 8.

42   Schonfeld to Chief Rabbi 7 July 1952. MS 183 307/2.

ing that it had been extracted in response to the Chief Rabbi's fears that governmental impatience might cause the money to be lost. Not surprisingly, when the notice was submitted for its statutory second publication, Schonfeld resubmitted objections to the trust funds plan on much the same grounds as he had in June.[43]

A new round of talks between the LBJRE and the JSSM was initiated. It was hoped that the Chief Rabbi's presence at these meetings would prove helpful. Much of the discussion centred on the question of the status of the new school in Camden Town: should it be a grammar or secondary modern school? The JSSM opposed the former option, as its own secondary schools were all grammar schools, and a new well-outfitted school would constitute serious competition. More disconcertingly, Schonfeld repeatedly returned to the basic issue of the disposition of the trust fund monies, and in an unprecedented attack on the proposed arrangements, alleged that the money was the JSSM's 'by right' and that in refusing to recognize these rights, his movement was being 'robbed'.[44]

Schonfeld's claim was outrageous. To argue that the old trust funds had in any way been money to which he was entitled was patently false. Families representing those funds, whose ideological orientation was very different from that of Schonfeld and his schools, had agreed to transfer the funds to a new foundation, responsibility for which would be entrusted to the LBJRE. It is unthinkable that they would have agreed to turn over the funds to Schonfeld, given his brand of separatist Orthodoxy.

Nevertheless, additional efforts were undertaken to find a formula that might satisfy Schonfeld. The JSSM was offered two places on the governing body of the proposed London Jewish Educational Foundation. In February 1953, Schonfeld wrote a letter to the Chief Rabbi confirming that in return for sufficient funds to cover the cost of achieving state-aided status for two of his schools, and the promise to assist the Yesodey Hatorah and North West London primary schools, he would withdraw his objections to the

43   Schonfeld to the Editor, *JC* 1 August 1952, 17; to Ministry of Education 14 September 1952.
44   Minutes, Meeting between LBJRE, JSSM and Chief Rabbi 1 December 1952.

proposed trust funds scheme.[45] This basic formula – a grant in return for withdrawal of his objections – became the basis for future negotiations. Woolf, impressed by the Chief Rabbi's desire to make rapid progress on both the trust funds and the co-ordinating body for Jewish education, suggested that they accede to the request for £15,000 in the hope that this might satisfy Schonfeld.[46]

Yet again, Schonfeld and Dr Jacob Braude, the JSSM chairman, reneged and continued to oppose the proposed disposition of the trust funds and the plan to rebuild the JFS. Schonfeld came up with a new objection: the two places reserved for the JSSM on the governing body of the proposed London Jewish Educational Foundation were for lay representatives, which by definition excluded him.[47] Moreover, he saw the promise to provide significant funding for his Hasmonean and Avigdor schools as absolute, but the LBJRE saw it as conditional on a vote of the new governing body and agreement of the governmental authorities. Schonfeld's responses were increasingly erratic, even disturbed. He wrote to the Chief Rabbi that he would 'make every effort to obstruct ... their unsavoury plot'.[48]

Schonfeld requested assistance from the Chief Rabbi in his bid to secure state-aided status for the Hasmonean school. The Chief Rabbi saw an opportunity to point out the inconsistencies in Schonfeld's stance, replying that 'an embarrassment must inevitably arise if I head a delegation on behalf of an organization of which you are the principal, which at the same time raises objections to a scheme which I approve.'[49] Days later, Schonfeld again wrote to the Ministry of Education asserting his continued opposition to the trust funds scheme. In addition to reiterating previous criticisms, Schonfeld challenged the Chief Rabbi's authority to mediate the controversy.[50]

45   Schonfeld to Chief Rabbi 16 February 1953.
46   Woolf to F. Samuel (vice president of the United Synagogue) 22 December 1952.
47   See note appended by Schonfeld to letter from Chief Rabbi 2 February 1953. MS 183 307/2.
48   Schonfeld to Chief Rabbi 8 March 1953.
49   Chief Rabbi to Schonfeld 11 March 1953.
50   Schonfeld to Ministry of Education 23 March 1953. MS 183 307/2.

Chief Rabbi Brodie's patience was running out. Deciding that the time had come to press ahead with the trust funds scheme and the rebuilding of the JFS, he wrote to the Ministry of Education refuting the JSSM's charges and describing the many attempts that had been made to resolve the controversy. On the basis of the July 1952 letter in which Schonfeld had promised not to obstruct the Chief Rabbi's final decision, Brodie requested that the Ministry approve the plans.[51]

The JSSM now resorted to what Gerry Black described as its 'last throw of the dice'.[52] Through its chairman, Braude, the JSSM requested that the Chief Rabbi convene a rabbinical court in decide the matter by Torah law (*din torah*), to preclude its being adjudicated by outside authorities. This was not only an attack on the LBJRE, but on the office of the Chief Rabbi. The LBJRE responded forthrightly:

> Your proposal to appoint three rabbis to adjudicate ... is not only a denial of the Chief Rabbi's decision, but appears to be an attempt to denigrate the office of the Chief Rabbi, to lower its prestige in the eyes of the Government department, and to rob it of the authority vested in it by the Anglo-Jewish community.[53]

Concern that the matter would be adjudicated by outside authorities was hypocritical, given that it was the JSSM that had initially lodged objections with the Ministry. The LBJRE and the Chief Rabbi gave the idea short shrift.

The demand for a '*din torah*' had a boomerang effect. Instead of the JSSM's securing a decision in its favour, the movement lost whatever public sympathy it still had. The *Jewish Chronicle* reproached Schonfeld and his movement for their demeaning proposal, and for Schonfeld's 'tone and approach', which was 'more likely to destroy than to build bridges'.[54]

In the summer of 1953, the Ministry of Education responded to the Chief Rabbi's request that it disregard the opposition of Schonfeld and his

---

51 Chief Rabbi to Ministry of Education 10 March, 26 April 1953.
52 Black, *JFS*, 204.
53 Rubin to Braude 8 May 1953. MS 183 481/3.
54 *JC* 3 April 1953, 14 (editorial).

allies. Though the Ministry did not wish to be 'uncooperative', it pointed out that, seeing as plans to rebuild the JFS were dependent on resolution of the trust funds question, the 'unfortunate dispute' with the JSSM meant that the Ministry could not endorse the school building plans.[55] In other words, the authorities were unwilling to disregard Schonfeld's objections, and would take no further action until both issues were resolved. A request by the Chief Rabbi to meet with the Minister of Education was denied, and despite additional efforts at negotiating a settlement with the JSSM, including a further compromise proposal by the LBJRE regarding JSSM representation on the governing body of the new Foundation, the stalemate persisted.

Meanwhile, Schonfeld endeavoured to advance his claim on the trust funds. In August, after reaching the conclusion that further negotiations with the LBJRE were futile, he requested a direct meeting with the original trustees,[56] and when this was denied, he sought to engage the Board of Deputies in the conflict. Though, given the contempt with which the Board of Deputies was held by right-wing Orthodoxy, this move was disingenuous, it was nonetheless clever, as the Board had for some time been interested in raising its profile in educational affairs.[57] The controversy was discussed at one of the Board's monthly meetings, and the chair of its Education Committee, Elsie Janner, wife of Labour MP Barnett Janner, proposed establishing an independent tribunal under its auspices. This idea was rejected by the Chief Rabbi, ostensibly because the negotiations were at a delicate stage, but probably because the Chief Rabbi was unwilling to cede any of his influence in the sphere of education.

There was a new development in the spring of 1954. Schonfeld wrote to the Chief Rabbi that if the JFS would not be a grammar school, 'then the main danger to our movement ... has been removed and the way opened

---

55   G. R. Hughes (Ministry of Education) to Wallach 21 July 1953.
56   Schonfeld to Chief Rabbi 24 August 1953. See also *JC* 30 October 1953, 12.
57   The Chief Rabbi's position was that the Board of Deputies had a legitimate role with regard to legal questions ensuing from governmental educational policies, but not in connection with educational matters in themselves. See ACC 2805/75.

for a reviving of the comprehensive settlement of the trust fund problem'.[58]
Chief Rabbi Brodie and Nathan Rubin called a meeting of the Voluntary
Schools Committee and decided to endorse the proposal that the new
school not be a grammar school. Brodie welcomed the plan as a solution
for children for whom there were no Jewish secondary-modern places.[59]
It was now possible for the parties to the conflict to meet and settle the
long-standing dispute. The offices of Edmund de Rothschild in New Court
were chosen for this finale, and following difficult negotiations, an agreement was reached.[60]

The accord reflected a series of compromises. For example, the LBJRE
accepted that the JFS would become a secondary modern school, while
Schonfeld and Braude withdrew their demand for the school to be relatively small in size. It was agreed that the school would have an initial
intake of 500 pupils, with potential for 1,000 places. (In fact, according
to government rules, the site could only be procured if the larger number
was enrolled.) Similarly, there was give and take on the issue of the new
Foundation's governing body. The sides agreed that it would be composed
of the Chief Rabbi and six representatives appointed by the LBJRE, including one representative of the existing Jewish day schools. In addition, two
representatives would be appointed by the JSSM, and three governors from
the former trust funds would be nominated. Thus although the JSSM's
presence fell short of what Schonfeld had been seeking, it was not excluded
altogether.

The final hurdle facing the agreement involved a promise of sufficient
funds to secure state-aided status for two JSSM schools, and the Yesodey
Hatorah and North West London Jewish Primary schools. Having agreed
that the sum of £50,000 would be required for this goal, Woolf promised
that the Foundation would set aside £10,000 from the transferred funds of
the old schools, and would support a community-wide appeal for a similar

58   Schonfeld to Chief Rabbi 18 March 1954.
59   Minutes, Voluntary Schools Special Sub-Committee 22 March 1954.
60   Meeting at E. de Rothschild's, New Court between Rubin, Woolf, Schonfeld and
      Braude. 11 May 1954. For the founding agreement, see Minutes, Governors of London
      Jewish Educational Foundation 19 July 1955.

sum. Moreover, it would request that the Central British Fund – the organization that supported Jewish refugees from Germany in the UK – transfer £5,000 immediately for the refugee children attending these schools, and £5,000 at a later stage. Satisfied with these promises, Schonfeld and Braude agreed to withdraw their objections to the trust funds scheme.

With the necessary agreements in hand, Rubin resubmitted the trust funds scheme to the Ministry of Education for its official publication. This time, there was no opposition, and in November 1954, the Ministry granted legal approval to the London Jewish Educational Foundation. With the funds now accessible, the Jews' Free School could be rebuilt. Four years later, in September 1958, the school was reopened in Camden Town. Schonfeld's opposition had delayed the opening of the school by several years. Part of the responsibility for the failure to resolve the trust funds controversy does, however, lie with the Chief Rabbi, whose attempts to avoid conflict had only strengthened Schonfeld's obstinacy.[61]

Late in 1956, a letter to the *Jewish Chronicle* from a leading JSSM figure bemoaned the lack of day-school places. Rubin seized the opportunity to remind the paper's readership that it was the JSSM and its upstart Jewish Day Schools Trust that bore the responsibility for this state of affairs.

> It was urged upon them that their action would inevitably lead to a considerable delay. Their objections, were however, not withdrawn until after two years. ... This led not only to a delay in the building of the school, but resulted in a considerable increase in the cost of the project owing to the reduction in the value of the trust funds from inflation and devaluation.[62]

Though Schonfeld's declared aim had been to enable more Jewish children to get a day-school education, his opposition to the trust funds scheme had effectively delayed achievement of this goal. It was a stain on his career that was not easily forgiven.[63]

61 See Newman, *United Synagogue*, 183.
62 See *JC* 19 December, 26 December 1956, 2 January 1957.
63 See *JC* 10 February 1984, 16 (editorial), and obituary, 18.

It is unclear why Schonfeld had a change of heart in March 1954. Black's explanation, that the cumulative criticism in the *Jewish Chronicle* had at last induced in Schonfeld a sense that he had gone too far, seems unsatisfactory, given Schonfeld's years of passionate and extreme opposition to the trust funds scheme.[64] The funding that Schonfeld finally received from the London Jewish Educational Foundation was hardly an improvement on the offer that had been made to him two years earlier. It seems more likely that Schonfeld had been holding out for more money, and only relented when additional funds were promised by an new source, namely, the Conference on Jewish Material Claims Against Germany. Chief Rabbi Brodie was chosen to chair the Conference's British committee, officially called the Cultural Advisory Committee (Britain), giving him a crucial role in the distribution of substantial sums. Surely it was no coincidence that Schonfeld's change of heart occurred very soon after the newly established Cultural Advisory Committee decided, at one of the its first meetings, to allocate $15,000 to the JSSM. This was to be the first of a series of allocations to the JSSM.[65] In this context, Schonfeld's claims of entitlement were valid. His movement had provided considerable assistance to school age refugees from Nazi Germany, and its work in absorbing children who had been physically and spiritually harmed by the Nazi regime was well-known.

---

64   Black, *JFS*, 203.

65   About $43,000 had been allocated to various ultra-Orthodox educational associations, many connected to Schonfeld's Jewish Day Schools Trust. See Report of the First Year of the Conference on Jewish Material Claims Against Germany, New York, 1954, 79. ACC 2805/126. The distribution of funds to the JSSM and fervently Orthodox groups was controversial within Anglo-Jewry. Both the LBJRE and the ZF Educational Trust (ZFET) demanded a share of these funds. Dr Fox of the ZFET went so far as to challenge the criteria for the allocations, alleging that the Chief Rabbi was giving preference to Agudah-type organizations, see ACC 2805/127. See Minutes, Cultural Advisory Committee 22 February, 1954. ACC 2805/126.

In March 1955 Schonfeld received notification of a further allocation of $20,000 to his primary and secondary schools, and in July 1955, the *Jewish Chronicle* announced that $56,000 had been tentatively allocated to London Jewish day schools, *JC* 15 July 1955, 1.

More than anything else, the trust funds controversy demonstrated that without a communal body to co-ordinate educational affairs, the expansion of day-school education would be plagued by ideological conflict and turf wars. As we saw, attempts had been made to create such a structure in 1941 and again during the trust funds debacle, but each time differences between the groups undermined the plan. New educational legislation was the impetus for further attempts in 1959, but they too failed. The groups' fears of jeopardizing their autonomy and influence seemed to outweigh the benefits of co-ordination.

Resolution of the trust funds controversy had another important effect. Prior to the re-establishment of the JFS, the only Jewish option for secondary schooling was the JSSM grammar schools. But now, parents whose children failed the 11 plus exam, ruling out grammar school, had the option of sending their children to a state-aided Jewish school instead of a secondary modern.

During its early years, most of those who attended the re-established JFS went on to blue-collar occupations, but in time, the numbers who acquired further education increased. However, the fact that the JFS was a secondary modern school obviously discouraged parents whose children were academically talented from sending them to the school. The JFS suffered from a poor academic image for many years, and it was only after the Labour government committed itself to ending selection at age eleven and eliminating the grammar schools that the JFS began attracting larger numbers of children with academic aptitude.[66]

One of the first tasks of the JFS Board of Governors was to appoint a headmaster. None of the six short-listed candidates were graduates of either the original JFS or a Jewish secondary school.[67] Dr Conway, the panel's choice, had attended the local grammar school in Llanelli, Wales. He graduated from University College, Swansea and began his teaching career in Liverpool, later becoming headmaster of that city's day school, Liverpool Hebrew School. His religious Orthodoxy, administrative experience, and academic credentials satisfied the JFS search committee.

66 Black, *JFS*, 208–9.
67 See files of the selection committee. ACC 2805/114 JFS 1958–61.

The founding of Carmel College

It would be accurate to say that until 1952, the initiatives in day-school education came either from the Hirschian Orthodox and haredi elements of Anglo Jewry, or individuals from mainstream Orthodoxy who challenged the accepted views on Jewish education. Rabbi Kopul Rosen, who created the first Jewish 'public' boarding school in the UK (it was also the last), exemplified the latter. He had long been an outspoken advocate of denominational day schools, but in 1947 determined that the time was ripe to take action. He initiated a discussion with an article in the *Jewish Monthly*, the journal of the Anglo-Jewish Association, whose subscribers were mainly members of the Jewish social and economic elite from among whom support for the project would presumably be drawn. Cognizant of the possible hostility with which his ideas might be received, he used a pen name, Jewnius.[68] The article was a rather cautious proposal; it met with a civil but hostile reception.

Kopul Rosen was born in the Notting Hill district of London in 1913 to a Hasidic family. He studied at Etz Chaim Yeshiva in the East End for seven years and was active in various Zionist youth organizations, such as Bnei Zion and Habonim. At the age of 22, he left England for the Mir Yeshiva in Poland, where he spent four years and received rabbinic ordination. Upon his return to England, he was appointed rabbi of the Higher Crumpsall Hebrew Congregation in Manchester. Shortly thereafter, his responsibilities were broadened to include the post of army chaplain for the Manchester district, which he held until 1943. Throughout this period he continued his Zionist activities, earning a reputation as a highly articulate exponent of Zionism. In 1944, Rosen was invited to be rabbi of Glasgow. His inauguration address concentrated almost entirely on Jewish education, calling on those present to make a greater commitment to day schools.

---

68   Jewnius, 'A Jewish Public School', *Jewish Monthly* 1:3 (1947), 10–15. It is not altogether certain that Rosen wrote the article himself, and it may be that it was the work of an ally.

'The first line of Jewish defence is not the sending of propaganda speakers to address non-Jewish audiences or to distribute pamphlets. The first line of Jewish defence is in the Hebrew classroom', he declared.[69] But within eighteen months, Rosen was again called upon to leave his position and assume greater responsibilities, this time as the head rabbi of the Federation of Synagogues. Chief Rabbi Hertz was an enthusiastic supporter of Rosen's appointment, as he felt it would strengthen Zionist work in London, which had reached a critical juncture. Two years later, following Hertz's death in 1946, a new Chief Rabbi was to be appointed. Rosen was a candidate, but his young age – thirty-five – was a disadvantage. When it became clear that Israel Brodie would be chosen, Rosen withdrew and devoted himself to the establishment of a Jewish 'public' school modelled on the classic English elite schools.

Rosen's article opened by bemoaning the dearth of devoted communal leaders and educators, a point on which Anglo-Jewry was in agreement. The Jewish community had been relying on the English 'public' school, which valued 'community before self' and sought to produce 'men of character', for its cadre of community leaders. Future generations, however, required schooling where the Jewish religious environment was 'grafted on to the public school tradition'.[70]

Given that Anglo-Jewry in general opposed separate Jewish day schools, there was little reason to think that Rosen's proposal would be greeted with enthusiasm by parents who patronized the private system. 'Jewnius' challenged the antagonism to separate schooling. Rosen was well aware of the increasing parental interest in the 'public' schools, primarily due to the academic benefits associated with them. For graduates of 'public' schools, entry to Oxbridge was a matter of course. Jewish parents were also eager for their children to have the opportunity to forge friendships with the progeny of the English upper class, on the assumption that such friendships would constitute a professional and social advantage. But there was concern that Jewish pupils were subject to quotas or tests of connection to

69   Ibid., 16.
70   Ibid., 10.

the schools' religious affiliations. Rather than objecting to these putative practices, Jewnius argued that such schools were perfectly within their rights as denominational institutions to limit the number of pupils from other religious communities.[71] Instead, he recommended that parents consider supporting his proposed Jewish 'public' school.

Attending a 'public' boarding school was not conducive to maintaining one's Jewish identity. These schools had no synagogues or kosher kitchens, precluding observance of many Jewish ritual obligations, nor could they provide adequate supplementary Jewish education. Parents who chose the 'public' school environment for their children were cognizant of the meagre Jewish education they would receive. For these parents, the top priority was affording their children the opportunity to live among, and learn the mores of, the English upper class.

Admittedly, there had been attempts at creating Jewish 'houses' within existing 'public' schools, whereby the Jewish boys participated in the classroom and general activities together with the other boarders, but had separate dining and residential facilities. 'Jewnius' considered these experiments unpromising: the Jewish houses at Harrow and more recently Cheltenham had closed, leaving Clifton the only ongoing success.[72] Rejecting the claim that such institutions offered a desirable synthesis, Jewnius argued that such arrangements were likely to create an atmosphere where 'antisemitism might flourish'.[73]

Jewnius invoked the experience of other denominations, which had recently decided to open their own 'public' schools, in particular, the Roman Catholics and the Quakers, who had concluded that it was better for them to establish their own institutions than to have their children attend Anglican 'public' schools. Catholic schools such as Stoneyhurst, Ampleforth and Beaumont admittedly lacked the long-standing traditions of other 'public' schools, but were respected and oversubscribed, Jewnius claimed. The

71   Ibid., 11.
72   Readers pointed out that there was also a Jewish House at the Perse School in Cambridge, see D. Kenrick and S. Greenberg, Letter to the Editor, *Jewish Monthly* 1:6 (1947), 57. However, it closed not long after.
73   Jewnius, 'Jewish Public School', 13.

Jewish community would do well to follow this precedent and establish their own public schools, he argued. The ideal school would meld the best of the English 'public' school tradition with 'religious instruction and training in accordance with the doctrines and precepts of traditional Judaism'.[74] Jewnius promised that every effort would be made to engage with other 'public' schools in athletic competitions and other activities.[75]

Jewnius's article provoked a lively response. No other subject at this time, including Zionism and the troubles in Palestine, attracted as much interest as the Jewish 'public' school debate. But apart from a letter from a JSSM official, no letter-writer endorsed the idea of denominational education, whether state or 'public'.[76] The chief objection, as we have seen, was the claim that these schools failed to prepare their pupils for interaction with the broader society. S. Goldblatt, a captain at Eton, warned of the 'dangers' of a Jewish public school:

> Can tolerance be taught and practised in a homogeneous community? A Public School is a world of its own – cut off from other schools, cut off from life; boys kept apart in this other world, during the years in which their characters are moulded and matured, may be unable to mix with people of different ideas and a different outlook when they pass on to a University and adult life.[77]

A similar position was taken by C. Lyon-Maris, headmaster of the Beaconsfield School in Buckinghamshire, the only preparatory school in England that prepared Jewish boys for entry into 'public' secondary schools. He alleged that withdrawing children from various activities on religious grounds and segregating Jewish from English boys would be 'accentuating differences, very undesirable at this time'. The Jewish parent had a duty, he argued, 'not only to acquaint his son with the tenets and practices of his religion ... but also to be a good citizen of his country and to be able to face life on parity with other citizens'. The Jewish pupil ought not 'keep himself aloof in a modern Ghetto, behind self-erected barricades of religious

74   C. Domb, *Memories of Kopul Rosen* (London: Carmel College, 1970), 100.
75   Jewnius, 'Jewish Public School', 13.
76   See A. Shapiro, *Jewish Monthly* 1:5 (1947), 57–9.
77   S. Goldblatt, Letter to the Editor, *Jewish Monthly* 1:5 (1947), 55.

practices'; creation of a Jewish public school would 'create antisemitism where it does not exist at present and prejudice the present friendly feeling of these schools towards Jewish boys'. The headmaster so disapproved of an exclusively Jewish school that he declared he would not prepare or train any boy to enter such a school.[78]

'Public' school students added their voices to the chorus of opposition to a Jewish 'public' school, arguing that Jewish education could be imparted while the Gentile pupils received their religious education. This, they claimed, was the 'happy medium between segregation and the equally dangerous assimilation'.[79]

The debate between those favouring a Jewish 'public' school and those opposed to it in some ways paralleled the debate over denominational education in the state system. Opponents of denominational schools also claimed that such schools were a form of separation and limited the scope for interaction between Jewish and Gentile children. They too argued that 'mixing' in schools was an important means by which each party would learn about the other, dissolving prejudices that might exist between the different groups. But denominational schooling was opposed chiefly because it was believed that the minority had an obligation to adapt its behaviour to match that of the majority, an objective that could best be achieved through the schools. Separating Jewish children deprived them of the opportunity to acquire this 'matched' behaviour, which was an important life skill. Conversely, proponents of Jewish day-school education, whether state or 'public', viewed it more as an ideal environment for learning and experiencing Jewish life. Far from creating children who would be insecure about their ability to integrate into the wider society, the Jewish schools would, it was argued, produce graduates who, being confident and unashamed of their identity, could interact easily with all.

Despite the largely negative response to his proposal, Rabbi Rosen was not deterred. Supporters, especially J. C. Gilbert, Alexander Margulies and Leslie Paisner, not only helped him raise the necessary funds, but also undertook to locate a suitable building for the proposed boarding

78   C. Lyon-Maris, Letter to the Editor, *Jewish Monthly* 1:4 (1947), 58.
79   'Two Malverians', Letter to the Editor, *Jewish Monthly* 1:4 (1947), 59.

school. So grateful was Rosen to Gilbert that he named the school in tribute to Gilbert's wife, Carmel. By March 1948, premises had been purchased at Greenham Lodge, Newbury, and shortly thereafter a headmaster was appointed. In September the school opened with fewer than thirty boys. The early pupils arrived at the school for diverse reasons: closure of the Jewish House at the Perse School, Cambridge; failure to gain entry elsewhere; parents who felt their children would do better in a small group or liked the idea of a Jewish 'public' school. A few were troubled children who had not succeeded at other schools, and whose parents took advantage of Carmel's eagerness to recruit pupils.[80]

Though an ardent proponent of modern Orthodoxy, Kopul Rosen was not a separationist like Rabbi Schonfeld, who, as we saw, established his own community and institutions. Another crucial difference between the two Anglo-Jewish Orthodox educators was that Rosen was an enthusiastic Zionist, playing a central role in the Mizrachi organization. This enthusiasm manifested itself in both the formal curriculum and the school's general atmosphere.[81]

In 1953 Carmel College, having been awarded provisional recognition by the Ministry of Education, moved to a new address at Mongewell Park, Berkshire. Two years later it was granted full recognition. By 1960 there were 300 pupils, and the construction of new buildings gave it a potential capacity of 500. A considerable number of pupils came from overseas, an indication that an Orthodox Jewish 'public' school was still of limited appeal to Anglo-Jewry.

By the early 1950s, Jewish day-school education had rebounded somewhat from its wartime low. This was mainly due to the growth and influence of the Orthodox communities within Anglo-Jewry: Carmel College and the JSSM schools were established by rabbinical figures and run on Orthodox lines. Even the soon-to-re-open JFS was to be administered by an Orthodox educational agency, the mainstream LBJRE. Soon, however, another ideological orientation was to make itself felt.

---

80 Domb, *Memories*, 103.
81 Rabbi Rosen became President of British Mizrachi in 1947, resigning in 1953 due to growing disillusionment with the association of religion and politics in Israel.

The Zionists extend their mandate to education

At the time of the Butler Education Act, the Zionist Federation of Great Britain (ZF) did not play a significant role in Anglo-Jewish education, but focused on lobbying the British government to establish a Jewish national home in Palestine, and, of course, fundraising. Once the State of Israel was established, however, the ZF became an organization whose purpose needed serious redefinition, as discussions in the Zionist periodicals of the era attest.

Some had argued for years that the ZF should take education more seriously. In 1928, when Wellesley (Pinchas) Aron had outlined a plan for the creation of a Jewish cultural youth movement, the ZF had responded with profound disinterest.[82] Persevering nonetheless, Aron had established the Habonim youth movement, which was soon organizing weekly activities, camps, and later, training farms for potential pioneers to Palestine. Despite the occasional call for a more concentrated effort in the field of informal Jewish education, this sphere was, like formal education, largely ignored by the Zionist movement, which preferred to expend its efforts on political machinations.

In 1948, the ZF's education department, headed by Levi Gertner, concentrated on teaching modern Hebrew. Gertner claimed there was high demand for instruction in spoken Hebrew, and sought to expand the number of Hebrew classes, fortnightly seminars, and summer schools. The department published a monthly journal in Hebrew, *Tarbuth*, and a study aid, *Dapim*. It also sponsored extension courses on Jewish and Hebrew subjects in cooperation with the University of London, and held extramural activities in conjunction with the Anglo-Palestine Club. By 1949, the ZF boasted that over 1,200 adults were participating in Hebrew classes under its aegis or held in cooperation with the London and Middlesex County Councils; in the summer of 1949, the education department sent its first delegation of teachers to a training course in Jerusalem.[83]

---

82   Oral Interview 2324, Wellesley Aron, Institute of Contemporary Jewry, Hebrew University 9 March 1983.

83   ZF Forty-Eighth Annual Report, Jan 1948-Mar 1949, 13–15; ZF Forty-Ninth Annual Report, Mar 1949-Mar 1950, 16–18. CZA F13.

By autumn 1949, the call for the establishment of ZF-sponsored day schools was gathering momentum, and leaders of the campaign took the opportunity to make their views heard. They issued their clarion call in the ZF's outreach magazine, *The Gates of Zion*. In an article entitled 'Israel, Zionism and the Diaspora', Dr I. Fox, a leading ZF member, called for a reorganization of Anglo-Jewish education on the basis of the day school, with Hebrew and secular subjects taught 'in the day time, in ordinary school hours and in a Jewish atmosphere'.[84] Rev. Jacob Goldbloom, a senior ZF member and pioneer of the *Ivrit b'Ivrit* approach – teaching Hebrew in Hebrew – at his renowned Redman's Road Talmud Torah, pleaded for Zionists to get involved in Jewish day-school education.

> The best way to safeguard Hebrew education for the growing generation is the Jewish Day school. ... The Zionist Federation is now duty bound to unite with other organisations (the London Board [LBJRE] and all other organisations willing to co-operate in this holy task) to establish a chain of Jewish day schools all over the country, where all Jewish subjects shall be taught in Hebrew only.[85]

A resolution to this effect was submitted to the ZF's executive council for consideration at the annual conference. However, implementation of the resolution would have been problematic – the ZF had neither the financial means nor the necessary experience to establish Jewish day schools – and the resolution was shelved. When a ZF committee investigated the building costs of a single day school, they estimated that £25,000–30,000 would be necessary, to say nothing of the maintenance and staffing costs.[86]

Throughout 1952 a growing number of voices called for ZF involvement in Jewish day-school education. The introduction to the ZF's annual report for that year stated, 'We must save our youth by establishing Hebrew kindergartens, Hebrew day schools, [and] introducing modern Hebrew in all other Jewish schools, and thus foster that love for Judaism and love for Israel which will result in *chalutziut* and *aliyah* to Israel'.[87] To provide

---

84   I. Fox, 'Israel, Zionism and the Diaspora', *Gates of Zion* 4:1, October 1949, 12.

85   Rev. J. Goldbloom, 'Tasks of British Zionists', *Gates of Zion* 4:3, April 1950, 4.

86   ZF Executive Council Minutes, Education Committee Report. 16 October 1950. CZA F13 1005 I.

87   ZF Fifty-Second Annual Report, Mar 1952-Mar 1953, 10. CZA F13.

the movement's leadership with the necessary background information, and suggest possible strategies for entering the educational arena, Lavy Bakstansky, the ZF's veteran general secretary, asked Gertner to prepare a memorandum on the state of Jewish education in Great Britain.

In the memorandum, Gertner did not recommend the immediate establishment of a network of separate Zionist schools; rather, he suggested beginning by entering into collaborative efforts with existing schools.

> One is drawn to the conclusion that rather than attempting small and insignificant efforts of our own and dissipating our energy by the establishment of a small kindergarten or a small elementary school, the task of Zionism lies in taking part in and influencing existing machinery which is financially solid and which is supported and maintained by the community as a whole.[88]

But to affirm that founding its own schools was indeed its ultimate goal, in 1953 the ZF passed a resolution to establish its own day-school movement:

> The Zionist Federation is extremely perturbed by the unsatisfactory standard of Jewish education in general. It therefore considers that it is the task of the Zionist Federation to create a movement backed morally and materially by the Federation to support existing Jewish Day Schools and to establish new ones in which Hebrew should be taught as a spoken and living language.[89]

Without adequate funds to advance this goal, however, the ZF contented itself with pursuing Gertner's strategy of beginning with collaborative efforts. A proposal to open a Hebrew-speaking kindergarten at Zion House in North West London was accepted and implemented; the kindergarten opened in May 1953.[90] A Day Schools Committee was established, headed by Fox. One idea it considered was the proposal that the ZF sponsor two or three teachers of modern Hebrew in JSSM schools, in

---

88   Levi Gertner, Memorandum on Jewish Education in this Country, 5 June 1952, 5. CZA F13 42.

89   Executive Council Resolutions to the 52nd Annual Conference of the ZF 1953, no. 29. CZA F13 1005 III.

90   *Jewish Observer* (*JO*) 22 May 1953, 17.

return for which it would receive representation on the school's board of governors. This was opposed on the grounds that the said schools' ideology was unacceptable. Instead, the committee preferred to explore the possibility of a partnership with the Hillel House primary school that operated out of the Ohel Shem synagogue in Willesden, London. The fact that this synagogue was affiliated with the Federation of Synagogues gave the project special appeal, as it suggested that the arrangement might set a precedent for further cooperation with other similarly-affiliated synagogues. An agreement was soon reached with the board of governors of the Hillel House school, whereby modern Hebrew, in the Sefardic pronunciation, would be introduced into its programme, as well as lessons on daily life in Israel. In what was to be the first of many similar agreements, the ZF received representation on the school's board of governors in return for assuming some of the school's financial responsibilities. The Barcai Zionist Society, an affiliate of the ZF, promised an annual donation of £1,000 toward the project.[91]

These successes in hand, Jewish day-school education became the mission that imbued the ZF with a sense of purpose, giving the ideology-driven organization a concrete focus. Bakstansky admitted as much when, in a private letter to Goldbloom, he stated that Jewish education was 'the most important work to which the Federation is now dedicated'.[92]

Yet the ZF had to overcome a series of obstacles before it could realize its dream of a day-school movement. The more prosaic of these were funding, a limited pool of teachers, and dearth of textbooks. These problems were partially relieved when the Jewish Agency promised to allocate funds to the ZF through its department of Education and Culture in the Diaspora.[93] After the ZF had imposed a voluntary educational levy on its

91 'Hillel House–Zionist Federation Agreement', 27 August 1953. CZA F13 767/1.

92 Bakstansky to Goldbloom 7 September 1954. CZA F13 Box 220.

93 See Bakstansky to Gertner 23 February 1954, regarding a £10,000 allocation for modern Hebrew instruction in existing Jewish day schools. CZA F13 Box 165. In 1956, this sum was deemed an annual grant by Gertner, who headed the London office of the Education and Culture in the Diaspora department, see Gertner to Bakstansky 20 April 1956. CZA F13 Box 179.

members, Edward Sieff, chairman of Marks and Spencer Ltd., gave the organization generous financial support.[94] Sieff's support allowed for the establishment of the Zionist Federation Education Trust [ZFET], founded in 1955 for the purpose of establishing, funding, and administering day schools. At this point, the chief impediment to the ZF's entry into the sphere of formal Jewish education was the response of the existing communal educational establishment.

As we saw, the day schools at this time were mainly affiliated with Orthodox frameworks. Schonfeld's JSSM was affiliated with the Adath Yisroel synagogues, which in turn were associated with the anti-Zionist Agudas Yisrael. Schonfeld's attitude to Zionism fluctuated. At this particular juncture, he seemed amenable to cooperation with the Zionist movement, presumably to counterbalance the influence of the LBJRE, his antagonist in the ongoing trust funds controversy.

In 1951, Schonfeld agreed to write an article for *The Gates of Zion* on Zionism and the Jewish day-school movement. He used the opportunity to castigate the community's laxity in educating its children, and pressed for the expansion of day schools:

> In addition to omitting the teaching of religion, we have brought up many of our children as semi-pagans – a lamentable betrayal of Israel. ... Had Jewish homes been permeated with a strong Jewish atmosphere, much of this annihilation of Judaism and Jewish values might have been averted. As it is, the need for drastic action is most pressing. ... Jewish Day Schools are a crying necessity, if the degeneration is to be averted.[95]

Schonfeld was not suggesting that day schools in and of themselves were a satisfactory solution to the crisis. This depended on the substance of the syllabus and the adequacy of its understanding of Zionism. In what was a clear attack on many members of the ZF, he claimed that Zionism was not a matter of 'occasional donations' and attendance at social functions or even a 'smattering of modern Hebrew' and familiarity with 'odds and ends of Hebrew culture'. According to Schonfeld, 'Zionism in its true

94   Minutes, ZF Education Committee 21 June 1955. CZA F13 Box 186.
95   Schonfeld, 'Zionism and the Jewish Day School Movement', *Gates of Zion* 5:2, 1951, 8–9.

sense means ... a policy of living Jewish lives in the Diaspora until *aliyah* comes true'.[96] In other words, Schonfeld's Zionism was inextricably linked to religious observance.

In 1953, Schonfeld accepted an invitation from the Zionist movement to participate in an Anglo-Israel club symposium on Jewish education. Joining him on the podium were Reverend Goldbloom and Rabbi Rosen, whose Carmel College had received some funding from the ZF.[97] Schonfeld took the opportunity, once again, to assail mainstream Anglo-Jewry's existing educational frameworks. He argued that 'vested interests' were misleading the community into believing that genuine Jewish education was being provided. Although the brunt of his attack was directed at the LBJRE, he also held the Zionist movement responsible, claiming it was led by 'assimilationists, snobs, and people who themselves did not want to be Jews'.[98]

The Zionists, too, had reservations about the LBJRE, contending that it functioned 'as if the State of Israel had not been established'. An anonymous article in the *Jewish Observer*, apparently the work of Gertner, criticized the LBJRE for failing to teach Hebrew as a living language, impart national pride, or identify with the celebration of festivals in Israel.[99] Dr Fox too took the LBJRE to task for these alleged offences:

> One might have expected that the [London Board], being engaged entirely in the sphere of Hebrew and religious education, might have felt the impact of such a unique event as the creation of the State of Israel, might have laid greater emphasis upon spoken Hebrew, upon history, upon life in Israel, its struggles and ambitions. The London Board however, was too busy with its own particular problems: lack of pupils, poor attendance at classes, lack of suitable teachers, finance, etc. ... The result was that apart from what individual teachers, if so inclined, taught their pupils about Israel, the children were not made aware of the existence of the new Jewish State.[100]

96 Ibid.

97 The ZF gave Carmel College £2,500 for bursaries in 1953. Bakstansky to Gertner 23 February 1954. CZA F13 Box 165.

98 *JO* 30 October 1953, 18–19.

99 'Have Anglo-Jewish Educationalists Recognised the Existence of Israel?' *JO* 6 June 1952, 12–13. The LBJRE's inviting Israeli Ambassador Eliahu Elath to distribute the awards at its subsequent prize-giving ceremony may have been a response to this criticism, see *JC* 27 February 1953, 11.

100 I. Fox, 'Some Problems in Hebrew Education', *Gates of Zion* 8:3, 1954, 2.

Fox condemned the LBJRE's approach to Jewish education, suggesting that it supported Jewish day schools so long as they served the purpose 'of anglicising the children of foreign Jews'. But, he claimed, once this goal had been achieved and the children had integrated into British society, such schools were 'vehemently opposed'. This 'assimilationist' view, he alleged, encouraged Jewish children to attend 'Christian' day schools so that they might adjust their lives to the prevailing Christian mores. Fox argued that this stance explained the LBJRE's support for Sunday Hebrew classes as the preferred framework for imparting the tenets of the Jewish faith, as it paralleled the format of Christian education and hence was deemed a legitimate form of segregation. By contrast, he extolled the Zionist educational outlook:

> We state quite categorically that we Jews *are* different from our neighbours. In fact, to preserve our group identity is one of the objects of Zionism in the Diaspora. We are different from our non-Jewish neighbours not only in our religious observances, customs, and tradition, but also in our history, in our racial origin, in our outlook, in our ideals, in our philosophical concepts of life, in our feeling of kinship with our brethren and in our attachment to the Land of Israel.

The goals of a Zionist education were to Hebraicize Jewish education and make the children bilingual and ultimately bicultural. Waxing poetic, Fox described a time when, through fluency in Hebrew, 'ancient and modern Hebraic culture would restore the soul of the Jewish people'. Hebraicization of the Jewish people would 'lead to a revival of Jewish culture, and participation with Israel in a renaissance of Jewish art, drama, music, poetry etc'. Fox proposed replacing the traditional supplementary Sunday school and evening classes with Hebrew day schools offering the best in secular education alongside Judaic and Hebrew studies. In this framework, the child's personality, 'will no longer be split between a Christian and Jewish half'.[101]

101   Ibid.

The Zionists 'conquer' the LBJRE

In 1952, Gertner had prepared a memorandum for the ZF on strategies for increasing its influence in the sphere of day-school education. He recommended that the ZF use its tried-and-true tactic of infiltration to change the LBJRE's ideological orientation.

Theodor Herzl had been the first to suggest this method, when in his message to the Second Zionist Congress, in 1898, he had called for a 'conquest of the communities'. But it was Lavy Bakstansky who first applied this theory in Britain, when he engineered the 1938 election of Selig Brodetsky as the first Zionist president of the Board of Deputies, the 'Anglo-Jewish parliament'. He repeated this feat five years later when, at a critical juncture for Zionist diplomacy – it would have been deeply embarrassing for the Zionist movement had the elected head of the Jewish community in England, which administered Mandatory Palestine, not been sympathetic to Zionism – he organized an effort to pack the Board with Zionist-leaning deputies.[102] Thereafter, a caucus was regularly employed to lobby Zionist sympathizers at the Board of Deputies, especially during its triennial election campaigns. In late 1942, the Zionists contemplated extending this policy to the United Synagogue Council elections. A veteran Zionist, Paul Goodman, called on members of the parallel ZF-sponsored Zionist Synagogue Council:

> To follow up the elections to the Board with elections of good Zionists to the United Synagogue Council. It is time that this important body of Anglo-Jewry becomes more Zionistically inclined. We cannot do it by convincing the existing leaders. ... It is almost a useless task, but we can do it by getting more Zionists on the Council.[103]

102　See Shimoni, 'Selig Brodetsky'.

103　Minutes, Central Zionist Synagogue Council 14 March 1946. CZA F13 1012. These machinations continued until 1949, when the disapproval of United Synagogue Council members impelled the Zionists to desist from actively seeking to influence the elections, see Minutes, Central Zionist Synagogue Council 9 May 1949, CZA F13 1012.

Returning to 1952, Gertner, in his capacity as honorary secretary of the Zionist Synagogue Council and executive member of the ZF, recommended, with Bakstansky's encouragement, applying these tactics on the education front.

Gertner's memorandum focused on the LBJRE's structure, paying close attention to the election of central committee members; it also assessed its financial resources, noting that most of its income was drawn from the United Synagogue's education levy, set at 33 per cent of synagogue membership dues. Although the LBJRE operated at a deficit, the United Synagogue covered the shortfall. In assessing the balance of power within the LBJRE, Gertner concluded that although the Chief Rabbi had considerable influence, overall the LBJRE was sensitive to public opinion, namely, views held by the members who sat on its various committees, or expressed in the Jewish press. Capturing the LBJRE, Gertner concluded, would allow the ZF to neutralize opposition to its goal of establishing day schools of its own, and secure cooperation with local synagogues. Moreover, the Chief Rabbi's status as LBJRE president would constitute an endorsement of these activities.

The memorandum also critiqued the LBJRE's substantive pedagogy and curriculum, despite the recent addition of Hebrew as a living language, and the promise to introduce modern Hebrew literature. Gertner doubted these steps would have much impact, given the curriculum's 'over-emphasis' on religious matters. He proposed adopting the *Ivrit b'Ivrit* method of teaching Hebrew, and the introduction of Sefardic pronunciation. He recommended that the Zionists demand of the LBJRE that its syllabus cover contemporary Jewish history, especially the history of the Zionist movement up to the establishment of the State.[104]

Implementing the Bakstansky-Gertner game-plan, in July 1954 the ZF organized a campaign to take over the LBJRE at the upcoming biennial elections. Bakstansky co-ordinated this campaign from his Russell Street office, aided by Fox, Woolf Perry, E. Chanan, and Salmond Levin. The plan was for Levin to submit his candidacy for the LBJRE chairmanship.

---

104 Gertner, Memorandum, n 88 above, 2.

Levin had suitable credentials, being a long-serving LBJRE member, its vice-chairman since 1952, and co-author of the Lipman-Levin report on the trust funds. Moreover, he was not a member of the Zionist inner circle, which was seen as an asset, as his candidacy would appeal to the LBJRE's more independent-minded members. Levin was ambitious, and although there was some question as to his popularity, all other considerations seemed to favour his candidacy.[105] A deal was struck whereby in return for Zionist backing, Levin would, upon election, implement a series of changes to the LBJRE modus operandi. Hebrew would be integrated into the curriculum of new day schools, the LBJRE would utilize materials produced by the Jewish Agency's Education and Culture Department, and Yom Ha'atzmaut, Israel's Independence Day, would be recognized in the supplementary schools as an additional holiday to be celebrated. Levin would also make significant changes in personnel, appointing Zionist figures such as Gertner and Fox to the LBJRE, and its day-school committee.[106]

Levin managed to win, beating incumbent Alfred Woolf by a mere seven votes, but his election was only one of a number of important changes at the LBJRE. Woolf Perry, the honorary secretary of the ZF, secured the parallel position at the LBJRE, and E. Chanan was elected honorary treasurer. Chanan had been a key figure in the Hillel House School negotiations. Clearly, then, the election results were a serious blow for the non-Zionist establishment within the United Synagogue, particularly because they had taken the unusual step of circulating a letter to the LBJRE's membership requesting re-election of the incumbents.[107] Yet although these elections seemed to usher in a new era for Anglo-Jewish education – and indeed, in 1956, Fox's election to the LBJRE, and the re-election of various Zionist representatives, was considered a show of support for the ZF's educational vision – as we will see, the long-term effects of the putative regime change were not dramatic.

105　See Perry to Bakstansky 25 June 1954. CZA F13 Box 27; Bakstansky to Levin, Perry, Chanan and Fox 25 June 1954. CZA F13 Box 8.

106　Perry to Bakstansky 20 July 1954, reminding Bakstansky of the need to 'tie [Levin] down' re the said commitments. CZA F13 Box 157.

107　See letter written by Nat Rubin, 28 June 1954. CZA F13 Box 130.

The United Synagogue fights back

One of the first tasks of the LBJRE's newly-elected honorary officers was
to appoint trustees to the recently-established London Jewish Educational
Foundation. It will be recalled that this body had been created to distribute the trust funds monies and coordinate the planning of Jewish schools
in London. When the list of trustees was compiled, the name of Alfred
Woolf, the LBJRE's past chairman and chief negotiator during the trust
funds controversy, was conspicuously absent. The insensitivity of the newly-
elected Zionist officers toward Woolf was immediately condemned both
at the LBJRE meeting and in the pages of the *Jewish Chronicle*. One correspondent attacked the 'autocratic procedure' by which the LBJRE had
appointed its trustees, another asked what could have motivated the decision 'that a predecessor with a distinguished record in the field of Jewish
education should be consigned to the scrap heap'.[108]

The episode generated tension between the LBJRE's honorary officers
and the United Synagogue, its main sponsor. Such ungentlemanly behaviour
at this most English of Anglo-Jewish institutions would not pass unop-
posed. By January 1955, Ewen Montagu, president of the United Synagogue,
mounted a campaign to re-examine the role of his organization in financing
the major part of the LBJRE's budget. Predictably, the Zionists saw this
as an attempt to undermine their victory at the LBJRE. Bakstansky sum-
moned leading supporters to devise a defence, for if the United Synagogue
withdrew its support from the LBJRE and established a new body, then
the ZF's takeover of the LBJRE would have been for naught.

Under the agreements signed after the 1945 communal conference on
educational reconstruction, it had been determined that United Synagogue
members would pay an education levy equal to one third of their dues
to cover the LBJRE's operation costs. Montagu alleged that this burden
was disproportionate, and responsible for the United Synagogue's serious
financial problems. In January 1955, he called on members of the United

108 *JC* 8 October 1954, 13.

Synagogue council to establish a committee of inquiry into the organization's relations with the LBJRE. Montagu's resolution was carried, and the committee's report confirmed that the financial contribution of United Synagogue members to the LBJRE was three times that of members of the other LBJRE-affiliated organizations. The report argued that it was essential that these other partners pay their proper part, if not an equal share. In particular, the inquiry called on the Federation of Synagogues to increase its contribution. The commission also examined the question of representation on the LBJRE, and found that it was 'not commensurate with the financial contributions and sacrifices of the respective parent bodies'. Further, it was also 'disturbed to find that there existed in the Board "pressure groups" pursuing sectional interests' – a clear reference to the ZF. It proposed to curtail the phenomenon by expanding the number of office holders and making representation proportionate to financial contribution.[109]

The commission's findings only strengthened the Zionists' conviction that the United Synagogue was set 'to destroy the London Board ... by wielding the massive threat of its cheque book, and replace it with a satellite educational body of its own'.[110] Despite the rancour, the United Synagogue, after the personal intervention of the Chief Rabbi, agreed to set aside the recommendations of its special commission and instead convene a communal conference to discuss the funding of the LBJRE. The *Jewish Observer* – the official organ of the ZF – lauded the decision as a 'decisive setback' for Montagu.

Yet it seems Montagu got over his anger at the ZF activists' tactics, or had a change of heart concerning Zionist involvement in Jewish education. As we will soon see, he was to play a central role in negotiations between the United Synagogue and ZF concerning the establishment of the Rosh Pinah School on the premises of the Edgware United Synagogue. When, a year later, the Chief Rabbi tried to downplay the significance of the Rosh Pinah agreement, Montagu defended the LBJRE's agreement with the ZF at a communal conference.

---

109 *JC* 1 July 1955, 8–9.
110 *JO* 24 June 1955, 8, 18–19.

In July 1955, the ZF learned that the premises of the Edgware Synagogue, whose rabbi, Saul Amias, was a staunch friend of the Zionist
movement, were to be sold. They immediately decided to purchase the
building for use as a Jewish day school. Bakstansky negotiated a price and
appealed to Nahum Goldmann, head of the Jewish Agency, for the necessary funds. Goldmann obliged and shortly thereafter a purchase agreement
was announced.[111] As the synagogue had belonged to the United Synagogue,
it too had been involved in the negotiations, focusing on the proposed
school's ideological outlook, and ultimately passing a resolution in favour
of the sale. The ZF promised to pay £20,000 for the property.

Conscious of the need to couch its educational efforts in religious
terms, the ZF assured the Chief Rabbi that the curriculum would be 'based
upon the tenets of traditional Judaism'.[112] Though the ZF demanded the
inclusion of modern Hebrew to be taught with Sefardic pronunciation, it
made no attempt to establish a secular Hebrew school on the lines of those
thriving in Israel. Such secularism had little support within Anglo-Jewry
or the ZF rank and file. The sides agreed that the ZF would 'not employ
teachers of secular subjects who seek to impart either an anti-religious or
anti-traditional bias in their instruction' and that in the event of disagree-
ments over religious questions, 'the Chief Rabbi would be the final arbiter'.
The *Jewish Chronicle* found little reason to criticize the accord and every
reason to commend it. Montagu expressed hope that the school would be
the first of many, and 'have a lasting effect on Anglo-Jewry, and help to
weld it together'. Chief Rabbi Brodie, too, welcomed the agreement, especially the ZF's promise that the curriculum would emphasize the religious
aspects of Judaism.[113]

---

111   18 November 1955. CZA Z6 978.
112   Details of the agreement were published in *JC* 30 December 1955, 6.
113   *JC* 18 November 1955, 12; 30 December 1955, 9.

Kulturkampf

Despite the apparent meeting of minds regarding the Zionist movement's involvement in Jewish education, there was, in fact, considerable tension. Several years before the Edgware school agreement, the Chief Rabbi, sensitive to the broader implications of cooperation with the ZF, had made a point of distancing himself from the Zionist movement. Late in 1952, a series of religious crises in Israel had offended Orthodox sensibilities worldwide, generating protests against Israel by British groups affiliated with Agudas Yisrael. Leading the protests was Harry Goodman, Agudas Yisrael's key activist and editor of its broadsheet *Jewish Weekly*. The protests intensified when the non-Zionist Aguda-related parties left the coalition government in Israel over two contentious issues: the conscription of women, and Ben-Gurion's alleged attempt to end the 'stream' system in Israeli schools. News that the sale of pork was permitted in Israel further antagonized even the non-haredi Orthodox sectors of Anglo-Jewry.

Chief Rabbi Brodie viewed these developments with concern. Though a supporter of the Zionist movement who had assisted in its political and philanthropic efforts, he had also expressed disappointment over the Israeli government's stances on religious issues. The new developments disturbed him, and he informed the embassy in London of his views. He requested of Ambassador Elath that 'those in authority be made aware of the tense feeling, which this news has aroused within the community. ... I feel that the announcement [concerning the sale of pork] as well as other anti-religious factors are making it difficult for those who think like me to be wholehearted [in our support]'.[114]

Brodie feared his association with the ZF's educational efforts might be misconstrued as approval of the Israeli government's stance on religious issues. Nevertheless, when the Israeli embassy invited him to visit the Jewish state, he accepted, seeking to see things first-hand. The embassy anticipated

---

114 Chief Rabbi to E. Elath [Israeli ambassador] 6 January 1953. All correspondence
      with the Israeli ambassador is from ISA 130.13 2585/3.

that upon return home from his fact-finding mission, Brodie would help quell the growing anti-Israel feeling by participating 'in a propaganda campaign throughout Britain'.[115] But the Chief Rabbi was not placated by what he saw, and shortly after his return, protested Israel's secular leanings.[116]

In autumn 1953, the Jewish Agency allocated £10,000 to fund modern Hebrew classes at existing Jewish day schools.[117] The Chief Rabbi attacked this development at the annual Mizrachi (Religious Zionist movement) conference, admonishing that 'not a single penny of Jewish Agency funds should be spent on Jewish education, whether in Hebrew classes, Talmud Torahs, day schools, secondary schools, public schools or kindergartens'.[118] Brodie opposed such funding because he feared it would lead to interference in the content and method of Anglo-Jewish education, and thus to a more secular approach. He was uneasy about the implications of couching Jewish identity in non-religious terms, and saw the controversies in Israel as arising from this approach.[119] His anxieties increased when Mapam, the left-wing Zionist movement, joined the ZF in February 1956, and a letter from Bakstansky promising that all agreements with the United Synagogue would be honoured did not allay his fears.[120]

In May 1956, Brodie addressed these issues at a conference on the subject of religious and Zionist schools. Commenting on a report about

---

115   E. Elath to Director General of Foreign Ministry, Israel 14 November 1952 (Hebrew).

116   See letter from Wallach, where he expresses the Chief Rabbi's 'concerns' about the government's 'religious backsliding', 27 April 1953; cable from Federation of Synagogues Va'ad HaRabbonim to Ambassador Elath 21 July 1953.

117   See Bakstansky to Gertner, 23 February 1954. CZA F13 Box 165.

118   JC 27 November 1953, 12. See also I. Jakobovits, *The Attitude to Zionism of Britain's Chief Rabbis as Reflected in their Writings* (London: Jewish Historical Society of England, 1981), 13.

119   Brodie reiterated his opposition to using Zionist monies to fund Jewish education in Britain at the 1954 Board of Deputies' Commonwealth Conference, where the idea of the Jewish Agency's establishing a teachers' college was discussed, and again following the Rosh Pinah agreement in December 1955. See JO 2 July 1954, 16 and JC 30 December 1955, 9.

120   Bakstansky to Chief Rabbi 11 June 1956. ACC 2805/66.

the recent Zionist Congress in Israel, he voiced dismay that a delegate had spoken in favour of Jewish day schools that were 'entirely unlike religious day schools', but rather, emphasized Hebrew and secular Israeli culture. The Chief Rabbi feared that such a tendency might take root in Britain, and suggested as much when he noted that the ZF membership 'might not be well-known for their religious observance, perhaps they might be distinguished for their non-observance'. Despite the undertakings he had received, he feared that there would be a tendency to teach Hebrew for its own sake, rather than as the language of Jewish prayer, Jewish law, and Jewish learning. 'It was not enough', he said, 'to teach the children to say in Hebrew, "This is a table", but [they should be taught] to say, "this is the table which is before the Lord."' Brodie was not against teaching about Israel, but maintained that 'the dominant note at all times must be the emphasis on religious beliefs and practice based on Jewish knowledge'.[121]

The Chief Rabbi's criticism of the ZF was echoed in *Jewish Chronicle* editorials, which took the view that the community would 'need to give very anxious consideration to all the implications of the sponsoring of Anglo-Jewish day schools by the Zionist movement'. A. Richtiger, the ZF chairman, lost no time in responding to the growing attack on his organization's involvement in day schools. Noting that there was general dissatisfaction with the state of Jewish education in England, and that the community was apprehensive about assimilation, he defiantly declared that 'we mean to continue this work and extend it to the limits of our own financial ability'.[122]

During the summer of 1956 tensions in Israel concerning religious issues reached new heights after the death, in a run-in with the Israeli police, of someone protesting Sabbath-desecration in Jerusalem. These developments were covered in the Anglo-Jewish press and seized upon by the anti-Zionist elements in the community. Harry Goodman led the attack, castigating the World Zionist Organization 'for spending enormous sums, which were completely changing the cultural, educational and reli-

121 *JC* 11 May 1956, 12.
122 *JC* 25 May 1956, 18; 1 June 1956, 8.

gious outlook of the Diaspora communities'.[123] Later that year, the Shotzer Rebbe, principal of the Gateshead Yeshiva, and the head of the UOHC, condemned the ZF and the Chief Rabbi for their activities in the sphere of Jewish education. A manifesto was circulated calling on parents to

> ascertain that the teachers and leaders of the schools in whose hands the education of their children is entrusted are observant and God-fearing people imbued with love of Torah and Mitzvoth. For only those who are themselves observant can impart Torah to our children, save them from the threat of assimilation, and lead them steadfastly along the road of our forefathers.[124]

The mounting opposition to the involvement of the ZF in Jewish education, much of which was voiced by the haredi and modern-Orthodox communities, could not be overlooked by the Chief Rabbi. As we saw, he had his own reservations about the Zionists' involvement. The confluence of the aforementioned developments in Israel and expansion of the ZF's educational activities led him to take the unprecedented step of demanding a halt to further ZF educational endeavours. He wrote to the ZF's general secretary as follows:

> Up to the present we have not had any Jewish Day School associated with a party ideology. It will be a sorry day for our community if we are to be further divided into parties in the sphere of education. It becomes most imperative therefore that any steps that your Federation has taken to extend its work should be halted until such time as I have had the opportunity of settling the issues with the Zionist Federation.[125]

Bakstansky and his honorary officers quickly replied to Chief Rabbi Brodie, accusing him of 'backtracking' on the Rosh Pinah agreement, and reminding him that during the negotiations, the United Synagogue repre-

---

123 *JC* 27 April 1956, p. 12. A year earlier, Goodman had asserted, 'The establishment of a secular Jewish State, with all its implications for Jewish religious life, may not be a matter for rejoicing or thanksgiving'. Goodman to secretary of United Synagogue 18 April 1955. ISA 130.13 2585/3. (It is interesting that the Israeli embassy got hold of a copy of this private letter).

124 *JC* 13 July, 9 and 31 August 1956, 6.

125 Chief Rabbi to Bakstansky 20 August 1956. CZA F13 Box 111.

sentatives had inserted the clause 'in all schools to be established by the ZF'. This, he suggested, implied that the Chief Rabbi was 'aware of our plans to establish as many day schools as our funds would permit, and it was certainly not a question of two or three day schools'. Bakstansky argued that it was now too late for the Chief Rabbi to reopen the issue, when not only had he signed the accord, but the ZF had observed its letter and spirit.

> My principal Honorary Officers deeply regret that they cannot possibly accept the suggestion that our work should be halted even for one single moment. They are aware of no new circumstances which have arisen now and which did not exist at the time of our agreement with the United Synagogue which would warrant any such proposal.[126]

This exchange did not end the matter. Chief Rabbi Brodie used his annual New Year Message, published in the *Jewish Chronicle*, to voice further criticism of the ZF:

> Education as a topic of discussion and argument seems to produce a crop of unusual but confident experts ... spokesmen of other organisations whose activities have been concentrated in other communal fields. ... We cannot afford, nor must we tolerate, any suggestion of 'trends' or political slogans in the aims and content of Jewish education which are liable to aggravate the spirit of factionalism.[127]

In his sermon at the Great Synagogue on the first day of Rosh Hashanah, Brodie extended his criticism, attacking the secular leanings of the State of Israel:

> Religious indifferentism, vehement positive secularism flies in the face of our religious historic outlook [and] cannot for long command the mystic and deeply felt affection of world Jewry. ... Notwithstanding the considerable bonds of language and a common attachment to the land of Israel, it is well to remember that the prime factor and leaven of Jewish unification and survival is and remains the Torah.[128]

---

126 Bakstansky to Chief Rabbi 21 August 1956. CZA F13 Box 111.
127 *JC* 14 September 1956, 5.
128 Ibid.

The Zionist movement's response was to extend its day-school activity. In July 1956, the ZF announced it had signed another day-school agreement, this time in the northern city of Leeds. There, the local Board of Jewish Religious Education had joined forces with the Leeds Zionist Council to establish the city's first Jewish primary school, to be named after the Zionist leader and former Leeds University math professor, Selig Brodetsky.[129] Three months later, yet another agreement to establish a primary school was announced, this one in co-operation with the Clapton Federation Synagogue in North-East London. This provoked an uproar not only from the fervently Orthodox, but also within that synagogue itself. Eighteen of its honorary officers supported the agreement, ten opposed it, and the vice-president of the Federation of Synagogues, with which the synagogue was affiliated, resigned his post, asserting that it was 'against the fundamental religious principles of the Federation to associate with a political party whose intrusion into Jewish education was resented by all Orthodox Jewry, and had been condemned by Orthodox rabbis.'[130]

Rabbi Schonfeld and his UOHC immediately joined the opposition, having already voiced disapproval of the opening of the Rosh Pinah School in Edgware, particularly since it was only a few hundred yards from their own Hasmonean primary school. When the local authorities moved to close down the JSSM-affiliated school because it had been established without the necessary permits, the local council cited the existence of the ZF school as evidence that Schonfeld's school was unnecessary. The announcement of the opening of additional ZF schools in Leeds and Clapton intensified the resentment. At the UOHC's annual meeting, all the speakers condemned the ZF's intrusion into day-school education. A public protest meeting held at the Stamford Hill Bet HaMidrash synagogue and attended by supporters of Agudas Yisrael, Mizrachi and the Federation of Synagogues, passed an antagonistic resolution condemning the 'anti-religious character' of ZF schools and their teachers' 'profane attitude' to traditional Judaism.[131]

---

129   JO 20 July 1956, 8; ZF Honorary Officers' Minutes. CZA F13 1008 III.
130   JC 12 October 1956, 5.
131   News and Views [Agudas Israel Organization of Great Britain] 26 October 1956, 1. ACC 2805/66. Unless otherwise specified, correspondence and archival material pertaining to opposition to the ZFET schools is from ACC 2805/66.

The opposition to the ZF schools gathered momentum. Several honorary officers of the Mizrachi organization, devoted Zionists themselves, attended the Stamford Hill protest meeting. Indeed, a number of Mizrachi members had attempted to overturn the decision regarding co-operation between the ZF and the Clapton Federation Synagogue. In other words, the ZF was now being opposed by its allies, a situation that reflected divisions within Israel, where the religious parties had recently left the ruling coalition over similar educational concerns.[132]

Sensing that a *kulturkampf* might be imminent, the Chief Rabbi called a communal conference. Tensions ran high, and it was clear that if one side attended, the other would absent itself. The Chief Rabbi was duty-bound to impress upon both sides the importance of their mutual participation, but there is no doubt that if he had to offend one side, he preferred to offend the Zionists and not the Orthodox. Again, this mirrored the scenario in Israel, where the national religious party had allied itself with the other religious parties and jettisoned its partnership with the secular Zionists.

Invitations to the conference were sent by the Chief Rabbi's office to those organizations and school movements involved in providing formal Jewish education in England. His accompanying letter opened with a statement of satisfaction at the interest being taken in Jewish day schools, alongside 'misgivings' about the emergence of uncoordinated and incompatible efforts in this field. He warned that if matters were allowed to continue unchecked, the looming *kulturkampf* might do 'untold damage to the fabric and structure of the Anglo-Jewish community'. He was therefore calling a conference, whose purpose was to

132   In a letter to the Chief Rabbi, B. Mindel of the Mizrachi organization stated, regarding the schools in Clapton and Leeds, 'We cannot abandon this most important field of activity to a non-religious body, whatever the safeguards'. 23 August 1956. And a letter to the Chief Rabbi from the World Mizrachi headquarters in Jerusalem expressed apprehension about ZF activities in Anglo-Jewish education and reflected bitterly on the organization's own struggles in Israel, see Gellerman to Chief Rabbi 16 September 1956.

(1) Ensure the essentially religious character of Jewish education in this country;
(2) co-ordinate all efforts in this field, while giving full scope to the diversity of
approach within the limits imposed by (1) above; and (3) ensure that available
resources are applied to the best advantage, by dealing with such problems as site-
ing and finance.[133]

This agenda was obviously an attempt to preserve the status quo and prevent the development of a secular ethnic – national orientation in Anglo-
Jewish education.

As anticipated, Schonfeld replied that the JSSM, which was affiliated with Agudas Yisrael, could not possibly 'associate in any way with
the Zionist Federation or their "schools". Our view is that they have not
a single proper school and further, even if they will have such a school or
schools, we should not condone their entry into the field by implicitly
recognizing their status'.[134] In the same vein, Bakstansky explained that
it would be inappropriate for the Zionists to join the conference, given
Agudas Yisrael's ongoing deprecation of Israel and Zionism.[135] Concerned
that the ZF's absence would be interpreted as a slight to the Chief Rabbi,
Bakstansky stressed that their non-participation in the conference, 'was in
no way meant as a sign of disrespect to the Chief Rabbi, whom we regard
as our Chief Rabbi and whose authority in religious matters we accept,
not only in our day schools, but in all our work'.[136]

In the end, the ZF did not participate, clearing the way for the participation of the Schonfeld camp. In his opening address, the Chief Rabbi
proposed the establishment of an umbrella organization to coordinate
Anglo-Jewry's efforts in the finance and planning of day-school education.
His hope was that this coordinating body would take steps to curtail the
proliferation of educational frameworks associated with political movements
– a formulation that, though general, referred to the ZF. Brodie warned that
without such a supervisory mechanism, there was a real danger of schism.

---

133   Wallach to Jewish education organizations 10 September 1956; Wallach to Bakstansky
      10 September 1956. CZA F13 Box 111.
134   Schonfeld to Wallach 17 September 1956.
135   Bakstansky to CR 17 September 1956.
136   Bakstansky to Chief Rabbi 24 September 1956.

Several delegates used the conference to chastise the ZF for its involvement in day-school education. Rabbi Babad of the UOHC, for instance, claimed that the sole raison d'être of day-school education was the imparting of religious education, hence such schools could not be run by those who 'could not be entrusted with religious education'. This sentiment was echoed by Schonfeld, who expressed support for the Chief Rabbi's minimalist interpretation of the Rosh Pinah agreement (he claimed it pertained to the Rosh Pinah school alone, whereas the ZF claimed it applied to all schools the ZF might establish) that had been concluded between the United Synagogue and the ZF. Ironically, it fell to Ewen Montagu to defend the Zionist movement's right to establish a school system if it so wished. It was a free country, he noted, where 'anyone who so desired could set up day schools'. More importantly, 'as regards the Edgware School, the United Synagogue had ensured the religious side of the Zionist school. ... In any case, the United Synagogue had signed an agreement and they had to abide by it'. Montagu's speech went on to criticize, albeit subtly, the Chief Rabbi's New Year's message, claiming it had not been conducive to the harmony the Chief Rabbi said he desired.[137]

Over the following months, the tension continued unabated. Following a speech by the ZF chairman that referred to funds received from the Jewish Agency, Brodie decided – pending an inquiry – to hold in abeyance his sponsorship of the Joint Palestine Appeal (JPA)'s Kol Nidre Appeal.[138] The leaders of the Zionist movement immediately understood the implications of the Chief Rabbi's withholding approval of a major JPA fundraising appeal, a radical step. Springing into action, they insistently explained that the money collected by the JPA was not used for Jewish day schools or other Zionist schools in Britain. Technically, this was accurate, because monies collected in England were not distributed locally, but sent to Jerusalem, where they were redistributed along with other funds

---

137 Minutes, Meeting Convened by the Chief Rabbi, 22 September 1956. CZA F13 Box 111.

138 See Chief Rabbi to Richtiger; Harwich to Chief Rabbi; Bakstansky to Sieff; Wallach to Harwich; May 1957 CZA F13 Box 117.

donated by Diaspora Jewry. Though the bulk of this money remained in Israel, certain sums found their way back to England for day-school work through the Education and Culture and Torah Education departments of the Jewish Agency. Hence, argued S. Harwich, the JPA's general secretary, the Chief Rabbi should voice his concerns to the Jewish Agency, and not penalize the JPA.

When the Chief Rabbi remained unmoved, Harwich and Bakstansky contacted leaders of the Mizrachi organization, which the Chief Rabbi was titular head of, urging them to remind the Chief Rabbi that their organization was a direct beneficiary of JPA funds. In a letter to Edward Sieff, President of the JPA, Bakstansky railed: 'They [the Mizrachi organization] cannot on the one hand be in the JPA and obtain from us 5½ per cent [of the JPA's intake] and in addition receive money from the Jewish Agency's Torah Education Department, and on the other hand, have their President, the Chief Rabbi, deny us the Kol Nidrei appeal'. This pressure, and Sieff's intervention, made the Chief Rabbi reconsider his position. Nine days after his threat to withdraw support for the JPA appeal, the Chief Rabbi relented.

A consultative council on Jewish day schools?

The need to present a united communal front during negotiations with the national authorities over future educational legislation was yet another factor spurring demand for a body to coordinate Anglo-Jewry's day schools. Moreover, there was growing awareness that Jewish schools were competing for limited communal resources. Some schools apparently hoped a council could help them preserve their influence and pre-empt competitors. All the day-school organizations claimed to support establishment of a consultative council, but when the need for compromise arose, each organization protected its own autonomy. The *Jewish Chronicle* argued emphatically that a council was necessary:

> Overriding everything else is the very real danger that we might see in Anglo-Jewish education the 'trend' system, so well known in Israel, of separate and competitive chains of schools each run on partisan lines. Such a system could lead to wholesale wastage of public money, to the site-ing of schools for reasons of competition and not of necessity, and to the injection of a partisan spirit into members of the community while still at school.

The newspaper pinpointed three organizations whose cooperation would be crucial: the JSSM, which it correctly anticipated would be 'the tougher proposition', the LBJRE, and the ZFET, which had been established in 1955 to fund and run the ZF day schools.[139] In the months that followed, the *Jewish Chronicle* actively lobbied for establishment of a community-wide coordinating committee, not only by giving the issue significant coverage and by interviewing communal leaders as to their stands on the subject, but also by explicitly censuring those it perceived as opposing the idea.

Almost immediately, the debate over establishing a coordinating committee became an arena for mutual recriminations between the Zionists and the JSSM. When the *Jewish Chronicle* asked communal leaders for their reactions to the proposed day-school council, Rabbi Schonfeld took the opportunity to renew his attack on the ZFET schools, declaring that he would not cooperate with them. Indeed, he maintained that the ZF had not established any 'Jewish day schools in the proper sense of the term', and asserted that he was being 'asked to cooperate with something that does not exist'.[140] ZF officials rebutted these attacks, and their chairman concluded that given Schonfeld's accusations, cooperation with the JSSM was 'a waste of time'.[141] Beatrice Barwell, vice-chair of the ZF's day-school committee, added her voice to the debate, stating that 'the absence of cooperation must be laid fairly and squarely at Dr Schonfeld's door, since his wild utterances, repeated ad nauseam, illustrate the bias of any proposals he sponsors'.[142]

139 'Day School Trends', *JC* 21 November 1958, 20.
140 *JC* 5 December 1958, 38.
141 *JC* 19 December 1958, 8.
142 *JC* 20 February 1959, 18.

Although the tensions between the Orthodox and secular political camps in Israel had abated somewhat, in Britain, mutual suspicions as to the other side's educational agenda persisted. An editorial in the Agudas Yisrael broadsheet exemplified such sentiments: 'The fact that the Rabbonim, the guardians of Torah life within our people, are against such schools is in itself sufficient proof that such schools jeopardize the influence of religion in Jewish life. Such schools concur with the aim of political Zionism to replace Torah by secularist and G-dless nationalism'.[143]

Other animosities also attested to the bitter rivalry between the various school organizations. For instance, the ZF had for some time alleged that it had been discriminated against by the Claims Conference, which had denied its applications for funding, whereas those of the JSSM and other ultra-Orthodox groups had been approved. In 1959, the LBJRE voiced similar concerns. Tensions also surfaced over the deepening crisis facing the JSSM's Avigdor School, the first Jewish school to lose state-aided status (see Chapter 1). Schonfeld accused the LBJRE of not trying hard enough to rescue the school, and even schadenfreude.[144]

Yet it was the governors of the JSSM, at Rabbi Schonfeld's behest, who first initiated a conference for the purpose of establishing a day-school council. Schonfeld envisaged the new body as a counterweight to the authority of the Chief Rabbi, the centrist-Orthodox LBJRE, and the expanding ZFET school network. He had always kept his distance from what he deemed the 'lukewarm Orthodoxy' of the United Synagogue and its affiliates, and its recent agreements with the ZFET reinforced his conviction that the aim of these organizations was to lead Anglo-Jewry away from religiously intense Judaism. The LBJRE's success in re-establishing the JFS, and the opening of a string of Zionist schools with the financial backing of the Sieff and Sacher families, deepened his resolve to maintain his movement's dominance in the day-school sphere. He looked to the various fervently-

---

143 *News and Views* 27 March 1959. ACC 2805/66. Unless otherwise specified, correspondence and archival material pertaining to the consultative council is from ACC 2805/66.

144 See Draft Letter [not sent] to Chief Rabbi 13 November 1959. MS 183 248/1.

Orthodox groups for support, even though these allies were more strictly separationist in their approach to communal affairs. Yet Schonfeld faced a dilemma. Though he wanted to strengthen his position as leader of both the Jewish day-school movement and the 'right-wing' Orthodox elements of Anglo-Jewry, he did not wish to fracture his relationship with the Chief Rabbi, who, as honorary president of the JSSM schools, lent him much needed respectability in the eyes of the local and national authorities.

In his invitation to Jewish day schools requesting their participation in creating a day-school council, Schonfeld cited the lack of such a body as the reason why consultations were not taking place between Jewish day schools and the national authorities, though there had recently been negotiations regarding denominational schools between the Churches and the Ministry of Education. Schonfeld was aware that the Chief Rabbi and the LBJRE had, in fact, been consulted over the proposed educational legislation.[145] Indeed, this was precisely what motivated his campaign to establish a new council: Schonfeld did not want to be represented by the Chief Rabbi and the LBJRE. He insisted that any discussions with governmental bodies over measures pertaining to day schools were the province of the schools themselves, and the Chief Rabbi had no authority to represent the schools in such negotiations.[146]

Schonfeld's opponents were leery of the JSSM proposals and drew attention to clauses in the draft constitution they perceived as designed to undermine their role in day-school education. His formulation of the criterion for membership, for instance, was exclusionary, restricting membership to 'Jewish day schools in Britain, both primary and secondary, whether state-aided or independent, which declare that they provide secular and Jewish Orthodox religious instruction'. Although all day schools at this time, including those of the ZFET, were under the religious supervision of the Chief Rabbi, there was concern that this stipulation would be invoked to

---

145 Meetings and correspondence had taken place between the Chief Rabbi's office and the Parliamentary Secretary to the Minister of Education in late 1958 and early 1959. ACC 2805/6/1/43.
146 Schonfeld to Chief Rabbi 17 March 1959.

disqualify the ZFET schools. A further proposal, that secondary schools be given two votes in council decisions and primary schools only one, also seemed designed to bolster Schonfeld's influence relative to other providers of day-school education. 'Dr Schonfeld remains his incorrigible self. ... Perhaps the goal [of the Council] is to give Dr Schonfeld a majority to wave at the Ministry of Education ... and a power to veto, to prevent action when that appeared preferable'.[147]

Despite these criticisms, Schonfeld and his fervently-Orthodox allies could legitimately claim that over half of their communities' children attended Jewish day schools, and that 21 of the 36 Jewish schools in England operated under their aegis. Their desire for a more representative forum than the LBJRE was thus understandable. The Chief Rabbi and the LBJRE realized this, but feared that having yet another Jewish organization represent the Jewish schools in dealings with the governmental authorities would cause unnecessary confusion. They also sensed that presenting a more strident Orthodoxy as the face of day-school education would deter many parents from enrolling their children. In an attempt to undermine Schonfeld's initiative, the Chief Rabbi and the LBJRE, with editorial assistance from the *Jewish Chronicle*, appealed for a postponement of the founding conference until the groundwork had been laid for a more balanced gathering.[148]

Schonfeld's alliance was undeterred by this opposition and went ahead with its conference, which endorsed the draft proposal with its restrictive membership criterion. The Council soon compiled a list of issues that they proposed to raise with the national authorities, including the demand that the defining criteria for denominational state-aided schools be amended, and that the intake of pupils into denominational grammar schools be left to the school governors alone. As we have seen, to receive aided status, supporters of a planned denominational school had to prove not only that

147 *JC* 6 February 1959, 18.
148 In an editorial, the *JC* supported the Chief Rabbi and Alderman Moss (Governor of the King David Schools in Manchester) in their call for postponing the conference. *JC* 13 March 1959, 20.

there was a sufficient number of parents who sought such schooling for their children, but also that an overall shortage of school places existed within the borough. Schonfeld's Council of Jewish Day Schools proposed that the latter requirement be dropped. Both the tone and substance of the document reflect a decidedly more aggressive approach than that espoused by the Chief Rabbi and the LBJRE.[149]

The Chief Rabbi responded to these events by convening his own conference, whose purpose was to demonstrate that only his office was capable of creating a broad day-school coalition. He permitted only organizations directly involved with day-school education to send observers, denying a request from the Board of Deputies that they too be allowed to attend. To prevent either the ZF schools or the 'right-wing' Orthodox schools from boycotting the conference if the other side attended, he created an 'observer status' for those unwilling to be formal participants.

Like his predecessor Rabbi Hertz, Chief Rabbi Brodie strongly resisted any Board of Deputies 'encroachment' on educational affairs. He considered education a purely internal religious matter, not a matter mandating involvement of an advocacy organization. Moreover, Nathan Rubin advised the Chief Rabbi's Office that if the Board of Deputies attended the conference, the ultra-Orthodox organizations would perceive the decision as granting legitimacy to the Reform and Liberal movements, and absent themselves from the proceedings. Writing to Elsie Janner, Chair of the Board of Deputies' Education Committee, the Chief Rabbi's secretary noted that because non-Orthodox bodies were represented on the Board of Deputies, the latter could not serve as a mouthpiece for the Jewish day schools, all of which were at least nominally Orthodox.[150]

In his introductory address at the conference, the Chief Rabbi attempted to placate those who worried the proposed council would encroach on the individual schools' autonomy. The Council's role would be to 'consult with other denominational educational bodies on matters

149 'Suggestions concerning Points to be Put Forward by the Council of Jewish Day Schools in Britain to the Ministry of Education' (1959–60).
150 Rubin to Wallach 3 November 1959; Wallach to Janner 21 January 1960.

of common concern and to advise and make representations to the central and local educational authorities in matters affecting Jewish denominational schools collectively'.[151] To detail the proposed body's mandate, the participants agreed to the Chief Rabbi's appointment of a working group made up of representatives of the principal players, included the chairmen of the LBJRE and the ZFET, two representatives of the JSSM, two representatives from provincial schools, Rabbi Munk of the Menorah Primary School and Nathan Rubin as secretary. It recommended that the proposed 'consultative council', as it was to be called, have one representative from each educational organization or school recognized by the Chief Rabbi as a Jewish denominational school. Meetings were to take place when legislation concerning denominational schools was proposed by the authorities, or a particular school requested the council's advice.

Although a JSSM representative had been present at the first meeting of the working party, he absented himself from the second following Rabbi Schonfeld's publication of a religious ruling that 'any participation' in the proposed establishment by the Chief Rabbi of a consultative day-school council 'is contrary to our schools standards and principles'.[152] Thereafter, the JSSM, Yesodey Hatorah, and Menorah schools took no further part in the council. Chief Rabbi Brodie responded by admonishing Schonfeld that 'if the JSSM stands aloof it will be the loser. In any case if the [JSS] Movement prevents the achievement of the modicum of unity in educational organizations, which our community so badly needs, I shall not be able to be formally associated with it any longer as its Honorary President'.[153] Schonfeld understood that in future he would not be able to rely on the good offices of the Chief Rabbi in negotiations with the governmental authorities, an outcome he had been trying to avoid. As we saw in Chapter 1, during this period the state-aided status of the Avigdor School was under review by the national and local authorities. The possibility that the

---

151 Minutes, Meeting to Establish a Consultative Body of Jewish Day Schools in Great Britain, 24 May 1959, 2.

152 Minutes, Working Party of the Consultative Body of Jewish Day Schools, 15 July 1959 and 27 September 1959, 1; Schonfeld to Governors of the JSSM 17 September 1959. MS 183 248/1.

153 Chief Rabbi to Schonfeld 9 November 1959.

Chief Rabbi would announce his withdrawal of support for the school might have injurious consequences. Schonfeld composed a relatively tame letter explaining why he and his school governors were opposed to the consultative council, the chief reasons being their refusal to recognize the Zionists as administering 'a religious day-school organization', and their objection to the fact that organizations, and not just the schools themselves, were to be involved in the proposed council. Schonfeld reminded the Chief Rabbi that a year earlier he had been 'among the first to draw attention to the dangers involved in such a political day-school movement', but it is clear from the letter's non-provocative tone that Schonfeld was anxious not to damage his relationship with the Chief Rabbi.[154]

Chief Rabbi Brodie did not act on his threat to resign as Honorary President of the JSSM, and continued to hope that Schonfeld and his allies might join the council at a later date. Expressing disappointment that the JSSM had not joined the council, the *Jewish Chronicle* announced the 'excellent news' that the Chief Rabbi had succeeded in establishing the Consultative Council of Jewish Day Schools. The newspaper regretted that the council's scope was limited to monitoring government legislation rather than exploring issues such as teaching methods and texts, but hoped that in time its responsibilities would be expanded.[155] In the final analysis, however, instead of a joint forum on day schools, what had been created were two parallel committees, each with a similar mandate, namely, advancement of Jewish day schools. Mutual suspicion, turf wars, and personal tensions had rendered creation of a single committee impossible. The Chief Rabbi complained that 'petty, trivial and nauseating approaches to Jewish education had thwarted constructive efforts'.[156] Yet given that Schonfeld's new committee was unknown and unconnected, the Chief Rabbi's office and the LBJRE remained, as before, the formal address for national consultations. A few years later, Nathan Rubin commented: 'All in all, we have been quite successful and have saved ourselves the bickering that would have gone on had we attempted to do this work through a large council'.[157]

---

154 Schonfeld to Chief Rabbi 18 November 1959.
155 *JC* 27 November 1959, 22.
156 *JC* 8 January 1960, 8.
157 Rubin to Chief Rabbi 19 December 1963. ACC 2805/112.

The existence of a joint council would not have made a major difference vis-à-vis national legislation: the Jewish community had little influence on decisions pertaining to denominational education. When the government discussed these issues with the ecclesiastical authorities, the small number of Jewish schools relative to those of the Anglicans and Roman Catholics meant that discussions with the Jewish community were basically a formality and a courtesy. As Rubin assured a concerned Jewish educator in Liverpool, 'We are quite safe in assuming that whatever financial advantages the Churches obtain from any amendments to the Education Acts, the Jewish community will enjoy. ... this was made quite clear by the Ministry at a recent meeting'.[158] The benefit of a consultative council was not to be found in its ability to influence government legislation, but rather its internal communal contribution: coordination of efforts in the planning of new schools, combating the teacher shortage, teacher training, and so on. A more ambitious project might have been devising a common approach to fundraising to enable day schools to secure state-aided status. Yet it was obvious to all that there was little hope the diverse streams in Jewish day-school education would pool their resources and work together unless the advancement of their mutual self-interest was assured.

The Goldbloom Department

Although the Zionists had contemplated establishing their own secondary school in the metropolis, the requisite outlay, and competition from existing schools, were a deterrent. Instead, the ZFET proposed to associate itself with an existing secondary school, namely, the re-established JFS, whose educational ethos was congenial. Indeed, the JFS taught Hebrew as a living language, and had established a variety of extra-curricular links

158   Rubin to E. Felton (Liverpool Hebrews' Educational Institution and Endowed Schools) 6 March 1959.

with Israel; JFS tours to Israel began in 1961. The headmaster, Dr Conway, was considering a pupil and teacher exchange with Israel, and promised scholarships for pupils studying Hebrew at the 'A' level.[159]

The proposed joint effort created a dilemma for the LBJRE, whose financial situation remained precarious. Members found it difficult to reject the ZFET's generous offer of a £50,000 contribution toward the school's building fund.[160] Moreover, the threat that, were the offer to be spurned, the ZFET might establish its own secondary school at a time when the JFS governors were contemplating expansion of the school could not be ignored. If the Zionists established their own school, parents who might otherwise have sent their children to the JFS would have an alternative, and further, because the JFS was a state-aided school, it would be legally bound to fill any vacant school places with non-Jewish children, thereby 'undermining the Jewish character of the school'.[161] On the other hand, concern that the ZFET might at a later stage attempt a takeover of the school in order to implement its perceived agenda of secular Jewish education generated vigorous opposition to the proposed partnership. Dayan Grunfeld, a much-respected member of the United Synagogue's Beth-Din, led the opposition, supported by other rabbinical court judges, Asher Fishman, the LBJRE's Education Officer, and the Hapoel Hamizrachi organization.[162] They appealed to the Chief Rabbi to use his influence to block the agreement, but his dual position as head of both the LBJRE and the Hapoel Hamizrachi placed him in a delicate situation.

---

159 See the section 'Israel in the Jewish Day Schools' in Chapter 5 below, and Black, *JFS*, 210–14.

160 In a memorandum to the Chief Rabbi, Rubin asserts, 'whilst it would have been preferable not to have had to consider accepting a sum of money from the Zionist organization, the amount involved and the name of the endowment are such that it would be unrealistic not to consider the proposal on its merits'. 24 September 1962. ACC 2805/112. Unless otherwise specified, correspondence and archival material pertaining to the Goldbloom Department is from ACC 2805/112.

161 Levin to Chief Rabbi 5 November 1963 and 3 December 1963.

162 'London Board Clash over Education'. *JC* 29 November 1963, 1, 14. See also A. Fishman to Rubin 5 November 1963.

Although the protracted negotiations between the LBJRE and the ZFET did lead to an 1964 agreement in the form of a trust deed that gave the ZFET a stake in the school – the Hebrew Department of the JFS would be run by a joint committee representing the two organizations – analysis of this text reveals that those who sought to limit the ZFET's influence had secured an important victory. The Hebrew Department was renamed the J. K. Goldbloom Department for Hebrew Studies in honour of the founder/headmaster of the Redman's Road Talmud Torah, pioneering educator, and Zionist leader. According to the trust deed, seven of the ten management committee members were to be drawn from the LBJRE, and the ZFET's request that it be represented on the school's board of governors was rejected. The LBJRE also resisted calls to give priority to JFS applicants who had attended Zionist primary schools, and reiterated that the school's policy was to give priority to graduates of any Jewish primary school. A clause stipulating that LBJRE appointees to the management committee could not include persons active in the ZF was clearly designed to prevent the latter organization from employing its familiar tactic of infiltration to 'capture' the Goldbloom Department. Further clauses were intended to placate the fears of Dayan Grunfeld and the religious Zionists, who worried that non-observant Jews might be elected to the committee, and insisted that if disputes arose over religious matters, the Chief Rabbi was to decide them.[163]

The Zionists' willingness to compromise with the LBJRE was further evidenced during a debate concerning the Goldbloom Department's aims. Among others, these would include encouraging 'contact between the pupils of the school and the Land of Israel'. The ZFET had sought to use the term 'State of Israel', but Dayan Grunfeld opposed this political term, preferring the traditional epithet, 'Holy Land'. After rejecting this locution because it is used in the 'Christian world', the LBJRE Chairman, with the support of the Chief Rabbi, won support for the compromise expression,

---

163   The terms of the agreement were published in *JC* 17 January 1964, 12.

still traditional but less explicitly religious, '*Eretz Yisrael*'.[164] This minor clash well illustrates the various sides' disparate ideological and pedagogic agendas, and differential capacities to impose their will.

The final hurdle to be cleared before implementation of the agreement was its acceptance by the LBJRE. Levin, the chairman, addressed the concerns of those opposed to the trust deed, focusing on the charge that the LBJRE was compromising its autonomy and educational approach. He insisted that 'the Board had given nothing away. ... and the school remained completely unchanged'. Countering those who claimed the Zionists were intent on changing the nature of Jewish education in Britain, he reminded LBJRE members of the existence of earlier agreements with the ZF that specifically mandated commitment to traditional Judaism. The ZF had respected both the letter and spirit of these agreements, and inspectors' reports 'had shown how successful the agreement had been in avoiding the kind of education that some people feared; there had been no indoctrination, no secularism, and no politics. What had been achieved was religious education with emphasis on living Hebrew and love of Zion'. Questions concerning religious matters had been referred to the Chief Rabbi, and teachers deferred to his authority. Levin reassured the board members that the Zionists were not engaged in a subversive campaign to inculcate secular nationalist and godless forms of Jewish identity. The motion passed easily, proving that the LBJRE clearly concurred with Levin that they had nothing to fear from the ZFET. The agreement was, as he described it, a matter of 'mutual self-interest'.[165]

Some might claim that the ZF, rather than fighting to achieve its goals, capitulated to the LBJRE. But it must be kept in mind that Zionism in England did not see its task as replacing the traditional religion-based Jewish identity with a secular national agenda. Education toward deepening a commitment to the Jewish people, both in the Diaspora and in Israel,

---

164 Levin to Chief Rabbi 13 November 1963. Ironically, the pendulum has now swung the other way, with 'Land of Israel' connoting an uncompromising right-wing political stance, while use of the term 'State of Israel' indicates sympathy with democratic and liberal values.

165 Minutes, LBJRE Meeting 13 January 1964.

through the Hebrew language and acquaintance with life in Israel, was seen as supplementary to, but not a replacement for, traditional Jewish education. Despite the fears of various Anglo-Jewish sectors, including traditionalists on the LBJRE, the strictly Orthodox, and the religious Zionists – the ZF was committed to a religion-based Jewish identity. Ben Azai of the *Jewish Chronicle* accurately summarized this paradox:

> No doubt there are many people in the ZF who never intended that their schools should always be opened in concert with the local synagogues, and who complained that there had been a 'sell out' to the Chief Rabbi and the London Board, but in typical Anglo-Jewish style, an organisation has grown up far more committed to tradition than would ever have been suggested by the personal degree of observance of some of its leaders. Of course this is hopelessly illogical. ... Nevertheless, this anomaly has continued in the United Synagogue for ninety years and will probably last a long time in the ZF also.[166]

At a 1962 conference on 'Jewish Life in Modern Britain', jointly sponsored by the Board of Deputies and the Hebrew University's Institute of Contemporary Jewry, one participant noted that 'Jewish religious education is not a matter of course and not the only possible focus of Jewish education'. He then elaborated on possible components of a secular Jewish education, including modern Hebrew, modern Jewish history, Hebrew literature, and study of the State of Israel. 'What strikes one most is the impression that the tremendous events which have happened to the Jewish people in our generation, and which have made so great an impact on Jewish life, have hardly made an impact on Jewish education in this country', he argued.[167] Most of the discussants completely ignored these comments, either because they feared an ideological clash, or because they considered them so alien to the Anglo-Jewish ethos that they did not merit consideration. With few exceptions, communal organizations continued to perceive Jewish education as solely a matter of imparting religious training, and not the nurturing of national or ethnic identity. This approach was clearly manifested in the supplementary religion classes offered by the various synagogue streams, as we will see in Chapter 3.

166   *JC* 8 April 1960, 25.
167   See Shaul Esh's comments in Gould and Esh, *Jewish Life*, 86–7.

Zionist education in the British context

Alliances forged by the Chief Rabbi and United Synagogue with the religious Zionists (Mizrachi) or the strictly Orthodox left the ZF isolated on several occasions. While it could claim genuine success in opening several new Zionist schools, 'capturing' the LBJRE, and winning a modicum of sympathy from the United Synagogue leadership, overall it did not fare well. Concerns over religious – secular tensions in Israel, and suspicion that the Zionists' goal was to cultivate a secular nationality-based Jewish identity, generated vociferous opposition to the Anglo-Zionist educational programme. The introduction of spoken Hebrew, use of Sefardic pronunciation, and the focus on modern history and life in Israel were deemed evidence of this policy. Yet these concerns were largely baseless, as the ZF agreed to uphold the consensus positions on religious issues. Nevertheless, the Orthodox leadership in whose hands Jewish education remained was not prepared to tolerate significant Zionist intervention in Anglo-Jewish education. The basic premise of the Anglo-Jewish religious establishment was that Jewish identity was a matter of religion, not folk-songs, not political independence, not speaking Hebrew as a vernacular.

The leadership of the United Synagogue, the old guard at the LBJRE, and the Board of Deputies, all believed that the nationalist secular model of Jewish identity, like the Hirschian separatist model upheld by Rabbi Schonfeld, provoked unnecessary tension with Anglo-Jewry's Gentile neighbours. The wider society was perceived as amenable to accepting religious differences and denominational affinities, but not particularistic ethnic or national identities. The strictly and fervently Orthodox, of course, were strongly opposed to an ethnic/national Jewish ethos, deeming it a profound distortion of Judaism and a prelude to assimilation.

The ZF was aware of these entrenched beliefs held by both the community and its leadership. It was thus willing to accept the condition that it defer to the Chief Rabbi on religious issues and promise to teach Judaism in accordance with the traditional understanding. Of course, this willingness to defer to the establishment was also a tactical consideration, inasmuch as explicit rejection of the religious basis of Anglo-Jewish identity would clearly have delegitimized the ZFET as an educational agency. The ZF therefore promoted its contribution to Jewish education as supplementing the existing religious approach, not supplanting it. The ZF hoped that its programmatic innovations and relevance would find an enthusiastic audience among pupils, and generate solidarity between Jews in Israel and those of the Diaspora. In essence, then, the communal reaction to the Zionist foray into Anglo-Jewish education was driven by fear: fear that a new and potentially problematic self-identity would be inculcated, disturbing the modus vivendi that Anglo-Jewry had painstakingly cultivated and sought to perpetuate.

Conclusion

During this period, the bulk of Anglo-Jewry was committed to integrating into the English middle class, and where this had already been achieved, to further upward economic and social mobility. For most members of the community, the key function of schools was to facilitate this process. Jewish education was typically a minor concern.

Only a small minority of parents chose Jewish day schools for their children because they offered a serious Jewish studies curriculum.[168] These were overwhelmingly strictly or fervently Orthodox families that sought to maintain firm social boundaries between their religious communities and the outside world. Although the number of Jews who identified with this separatism was growing, they remained a minority within Anglo-Jewry. As we have seen, two different ideological approaches to education emerged

---

168   When Bakstansky complained of the insufficient time allocated by the ZFET schools for the study of Hebrew, Gertner responded, 'Our schools must aim at affording ... pupils the best general education possible. By doing so we can gain the confidence of parents and induce them to send their children to our schools'. Gertner to Bakstansky 25 June 1968. CR C3 2.

among the very pious: that of the ultra-Orthodox schools such as Yesodey Hatorah, which prided themselves on strict separation from both the mainstream of Anglo-Jewry and the wider society, and that of Schonfeld's JSSM, which was prepared to engage with English society and Anglo-Jewry, but imposed boundaries limiting the scope of this interaction.

The attempt to bring the latter into partnership with the LBJRE and the ZF was, from the outset, fraught with obstacles. The strictly Orthodox perceived the LBJRE as religiously lax and the Zionists as stealthily teaching a new, secularized Jewish identity. For their part, the Zionists refused to cooperate with groups that did not recognize the legitimacy of the Jewish state and campaigned against its policies. The clashes in Israel over Sabbath observance, conscription of women, and the sale of pork, reverberated in England, adversely impacting efforts to achieve cooperation on logistical issues. Ultimately, the various sectors that sought to forward a common interest – the promotion of Jewish day schools – could not all be brought under the same umbrella. Indeed, this was true not only with respect to day-school education, but also vis-à-vis supplementary schools, as we will now see.

CHAPTER 3

Supplementary Schools

Anglo-Jewish education underwent a major transformation between 1958 and 1979. The number of children participating in Sunday and or after-school classes – popularly called Talmud Torah, Hebrew, or *cheder* classes – dropped by almost a third, almost all this loss being due to enrolment at day schools.[1] In 1958, 12, 618 children were enrolled in Hebrew classes, by 1978 this figure had declined to 9,067. During the same period, day-school attendance rose from 3,890 to 8,196.[2] Although, in terms of numbers, Hebrew classes remained the chief channel for provision of formal Jewish education, the gap was small, and closing quickly: it would take less than a decade for the day schools to overtake Hebrew classes.[3] This chapter will contextualize and explain this shift in the delivery of Jewish education, and explore the history, pedagogic philosophy, and logistics of the Sunday and afternoon school framework.

---

1   Private lessons will not be included in the discussion of Sunday/afternoon schools, as there is little documentation. But they were not a negligible phenomenon. In Redbridge, e.g., about 6 per cent of Jewish children received most of their Jewish education from private lessons; see Kosmin and Levy, *Jewish Identity*, 20–1.
2   The figures for day school attendance are from J. Braude, 'Jewish Education in Britain Today', in S. Lipman and V. Lipman (eds), *Jewish Life in Britain 1962–1977* (New York: K. G. Saur), 121; for Hebrew class attendance in 1958, from Fishman and Levy, 'Jewish Education', 73; and for Hebrew class attendance in 1978 from the LBJRE's annual report, to which figures for the Reform movement's schools, which were not under the aegis of the LBJRE, were added.
3   In 1986/87, the number of children attending Jewish day schools outnumbered those attending part-time frameworks for the first time. See *Securing Our Future* (London: JEDT, 1992), 7.

Apart from the strictly Orthodox, all the Jewish religious streams offered part-time Jewish education to children aged five to sixteen. The United Synagogue, in co-operation with the Federation of Synagogues, had established the London Board of Jewish Religious Education (LBJRE) to coordinate, fund, and prepare curricula for its synagogue schools and Talmud Torahs. Both frameworks were afternoon schools colloquially referred to as 'Hebrew classes', but whereas the latter met three or four times a week, for a total of eight to twelve hours, the former met for only about half that time, meeting, on average, three to six hours weekly. In both frameworks, the syllabus focused on prayers, *Chumash* (Pentateuch), and the classic rabbinical commentaries. While the Reform and Liberal movements did not offer Talmud Torah style afternoon schools, they did provide Sunday classes and in some cases, mid-week sessions as well.

Most of the children enrolled in after-school frameworks attended classes under the aegis of the LBJRE, with which about 80 per cent of London synagogues were associated.[4] In 1961, for instance, 11,500 of the approximately 13,500 children attending after-school frameworks were in classes registered with the LBJRE.[5] Over the next two decades, however, membership in the United Synagogue, and its centrist-Orthodox affiliate the Federation of Synagogues, declined markedly, by 1983 accounting for just 66 per cent of Anglo Jewry; the Hebrew classes under its aegis experienced a corresponding drop in attendance.[6] By contrast, the steady growth of the Progressive communities, particularly the Reform movement, was accompanied by a corresponding expansion of their Hebrew classes. In 1961, the Reform and Liberal movements had about 1,000 children in their London Sunday schools, in 1979 the figure for the Reform movement alone was 3,800.[7] During the same period, attendance at LBJRE schools fell from about 9,000 to 6,000 (see Table 4).

---

4   The United Synagogue had about 40,000 male members, the Federation of Synagogues, 10,000. The Reform and Liberal Synagogues had a combined membership of 15,000. Thus of 65,000 male members of synagogues, 50,000 were affiliated with centrist Orthodoxy; see Cohen, 'Trends in Anglo-Jewish', 61.
5   Fishman and Levy, 'Jewish Education', 73.
6   Kosmin and Levy, *Jewish Identity*, 38; Prais, 'Polarization or Decline?', 6; Alderman, *Modern*, 371.
7   Fishman and Levy loc. cit.; J. Moonman, *Anglo-Jewry: An Analysis* (London: Institute of Jewish Affairs, 1980), 17.

These figures attest to the growing diversification of Anglo-Jewry, and, taken in conjunction with statistics on the growth in Jewish day-school places, to the fact that most of those who 'moved up', so to speak, to day-school education, came from the mainstream Orthodox sector.[8]

Table 4 Children aged 5–16 attending classes registered with LBJRE, 1958–78

	Synagogue classes	Talmud Torahs	Total
1958	10,130	1,488	11,618
1960	9,469	1,170	10,639
1962	8,783	1,131	9,914
1964	8,153	884	9,037
1966	7,677	*	7,677
1968	7,403	*	7,403
1970	7,604	*	7,604
1972	7,085	*	7,085
1974	6,647	*	6,647
1976	6,609		6,609
1978	6,249		6,249

*The figures for Talmud Torah attendance were merged with those for
synagogue classes in 1966.[9]
Source: LBJRE Annual Reports

Table 4 reveals the steady decline in the overall numbers of those enrolled in after-school frameworks, and particularly, the closure of Talmud

8   The Redbridge survey listed the percentages of children aged 5–14 years in the various Jewish education frameworks by parental synagogue affiliation. None of the children affiliated with the Progressive synagogues attended Jewish day schools, whereas some 17 per cent of those affiliated with Orthodox synagogues attended such schools; see Kosmin and Levy, *Jewish Identity*, 21.
9   The Federation of Synagogues withdrew from the LBJRE in 1966, thus its approximately 1,040 pupils are not included in these figures between 1966 and 1978, when the Federation rejoined the LBJRE.

Torahs. The latter phenomenon can in large measure be attributed to the exodus from inner London to the suburbs. The Talmud Torahs had been established by Eastern European immigrants at the turn of the century, first in East London and later in North London, but as the population moved to the suburbs, the more popular educational framework was that of Sunday and mid-week Hebrew classes. Furthermore, Hebrew classes began to supersede the home and synagogue as the dominant vehicle for the inculcation of Jewish knowledge and tradition. With the accelerated integration into mainstream society of the first and second generations of English-born children of Eastern European Jewish immigrants, the home often lost its effectiveness as a model of Jewish life and culture, either because the hold of tradition was weakening, or because of its perceived dissonance with the outside world.[10] Hebrew classes thus bore the responsibility of transmitting a Jewish heritage whose teachings were increasingly at odds with the religious observance and norms of the home environment. Many a rabbi and Hebrew class teacher noted sadly that when the conduct they sought to foster ran counter to that prevailing in the home, the home 'almost invariably' won out.[11]

The overall decline in the number of pupils participating in part-time classes also reflected a decline in the Jewish birth rate, which in turn reflected the general decline in birth rates in Britain following the post-war baby boom. However, after 1964 the contraction of the Jewish child population can be attributed to more specific demographic trends among Anglo Jewry: relatively late marriage, out-marriage, and smaller families.[12]

These phenomena deepened over the years. Fewer and fewer children were enrolled in Hebrew classes, while Jewish day-school enrolment rose. Table 5 illustrates this dramatic shift:

---

10   See J. Gould, *Jewish Commitment: A Study in London.* (London: Institute of Jewish Affairs, 1984), ch. 2.
11   Tony Brown, 'When Parents Try our Patience', *JC* 29 October 1976, 22. Brown was Director of the LBJRE at the time.
12   See Prais, 'Polarization', 3–16.

Table 5 Trends in Anglo-Jewish education for children aged 5–17, 1962–86[13]

Year	1962–3	1967–8	1975–6	1986–7
Enrolment in Hebrew Classes	21,075 36%	24,843 42%	17,346 32%	11,957 25%
Day-School Enrolment	8,854 15%	9,015 15%	10,908 20%	12,085 25%

Source: *Securing Our Future*, 7.

Table 5 might seem to indicate that in the period in question, almost 50 per cent of Jewish children aged five to seventeen received no formal Jewish education, but this inference is false. Most parents believed that the critical period for Jewish education was from age seven to thirteen, and a corresponding adjustment of the age bands reveals that between 75 and 80 per cent of children received some formal Jewish education.[14]

LBJRE Hebrew classes

The starting age for the LBJRE's part-time classes varied from one synagogue centre to another, but was generally around five. Most children began, however, a few years later. Although as a rule classes were available for children up to the age of about sixteen, for the most part boys left these classes following their Bar-Mitzvah; girls often left a year earlier, when they were twelve. On average, boys attended Hebrew classes for four or five years, girls for even less.

13 Fishman and Levy, 'Jewish Education', 74.
14 A 1962 study found that just 8 per cent of pupils remained beyond the age of thirteen, see ibid., 73. Despite attempts to establish teenage study centres, the figures for the post-Bar-Mitzvah age group had changed only marginally by 1977, see Braude, 'Jewish Education', 121. The 1978 Redbridge survey found that only 7 per cent of fifteen to nineteen year olds affiliated with Orthodox synagogues had attended Hebrew classes past age thirteen, see Kosmin and Levy, *Jewish Identity*, 21.

Classes usually met on Sunday morning, and twice mid-week, for sessions lasting about an hour and a half. Mid-week attendance, however, was typically just a third of Sunday attendance, a situation much bemoaned by the LBJRE. The school year was also fairly short, fluctuating between a maximum of forty-five and a minimum of thirty-five weeks, since many of the classes were held in local council schools, which were closed during school holidays.

Critics of part-time Jewish education frequently expressed dissatisfaction with the limited number of teaching hours and the disparities in the educational outcomes that resulted from the discontinuous attendance. Obviously, children who attended both during the week and on Sundays were more likely to attain higher levels of achievement than those who were present on Sundays only. Attempts to rectify this situation by enforcing mid-week participation were unsuccessful, generating acrimony and controversy. Other proposals, such as streaming ability levels and bringing children together from wider catchment areas, were often difficult to implement.[15]

To the great chagrin of the LBJRE's educational and religious leaders, parents preferred this minimal Jewish education. Though at times critical of its methods, curriculum, standards and facilities, the vast majority were satisfied with the Sunday-school/Hebrew classes framework.[16] A study conducted in 1969–70 found that 74 per cent of the respondents had attended such classes and 79 per cent reported that their children were or would be enrolled in Hebrew classes. For many, the Sunday-school system was perceived as paralleling the Anglican religious education system that had been popular a generation earlier among the general population. If grammar and public schools were the models for secular education, by the same logic, Sunday schools were to be emulated as a framework for imparting religious education.

15   S. J. Prais, 'A Sample Survey on Jewish Education in London, 1972–73', *Jewish Journal of Sociology* 16 (1974), 143–4.
16   Gould, *Jewish Commitment*, 30; Kosmin and Levy, *Jewish Identity*, 21.

This pattern began to change starting around the late 1960s. Jewish parents increasingly sought a more intensive, less intermittent Jewish environment for their offspring, namely, day school. This phenomenon will be addressed in the next chapter; here, I will just point out that it was not, in the main, a response to parental dissatisfaction with Hebrew classes.

Syllabus and syllabus reform

The 1962 LBJRE Hebrew Class syllabus for pupils aged twelve and under lists five areas of study: Hebrew language, Hebrew grammar, history, geography, and religious precepts.[17] The 'Hebrew language' component actually referred to reading and translating key Bible stories, such as the story of Noah and the Flood. Core prayers, such as the 'Amidah', 'Shema' and 'Birkat Hamazon' (grace after meals) were also taught, as well as various prayer services, particularly those recited at the beginning and end of the Sabbath (Kabbalat Shabbat and Havdalah). Another text taught in the original by translating it into English was the Passover Haggadah. This component of the curriculum reflects a Judaism based on the individual's relationship with God via commitment to prayer and ritual.

Although the grammar component called for familiarity with the structure of the Hebrew language, particularly the formation of nouns and adjectives, little emphasis was placed on Hebrew as a living language. The objective was to enable children to read biblical and liturgical texts in the original and be able to translate them word-for-word, rather than to understand their deeper meaning and intent. The impression that Judaism was an ancient religion was reinforced by the very limited scope of the Jewish history component of the syllabus, which concentrated on the First Temple period, and to a lesser degree, the Second Temple period. Students were taught nothing of Jewish life in the Middle Ages, nor of the

---

17   The complete syllabus can be found in Gould and Esh, *Jewish Life*, 80–3.

dramatic developments in modern Jewish history such as the Holocaust and
the establishment of the State of Israel. Examination of the sub-sections
of this curricular area reveals an underlying 'great men' approach to history, greatness being defined almost completely in terms of brilliance in
Torah study, an approach far removed from that characteristic of history
as taught in local council schools.[18] The geography component may have
been intended to fill the lacuna in contemporary affairs, as its mandate
was to teach 'the elementary geography of the Holy Land and the State of
Israel'. Lastly, the section of the syllabus addressing religious knowledge
focused on observance of the precepts (*mitzvot*), especially those related
to the Sabbath, dietary laws (kashruth), phylacteries (*tefillin*), ritual fringes
(*tzitzit*) and the placing of a mezuzah on the doorposts of the home.[19]

Although no statement of purpose accompanied the syllabus – a platform outlining the goals of the LBJRE Hebrew classes was formulated
only in 1972 – the aim of these lessons was clearly to inculcate religious
beliefs and foster religious observance in the spirit of Orthodox Judaism.
The objective was to familiarize children with the synagogue service and
core religious observances, with only minimal discussion of their rationales
and Judaism's general ethical teachings. Nor were the cultural, ethnic and
national dimensions of Judaism covered in the curriculum. This was in
keeping with the position of the United Synagogue, which upheld a Jewish
identity that could be accommodated within the parameters of what were
perceived as legitimate religious differences within British society.

Although there was no organized opposition to the LBJRE syllabus,
two main criticisms were frequently voiced, namely, that what was taught
was inappropriate and irrelevant to the lives of the pupils, and that it was
taught in an off-putting and ineffective manner. The critics tended to be
young and situated at the 'left' pole of Anglo-Jewish Orthodoxy. Rabbi
Chaim Pearl, who later emigrated to the United States, where he headed
a Conservative congregation, and Rabbi Kopul Rosen, founder of Carmel

18   Although the syllabus for children over fourteen did include material on key Jewish
      figures from the Middle Ages to the twentieth century, as noted above, few children
      continued at Hebrew classes beyond Bar-Mitzvah age.
19   LBJRE Annual Report, 1963, Appendix B, 82.

College, were among the most outspoken adversaries. The *Jewish Chronicle*, which had supported Rabbi Louis Jacobs in his theological conflict with the Orthodox mainstream, came out in support of the views of Rosen and Pearl regarding the LBJRE syllabus.[20]

As early as 1961, speakers at the annual meeting of the Central Council for Jewish Religious Education had expressed dissatisfaction with the syllabus and teaching methods of the Hebrew classes. Rabbi Pearl characterized the practice of having once-a-week pupils study the Pentateuch and prayer service almost exclusively as 'a sheer waste of time'. Dr Goldman, the chairman of the Council, condemned the system as 'contrary to all sound principles of teaching', and Rabbi Kopul Rosen and Beatrice Barwell, head of the National Union of Hebrew Teachers, pleaded for the repudiation of 'conventional theories and outmoded routines'.[21] In 1963, Dayan Grunfeld, a member of the United Synagogue rabbinical court, called for an inquiry into the substance of Jewish education. Despite the recurring protests, no inquiry was launched, and little was done to effect change. The only real response was the informal debate that took place on the pages of the *Jewish Chronicle*.

The major demand voiced by those opposed to the syllabus and the pedagogic thinking behind it was that it be made more relevant to the children's needs and interests, and to contemporary Jewish life. An editorial described the system as 'unpardonably stupid and inevitably disastrous', and, recommending that the aims of the Hebrew classes be rewritten with a view to familiarizing children with Jewish festivals, religion, and history, argued that the Bible should be taught, 'not word for word ... but by reading and narration'.[22] Pearl too emphasized this point, deploring the fact that children who could barely read Hebrew struggled to parrot translations of chapters from the Torah: 'does a foreign student learn English by reading Chaucer and Shakespeare before all else?'[23]

20 The 'Jacobs Affair' is discussed below; see Alderman, *Modern*, 361–4; Cesarani, *Jewish Chronicle*, 217–22.
21 'Obsolete Methods', *JC* 24 March 1961, 28.
22 *JC* 30 August 1963, 7.
23 *JC* 31 January 1964, 7.

The traditional syllabus and methodology did have defenders. Israel Slotki, a much-respected veteran teacher in the Manchester Talmud Torah system, argued that the Hebrew class syllabus reflected the key goals of the United Synagogue, and as such fulfilled its mandate:

> The main purpose of our synagogue and religious classes in the Diaspora is to bring up Jews and Jewesses who would practice in love and devotion the religion they have been taught, who would attend synagogue, keep the festivals, and lead a good Jewish life in true loyalty to their faith and country. Some knowledge of our traditional literature is a sine qua non, whatever the method adopted.[24]

And not surprisingly, the LBJRE's chairman, Salmond Levin, issued a categorical defence of its policies. 'Our Orthodoxy and syllabus stem from the same place, from Moses and Sinai. It has come down to us through the years, unchanged and unchanging'.[25] Seizing upon this conservatism, the *Jewish Chronicle* attacked Levin and his Board in a scathing editorial:

> For Mr Levin to hide the LBJRE's unsatisfactory performance behind Moses' mantle and to claim that the Board's syllabus came down from Sinai unchanged is comic, if it were not also tragic. Instead of sycophancy and self-congratulation, Mr Levin and his colleagues should examine their own responsibility for the deplorable state of Jewish education in the Orthodox community.[26]

Educators, too, castigated the LBJRE syllabus, particularly its failure to cover modern Jewish history and its outdated methodology for teaching Hebrew. A Hebrew University expert noted that the events that had so dramatically impacted the Jewish people in the preceding decades went virtually unmentioned in UK afternoon schools. He also decried the way Hebrew was taught, in light of the advances that had been made in Israel, where the ulpan method had been remarkably successful in teaching Hebrew to immigrants from around the world. He observed that the study of the Hebrew language and the traditional texts written in it was still being conducted as if Hebrew were only a sacred language used solely

24   *JC* 24 July 1964, 35.
25   *JC* 12 June 1964, 12.
26   *JC* 12 June 1964, 7 (editorial).

in the synagogue: pupils were still learning the language as their fathers and grandfathers had, namely, by translating Scripture word by word.[27]

In early 1968, criticism of the LBJRE's Hebrew classes came to a head. A motion calling for the creation of a commission of inquiry to investigate the LBJRE was placed on the agenda of a United Synagogue meeting. A distinct lack of confidence in the LBJRE was expressed, and among other things, it was demanded that no member of the LBJRE be invited to sit on the proposed commission of inquiry. Sir Isaac Wolfson, president of the United Synagogue, urged the motion's sponsors to withdraw it so that he and the Chief Rabbi, in conjunction with the LBJRE, could establish their own inquiry, but his proposal was rejected. A resolution promising an extensive inquiry into all aspects of Jewish education in London was passed.[28]

A few months later, Levin resigned his chairmanship of the LBJRE, after fourteen years in the position. Hopes for reform were pinned on the LBJRE's biennial elections, scheduled to be held in late 1968. Asher Fishman, an active community leader who also served in other capacities, and had been a LBJRE member for eighteen years, was elected chairman, and, despite the tradition of unusually long terms of service, several new officers were elected as well. One of the new officers was Sidney Frosh, who was to play a central role in the restructuring of the United Synagogue, and served as the first chair of the LBJRE's day-school committee.

Immediately upon their election, this new cadre of lay leaders published a boldly titled plan for Jewish education, *A Time for Action: The Board's Plans for Today and Tomorrow*.[29] Most of their proposals focused on bringing change to the much-maligned Hebrew classes system, yet the honorary officers shied away from significant innovation. The preamble to the plan affirmed past goals:

27 Gould and Esh, *Jewish Life*, 88.
28 'Attempt to Disband Education Board', *JC* 2 February 1968, 1, 18. Seven months later, the commission had yet to be established, though the Chief Rabbi had nominated two American experts to join a panel of local community figures; see Chapter 5 below.
29 LBJRE Annual Report, 1969, Appendix A, 35–43.

> The paramount need of today, as it was yesterday, is to intensify our pupils' knowledge of practical Judaism, and to instil in them not only Jewish learning but also a love for and desire to practise authentic Judaism in all its facets. Jewish education is based firmly on Jewish tradition, and the *Chumash* [Pentateuch] and the *Siddur* [prayer-book] are and must ever remain the basis of our education.

In the same vein, Fishman, in his inaugural speech as LBJRE chairman, reiterated this commitment to the *Chumash* and *Siddur* as the basis of Hebrew class education, telling the delegates: 'It must be a case of old wine in new bottles'. The officers did, however, pledge to introduce new pedagogic methodologies, keep pace with developments in general educational thought and practice, and to take 'fully into account the impact upon World Jewry of the establishment of the State of Israel'.

More specifically, it was resolved that Hebrew would become the medium of instruction, with Hebrew comprehension ultimately reaching a level where the old method of word-by-word translation would be rendered superfluous. Much to the satisfaction of the Zionists, the Board promised that Hebrew would be taught in the Israeli ('Sefardic') pronunciation, not the traditional Ashkenazic pronunciation used in the United Synagogue prayer services. A more utopian goal was that children aged seven and older would be obliged to attend midweek as well as Sunday classes. Children who did not meet this requirement were to be refused permission to sit for the LBJRE's 'Bar-Mitzvah test', and consequently would not be allowed to read from the Torah at an Orthodox synagogue. Also introduced was a syllabus for a 'Daughter of Valour' examination for girls that would parallel the Bar-Mitzvah test (the United Synagogue, being Orthodox, did not endorse the institution of the Bat-Mitvzah, which had been implemented by the Progressive streams); its emphasis was to be 'the duties of a Jewish woman'. In addition, teaching methods were to be upgraded through the introduction of new textbooks, films, activity booklets, and other innovative pedagogic materials.[30]

The response to the proposals was mixed. The plan to introduce instruction in Hebrew and Sefardic pronunciation won considerable support, as many felt it heralded the demise of the old system of learning by rote

30   Ibid, 35.

translation. On the other hand, while recognizing the disadvantages of Sunday-only attendance, many felt that compulsory mid-week attendance was impracticable. The popular *Jewish Chronicle* columnist Chaim Bermant, who wrote under the name Ben Azai, predicted that the policy would drive families for whom Jewish education was not particularly important away from the United Synagogue and into the arms of the Reform movement. He thought it wiser to first pursue a community-wide accord between all organizations providing part-time education mandating thrice-weekly attendance by all children.[31] Implementation of this proposal, however, would require cooperation between the Orthodox and the Progressive streams. Given that the former had an ironclad policy of non-cooperation with the latter, Ben Azai's proposal was as impractical as the proposal it was intended to replace.

Moreover, parents were generally hostile to the idea of compulsory mid-week attendance, giving a variety of reasons for their opposition. Some said they would be unable to accompany their children to mid-week Hebrew classes as they themselves would be at work or otherwise engaged. Others felt that mid-week attendance would adversely affect their children's social life and extra-curricular activities, such as Girl Guides, piano lessons, and the like. By giving religious education undue weight, they claimed, it would be disturbing an implicit balance.[32] Some objected on the grounds that they considered Hebrew classes dull and tedious. Before long, the proposal to compel mid-week attendance was dropped, and though it resurfaced a few years later, it was not adopted.[33]

Parental attitudes are also reflected in the saga of the LBJRE's 1972 attempt to impose a system of direct fees on a per term basis. When the LBJRE was initially established in 1946, its dominant partner, the United Synagogue, decided that instead of making the Board dependent on charity, member synagogues would be subject to an education levy equal to one-third of their membership fees. Its partner, the Federation of Synagogues, agreed to impose an equivalent education levy. Within three years, however,

31   *JC* 14 March 1969, 7.
32   *JC* 21 March 1969, 26.
33   Memorandum on Hebrew Education and the LBJRE, May 1973. CR C3 3, 2.

the United Synagogue, seeking to contain a growing deficit, had reduced
the education levy to 25 per cent. Its deficit continued to grow nonetheless,
and by 1959 had reached record proportions, primarily due to increased
building in the suburbs. Much to the chagrin of the LBJRE, the United
Synagogue decided that synagogues involved in building projects would
receive rebates on their education contribution. By 1968, the education
levy had eroded to 17 per cent, and some, alarmed at the United Synagogue's precarious financial situation, openly called for the disbandment
of the LBJRE and its replacement by an autonomous United Synagogue
education department.[34] It was against this background that in 1972 it
was proposed that direct fees be charged for Hebrew classes. Initially, the
LBJRE rejected the plan, but at a subsequent meeting, the motion passed
by a large majority.[35]

No sooner had the *Jewish Chronicle* run the headline 'Free Education
Ends Next Month' than synagogue office personnel and parents organized
to oppose the plan. The secretaries of local synagogues voiced anger at the
fact that new responsibilities had been thrust upon them without prior
consultation, and synagogue management committees voted against the
plan. A veritable revolt broke out as one synagogue centre after another
announced non-compliance with the direct fee plan. Predictably, throughout London, parents expressed dissatisfaction with the proposed regimen.
A public meeting called by the LBJRE to discuss the matter attracted
an unusually large audience, the vast majority of whom opposed the fee
system.[36] Parents, particularly those who were just marginally involved in
Jewish life, did not want to take responsibility for paying for their children's Jewish education. There was real concern that parents would withdraw their children from Hebrew classes rather than pay the fees, and
the LBJRE retracted the decision to charge fees. In the words of a *Jewish
Chronicle* editorial, the community would first have to 'educate parents
to their responsibility'.[37]

---

34   Newman, *United*, 191–2.
35   *JC* 14 July 1972, 8; 4 August 1972, 1, 5.
36   *JC* 13 October 1972, 9.
37   *JC* 27 October 1972, 24.

For many, the tradition of paying directly for education was as yet unfamiliar. But undoubtedly, it would have been easier to gain parental support for the plan had the quality of the Hebrew classes been higher. The LBJRE's inability to implement direct fees at this time, like its inability to impose compulsory mid-week attendance, attests to a widespread lack of confidence in its services.[38] And indeed, despite the enthusiasm they exhibited upon taking office, the new leadership of the LBJRE did not produce a turnaround in the community's attitude to Hebrew classes.

Nor did publication of a statement on the new pedagogic policy with regard to Hebrew language instruction placate critics in the Zionist camp, who viewed it as little more than an articulation of the values inherent in the traditional curriculum, to which had been appended a declaration of identification with 'Israel, its people and language, and Jews throughout the world'.[39] This was considered an insipid acknowledgement of the dramatic developments that had taken place in Israel since 1967 and their impact on world Jewry. Though they had applauded when Fishman, shortly after being elected, asserted that 'Torah comes from Zion and not from Gateshead', the Zionists were sceptical as to whether this view was shared by the Hebrew class instructors. Too many of them, it was argued, were products of ultra-Orthodox educational institutions and did not see Israel as a key facet of Judaic instruction. Zionist critics of the LBJRE's approach decried its 'reactionary attitude towards Israel', and anticipated that despite the declarations, the Hebrew classes would not change much.[40] In 1975, Beatrice Barwell, presenting an evaluation of Jewish education in England, alleged that nothing had changed vis-à-vis the teaching of Israel:

> Not all of them have availed themselves of the permission eventually given to use the Israeli pronunciation of Hebrew ... neither do they conscientiously bring Jewish history up to date by including in-depth the Holocaust and the establishment of

---

38 The direct fee plan was implemented in 1975/76, but many parents failed to pay the fees. At its annual budget meeting, the LBJRE reported that some £20,000 in fees were outstanding.

39 LBJRE Annual Report, 1973, 3.

40 *JC* 3 December 1971, 11.

the Jewish State ... nor is ... the joy of Yom Ha'atzmaut meaningfully taught as the newest *chag* [festival] in our calendar.[41]

Although Anglo-Jewry's relationship with Israel had intensified after the Six-Day War, this was hardly reflected in the Hebrew classes' curriculum. The long-standing mandate of preparing children for observance of religious precepts and rituals continued to mould the education provided by the Hebrew classes. Indeed, in 1972, the LBJRE described its objectives as follows:

> That children learn the various commandments, both religious and ethical, that they learn the language and background of our literature, both religious and historical; that they be able to understand the meaning and significance of prayers and be fluent in the synagogue ritual; that the education arouse in pupils a sense of the unique character of the Jewish people and the nature of its mission to the world, and finally, to instil in our pupils a sense of identification with Israel, its people and language and with Jews throughout the world.[42]

Thus while Israel was indeed part of the curriculum, religious observances remained its main focus.

The need for change was evident not just in the content and methodology of the Hebrew classes, but also the teachers. Recruiting, training, and retaining an enthusiastic and knowledgeable cadre of teachers was by no means easy. Throughout the period under discussion, the dearth of qualified staff remained a source of frustration.[43] Few of the teachers employed were graduates of professional training courses; those who were invariably complained of the poor remuneration for their services.[44] Indeed, wages

---

41   B. Barwell, 'Facets of Anglo-Jewish Education: Review and Evaluation', in D. Noy and I. Ben-Ami (eds), *Studies in the Cultural Life of the Jews in England*, Folklore Research Center Studies 5 (Jerusalem: Magnes, 1975), 38.

42   LBJRE Annual Report, 1973, 3.

43   As we will see in Chapter 5, this was also a problem for the day schools.

44   The headmaster of the Ilford District Synagogue complained to the Chief Rabbi in 1971 that it had been three years since salaries for Hebrew teachers had been raised, making it difficult for him to staff his school. It had taken four months to replace a teacher who left, and when someone was finally hired, he left just nine months later

for Hebrew class teachers were shockingly low. The pages of the *Jewish Chronicle* document efforts to increase the remuneration, but the LBJRE generally claimed its resources made this impossible. The National Union of Hebrew Teachers, founded in 1945, lobbied for improved compensation, to no avail.

Under the circumstances, Jewish education held little appeal as a career.[45] As a result, many of the teachers were just teenagers themselves. Some were sixth form students, others were graduates or students of the Gateshead Yeshiva who supplemented their stipends by working as Hebrew class instructors. The latter, though in many cases very devoted, were unlikely to serve as effective role models for children whose home environments were assimilated, and to whom strict observance of the religious precepts was completely alien. Over time, recourse to hiring Israelis as Hebrew class teachers became increasingly common, but complaints concerning their proficiency in English and ability to maintain discipline in the classroom abounded.[46] Yet the discipline problem was endemic to the Hebrew classes, and by no means experienced only by the Israeli teachers. The pupils, whose peers were outside playing or at home watching television, often found it frustrating to be expected to master material that, presented, as it was, in a tedious and mechanical manner, failed to engage them, and generated hostility rather than enthusiasm for their heritage.

The minutes of the LBJRE's meetings attest to the fact that the organization rarely dealt with the aims of and optimal methodologies for part-time Jewish education. Rather, meetings focused on pragmatic issues, and in particular, balancing the budget. While financial constraints indeed impeded expansion and creativity, the leadership demonstrated little passion for its pedagogic mission. Attendance at the LBJRE's meetings was sparse, a fact commented on frequently by the *Jewish Chronicle*'s Ben Azai. In 1965, for instance, he reported that the LBJRE met four times; only 12

---

to become head teacher at the Mile End Synagogue school. Tellingly, the individual in question was a yeshiva student, not a trained teacher at all. See Bernard Green to Chief Rabbi, 2 January 1971. CR C3 4.

45 Barwell, 'Facets', 38.
46 See Prais, 'Sample', 152.

of its 170 members attended all four sessions, and 57 failed to make a single appearance. The figures were similar in 1973, when of the board's 140 members only 5 attended the five sessions held, and 60 did not put in a single appearance.[47] Membership on the LBJRE engendered a sense of status and was perceived by some as a stepping-stone to the United Synagogue's inner circle, but most members had no real interest in improving the Hebrew classes. At almost every level, the system was plagued by a lack of commitment and energy, and in some cases, indifference and even hypocrisy.

Undoubtedly, the lack of energy, innovation, and enthusiasm that pervaded the Hebrew classes system was to a great extent attributable to the framework's underlying philosophy. The premise that the chief pedagogic objective was to inculcate religious beliefs and promote religious observance was taken to imply that the Hebrew classes were not a forum for questions and open-ended discussion about source texts, traditions, and basic religious principles.[48] This engendered much discontent among the pupils. The phenomenon was attested to in various studies and reports, and anguished over in interviews, articles and letters in the Anglo-Jewish press. In 1973, the Board of Deputies' Research Unit had fifteen-year-olds complete a lengthy questionnaire that covered, among other things, part-time education. Many of the respondents expressed frustration with the old-fashioned teaching methods, and complained of being bored due to the focus on teaching Hebrew reading regardless of comprehension. 'Although I can read fluently, I don't understand a word of it' was a typical complaint.[49] A reporter sent by the *Jewish Chronicle* to the Kenton Synagogue classes in 1974 was told repeatedly that the emphasis on translation was tedious. One child commented, 'I'm bored because all we're doing is translating someone's Bar-Mitzvah portion'. And in a letter to the *Jewish Chronicle* reflecting on her Hebrew class days, one young woman wrote, 'Classes dragged on, the teaching methods were dull in comparison to school,

47   *JC* 30 July 1965, 8; 9 November 1973, 13.
48   In the words of one observer, 'instructors were untrained and ill-paid. Questions were unwelcome, discipline severe'; see D. Englander, 'Integrated but Insecure: A Portrait of Anglo-Jewry at the Close of the Twentieth Century' in Parsons, *Growth*, 1:106.
49   See Prais, 'Sample', Appendix B, Comments by Pupils, 152–3.

and too many subjects were learned parrot fashion'.[50] The Hebrew classes, being supplementary in nature, were inevitably compared with the state or 'public' schools the children attended for their secular studies. Many of these schools routinely used sophisticated audio-visual methods to teach foreign languages. Recordings, tapes, and later, language labs and video, made language learning in such schools interactive and more interesting than the frontal text-based method used in the Hebrew classes.

Despite the persistent criticisms of the teaching methods and standards at the LBJRE's Hebrew classes, little changed in the 1960s and 1970s. Chief Rabbi Brodie did not involve himself much with curricular and methodological matters, his primary concern being to ensure that those employed in this framework met strict standards of religious observance.[51] Though his successor, Rabbi Immanuel Jakobovits, made education his top domestic priority, he preferred to devote his energies to the day-school sector, where he believed there was a greater chance of imbuing students with a deep and abiding commitment to Judaism, and left the Hebrew classes system unaltered. American Jewish education experts who visited London in 1968 supported his approach.

Their findings, together with research conducted by the Chief Rabbi's office, were published as a plan of action entitled *Let My People Know*. In a single paragraph in the preamble, the Chief Rabbi dismissed Hebrew classes as having failed in their mission. Since some 80 per cent of those receiving Jewish education in this framework abandoned their studies 'at an age when they cannot but remain juvenile Jews for the rest of their lives', he wrote, it was not surprising that 'so many of our young people find Jewishness too crippled and underdeveloped to sustain their loyalty to our faith, community, to Israel and indeed to the moral values of society'.[52]

---

50   *JC* 14 June 1974, 8; 18 November 1977, 33.
51   See 'Sunday School Teacher Applications and Recommendations 1962'. ACC 2805/112. Apart from details concerning applicants' marital status, training, synagogue membership and youth movement affiliation, all approved applications have the phrase 'strictly Orthodox' added and underlined. Chief Rabbi Jakobovits did not change this criterion, see CR C3 4 (1971).
52   *Let My People*, 3.

In addition to condemning the Hebrew classes without engaging in a serious discussion of the reasons for this failure, *Let My People Know* declared that future efforts in the field of Jewish education would be largely directed toward developing the day schools. At a LBJRE meeting, Jakobovits stated that 'many graduates' viewed their Jewish educational experience 'with resentment or contempt'.[53] This disparaging attitude added to the mounting demoralization of those involved in part-time Jewish education: the leaders of mainstream Orthodoxy were losing faith in the Hebrew classes they themselves sponsored.

Reform and Liberal religion classes

Let us now consider the classes run by the Progressive (Reform and Liberal) movement synagogues, which were historically committed to the Sunday classes framework. The Progressive movements opposed Jewish day schools, which they regarded as separatist and thus antithetical to their integrationist ideology, an ideology with roots in an era when the civil emancipation of the Jews was not taken for granted. Jewish day schools were seen as infringing the cherished principle of open interaction with non-Jewish society. Instead, Sunday or afternoon religion schools, as they were popularly referred to (though officially called 'religion classes'), were viewed as the appropriate framework for Jewish education. Schools were affiliated with particular synagogues, and were autonomous rather than movement-directed with regard to their educational policies. Generally, the curriculum focused on the Bible, ethical principles, and social questions, rather than on ritual precepts.

The Reform and Liberal religion classes underwent dramatic expansion during this period. This growth highlighted a deepening polarization within Anglo-Jewry, as centrist Orthodoxy lost members to, on the one

---

53   16 November 1978. CR C3 8 Speeches, 2.

hand, the ultra-Orthodox camp, and on the other, the Progressives. Migration to the suburbs was often the catalyst for such change; in Redbridge the trend was for parents to forgo synagogue membership after their sons' Bar-Mitzvahs.[54] The Reform movement, by contrast, was, demographically speaking, healthy, with more marriages than deaths.[55] In 1970, the two groups associated with Progressive Judaism accounted for slightly over a fifth of UK male synagogue members, by 1990, they accounted for almost a third.[56] In part, these shifts in affiliation occurred due to a sense of estrangement from the United Synagogue, which had veered to the right religiously and abandoned its historic commitment to 'progressive conservatism', a term employed by Chief Rabbi Hertz to reflect the tradition of membership in an Orthodox synagogue along with easy-going or lapsed religious observance.[57]

The clearest expression of the rightward shift within Orthodoxy was the Jacobs affair, in the wake of which something akin to American-style 'Conservative Judaism' – though not defined as such at the time – was established in Great Britain. A brief review of the Jacobs affair is thus essential for understanding the shifts in British Jewry's religious affiliations from the 1960s through the 1980s.

Rabbi Louis Jacobs had served as an assistant minister at the Golders Green Synagogue, and had a reputation as a promising rabbinical figure and Talmud scholar, when, in 1954, he accepted the post of rabbi at the (United Synagogue) New West End Synagogue. In a book entitled *We Have Reason to Believe*, published in 1957, however, Jacobs argued against the thesis that God had given every word of the Torah to Moses at Sinai.[58] At the time, the book was not particularly controversial, and the Chief Rabbi had no problem approving Jacobs's appointment as a lecturer in Pastoral Theology at Jews' College in 1959. Jacobs resigned as rabbi of the

---

54 Kosmin and Levy, *Jewish Identity*, 21.

55 B. Kosmin, The Structure and Demography of British Jewry in 1976, mimeograph, WZO, 1976, 6–7. JNUL; LMA.

56 Prais, 'Polarization', 6.

57 This term is discussed in Alderman, *Modern*, 215.

58 L. Jacobs, *We Have Reason to Believe* (London: Vallentine Mitchell, 1962).

New West End synagogue upon taking up the position at Jews' College. Rabbi Isidore Epstein had served there as principal for years, but was due to retire in 1962; there was an informal understanding that Jacobs would succeed him. But in 1961, Chief Rabbi Brodie rejected Jacobs as a candidate for principal of the College, apparently under the influence of the London rabbinical court, which was alarmed by Jacobs's book, and Dr Epstein, who resented being forced into retirement. In response, Jacobs resigned. In 1963, the position of rabbi at the New West End Synagogue became vacant, and Rabbi Jacobs was invited to reoccupy it. United Synagogue regulations mandated that all appointments of this nature had to be approved by the Chief Rabbi. Rabbi Brodie declared that he would approve the appointment only if Jacobs published a statement retracting his comments on Divine revelation. Jacobs refused to comply, and at an extraordinary meeting, won the confidence of his old-new congregation. In response, the United Synagogue called a special meeting of its own to determine its reaction to this slighting of the Chief Rabbi and the United Synagogue. It was chaired by Sir Isaac Wolfson, president of the United Synagogue, whose election to that office can also be seen as reflecting the rightward shift of mainstream Orthodoxy in Britain. At the meeting, the United Synagogue decided to summarily dismiss the honorary officers of the New West End Synagogue and its Board of Management.[59]

Although the debate did not lead, as some had feared, to the dismemberment of the United Synagogue, it has been argued by the United Synagogue's own historian that the Jacobs affair was evidence of a 'takeover' at the United Synagogue by a new generation. 'They were a very different breed of Jews from the Grand Dukes, who were representatives of the older, pre-immigration families and whose affiliations with the United Synagogue were matters of tradition and responsibility but not theological identification'.[60] Another consequence of the Jacobs affair, and a similar reflection of the polarization within the community, was that some members of the United Synagogue decided to take a stand 'against the religious

59   Bermant, *Troubled Eden*, 143.
60   Newman, *United*, 186.

fundamentalism of which the Chief Rabbi appeared to be a prisoner'.[61] Not longer afterwards, the premises of the former St John's Wood Synagogue, by a felicitous coincidence, came on the market and were acquired by Jacobs's supporters, becoming the home of the New London Synagogue, under the leadership of Rabbi Louis Jacobs.

It is doubtful whether many left the United Synagogue over its handling of the Jacobs affair; it is more likely that most who left were motivated by broader concerns. For many, Reform and Liberal Judaism had both theological and pragmatic appeal. As the feminist agenda became an increasingly important element in the public discourse, women found themselves alienated by the Orthodox synagogues. Whereas in the United Synagogue, women could serve neither as rabbis and lay prayer leaders, nor in other ritual capacities, in the Reform and Liberal movements egalitarianism was fast becoming the norm. There was also frustration, in some quarters, over the lack of decorum – specifically, the incessant chatter – during services at the Orthodox synagogues. Some resented chastisement about their inadequate observance of the precepts, and preferred the more accommodating approach of the Reform and Liberal movements. Practical concerns also played no small part in the shift in synagogue affiliation: many established synagogues were located in neighbourhoods that were no longer convenient. Moreover, the Reform and Liberal movements had a flexible attitude to conversion and were more welcoming to non-Jewish partners. The organizational structure of the movements also differed: the United Synagogue was traditionally a centrally-run, top-down system, whereas the Reform and Liberal movements were associations of autonomous synagogues.

Influenced by refugee scholars who arrived before and after the Second World War, particularly the charismatic and pro-Zionist Rabbi Leo Baeck, the Reform movement had abandoned the anti-Zionism of its early days. Following the Six-Day War and the Yom Kippur War, it reconsidered its public position on Zionism and the State of Israel, and in 1975 joined the World Zionist Organization. There was also a certain return to traditional

---

61 Alderman, *Modern*, 363.

religious ritual: prayers omitted from earlier editions of the prayer-book were reintroduced, as were immersion in a ritual bath for converts and observance of the second day of Rosh Hashanah. Canonicals were abandoned, replaced by woollen prayer shawls, Hebrew was reinstated, and it was decided that only kosher food would be served on synagogue premises. These changes reflected a shift from the Progressive movements' former universalistic tendency to a post-Holocaust particularism.[62]

These developments swelled the ranks of the Reform movement, and as most of the new members were young couples with children, it was soon necessary to expand the movement's educational frameworks. In contrast to the Orthodox synagogues, which preferred the terms 'cheder' or 'Hebrew school' for their educational institutions, the Reform congregations favoured the rubric 'religion school' because it implied study of the Jewish faith as a whole. Both boys and girls were expected to attend until at least the age of thirteen. Girls were offered a Bat-Mitzvah ceremony that was 'the same in every detail' as the boys' Bar-Mitzvah ceremony.[63] The religion schools offered classes for fifteen and sixteen year olds, and for some Progressive movement rabbis, the litmus test of their success was the number of teenagers who continued to participate in religion schools up to this age, when parental pressure was no longer the sole factor determining attendance.[64]

In 1968, at the height of the LBJRE crisis, the Reform movement was taking stock of its own educational system. But whereas the LBJRE's difficulties were broadcast on the pages of the *Jewish Chronicle*, the Reform movement's self-assessment was confined to its quarterly magazine, *Living Judaism*. Describing the general state of these classes, Benaiah Bardi, headmaster of the religion school at the Edgware and District Reform Synagogue, and a member of the Reform movement's Central Education Committee, painted a picture that called to mind the situation faced by the LBJRE:

62   J. Romain (ed.), *150 Years of Progressive Judaism in Britain 1840–1990* (London: London Museum of Jewish Life, 1990), 48.

63   J. Romain and A. J. Kershen, *Tradition and Change: A History of Reform Judaism in Britain 1840–1995* (London: Vallentine Mitchell, 1995), 240.

64   S. Herman, 'Education in Synagogue Religion Schools', *Living Judaism* (Summer 1968), 72; D. Marmur, *Reform Judaism: Essays on Reform Judaism in Britain* (London: Reform Synagogues of Great Britain, 1973), 191–2.

The facts are startling. High calibre specialist teachers are almost non-existent, there is no standard syllabus, and some schools have no syllabus at all. On the whole, teaching methods are old fashioned and ineffectual. Parents are often apathetic, and children are often bored. The net result is that some learning takes place, but no true education.[65]

Living Judaism devoted most of its summer 1968 issue to Jewish education and the Reform movement. Contributions addressed the religion schools' objectives, curriculum, and teaching methods. The discussions attest to awareness of the educational ramifications of Britain's open secular society. Rabbi John Rayner, Director of Studies at Leo Baeck College, the Reform movement's rabbinical seminary and teachers' college, noted that in pre-emancipation societies, Jewish boys of thirteen recognized that as full-fledged members of the Jewish community, they assumed new responsibilities. For these youngsters, acquiring the know-how of being Jewish was a social necessity. By contrast, in contemporary society thirteen year olds were often unaware of, or doubted, the importance of their Judaism. The central concern of the religion school teacher was thus now 'motivation' and not only 'knowledge', he argued.[66] Elsewhere, this view was endorsed by Tony Bayfield, rabbi at the North West Surrey Synagogue. Invoking Harold Loukes, a scholar of Christian education, he called for a less dogmatic approach to Jewish education, in line with the contemporary, more sceptical and thoughtful youngster.

Religious education in a secular society must be conceived in totally different terms from religious education in a religious society ... the authoritative transmission of a received tradition must give way to the open search for a *living* truth ... a hope of opening young eyes to look for themselves.[67]

Reform rabbis were trained to be conscious of their pastoral duties, and did not close their eyes to their congregants' actual religious practices and knowledge. The rabbi of the North Western Reform Synagogue

---

65 B. Bardi, 'New Dimensions in Religious Education', *Living Judaism*, Summer 1968, 80.

66 Ibid.

67 T. Bayfield, 'Trends in Jewish Education Today', *British Journal of Religious Education* 3:4 (1981), 132.

described many as either 'completely' non-observant or as having reduced observance 'to the level of nostalgia'.[68] Although this is an exaggeration, as evidenced by a community-sponsored poll and a later survey conducted by the Board of Deputies, these comments reflect the perceived magnitude of the religion schools' educational mission.[69]

The Reform movement had established a Central Education Committee as early as 1959, but there was opposition to a compulsory religion school syllabus. Synagogues were encouraged to create their own curricula, though some requested assistance in doing so. In this spirit, the reflections on the religion schools' curriculum in *Living Judaism* were intended to foster dialogue, not to dictate an ideological agenda. Rabbi A. Herman, minister of the Southgate Synagogue, suggested dividing the curriculum into three sections: theology, sociology, and skills. Bible stories, short prayers, festival celebrations, comparative religion studies and contemporary theological problems, he argued, should be used to enable students to reach an understanding as to 'what God means to us as individuals and as a Covenant Community'. The sociology section would focus on history and customs, but would be set within the context of world history rather than detached from it, as was popular in the Hebrew class and day-school frameworks. Also departing from the approach characteristic of the Orthodox schools, he recommended placing more emphasis on the events of recent times. The 'skills' section would include Hebrew reading and comprehension, as well as knowledge of – and participation in – synagogue services.[70]

Rabbi Rayner's recommendations were different. He proposed giving greater emphasis to comparative studies – particularly the differences between Judaism and Christianity – and explaining the unique virtues of Judaism vis-à-vis the faiths of mainstream society. He argued that the

---

68   Marmur, *Reform*, 192.

69   The Redbridge survey revealed that about 60 per cent of Reform respondents had a mezuzah, and a similar number ate matza during Passover. Some 50 per cent lit candles on the Sabbath eve, though only half that number recited the Kiddush; see Kosmin and Levy, *Jewish Identity*, 13. A 1971 poll found that 19 per cent of Reform and Liberal Jews kept a kosher home; the corresponding number for United Synagogue members was 82 per cent, see *JC* 22 January 1971, 1, 10.

70   Herman, 'Education', 73–4.

enormous influence of mainstream culture had to be countered with the message that Judaism had unique virtues of its own. Rayner also maintained that the differences between Jewish and Christian ethics, a subject he felt had been unduly neglected in the past, should be discussed in religion schools. Both Rayner and Herman favoured a curriculum quite different in focus from that of the LBJRE. In particular, they evinced less interest in teaching Judaism's ritual precepts, emphasizing instead its ethical teachings, often in a comparative context. The LBJRE typically did not allocate time to discussion of other religions, perhaps because the available time was deemed barely sufficient to teach Judaism, let alone other faiths.

Despite the genuine interest in revamping the curriculum, the recommendations were not implemented to any great extent. Bayfield found that most of the classroom time in the Reform Synagogue religion schools was spent on Hebrew, Bible, Jewish history, ethics and prayer, a regimen not too far removed from that of the United Synagogue Hebrew classes.[71] Apparently, the suggested changes could not be carried out because the various centres were autonomous and staffed by teachers who, in the main, lacked professional pedagogic training. Without systemic policy changes and special training programs for teachers, there was no practicable way to implement the recommended changes, despite their aptness.

With respect to pedagogic approaches and teaching methods, an area much criticized vis-à-vis the Orthodox Hebrew classes, and also deemed problematic by observers of Progressive education, here the impetus for change came from the rabbis themselves. Reform rabbis tended to have backgrounds in psychology, sociology and education, and sought to introduce a more flexible, open-ended and child-centred approach in the religion schools.[72] They also called for the standard methodological improvements, such as use of audio-visual learning technologies in the classroom, interactive teaching through drama, and so on. One headmaster envisioned a time when 'the boring days of talk and chalk would be gone forever and religious education would become an adventure'.[73]

---

71 Bayfield, 'Trends', 131.
72 Bayfield, e.g., encouraged teachers and educators to consider Piaget's child development theories when writing curriculum and developing lesson plans.
73 Bardi, 'New', 81.

Rayner suggested that the most committed and devoted members of the community should be encouraged to minimize their involvement in the synagogue councils and management committees, and instead devote their time to teaching the movement's children. Members who took up this challenge would lead by personal example, dedication and passion. Fearing that inexperience and lack of specialized training might hold back potential candidates, he recommended that a training programme be established at Leo Baeck College.[74] Other proposals were more familiar, calling for better compensation for teachers, and raising their profile in the community. Though the Reform movement was committed to the autonomy of each synagogue, its 1974 annual conference endorsed establishment of an effective central education department with a full-time director at its helm. Financial limitations delayed implementation of this decision.

Ironically, two of the movement's traditional rivals ended up funding the infrastructure for the changes. One was the Chief Rabbi's Jewish Educational Development Trust (JEDT), which had been established to further a variety of educational projects, primarily day schools. Given the hostility to Reform Judaism traditionally manifested by the Chief Rabbi's office, it is hardly surprising that considerable hesitation accompanied a proposed grant to fund the Reform education office. But in 1977 the JEDT did award it an annual grant of £12,500 for three years. Similarly, the Pincus Fund for Jewish Education in the Diaspora, under the aegis of the WZO, awarded a grant of £25,000 to the Teachers' Training Department of Leo Baeck College. Established in 1978, the unit's first director was an Israeli who had been selected from a wide field of candidates, highlighting how much the Reform movement had changed since its anti-Zionist days.[75]

74   J. Rayner, 'Progressive Judaism in the Religion School', *Living Judaism*, Summer 1968, 77.

75   Romain and Kershen, *Tradition*, 240–1. The growing embrace of Zionism was also reflected in the transformation of the Reform movement's youth groups. In 1977, for the first time, the Reform movement requested and received the services of an emissary (*shaliah*) from Israel; a tradition that continued thereafter. In 1981, Ian Wainer, a graduate and former employee of the Zionist youth movement Habonim, became director of the Reform movement's youth organization (RSY). Helped by a few key counsellors, several of whom had studied in Jerusalem at the Institute for

Despite the innovations that were introduced, and the Reform movement's well-entrenched aversion to day-school education, a small but growing number of voices began to call for the establishment of a Reform day school, in no small part because they had reached the conclusion that the religion school system had failed. Among those calling for a day school was Rabbi Selvin Goldberg of the Manchester Reform Synagogue, who had first broached the idea in 1965.[76] However, four years were to pass before a feasibility study was commissioned. To gauge members' views on the idea of a Reform day school, *Living Judaism* enclosed a questionnaire in its Winter 1970 issue. Only 4 per cent of its readers returned the survey, and of them, only 30 per cent were in favour, leaving the movement in no doubt that the time was not yet ripe for a Reform day school. One or two of the movement's leaders continued to keep the idea alive, particularly Rabbi Dow Marmur, who, given the hostility to the day-school idea, was remarkably outspoken. 'There is no evidence that a child from a Jewish day school, even those already operating, is isolated and ill suited to the open society. It is scandalous that this Movement has refused even to debate the subject seriously and that there are so few in our midst prepared to promote this cause'.[77] 'Part-time Jewish education is insufficient, even when begun at nursery school level and continued into the youth club and adult life. ... To achieve a degree of enlightened Jewish commitment an integrated system of education is essential, and only the Jewish day school can provide it'.[78] At his own synagogue, Rabbi Marmur opened a nursery school, beginning something of a trend. By 1977, there were three Reform nurseries in operation. The chairman of the Reform Synagogue Board of Governors considered this an indication that the time had come to raise the question of a primary day school in North West London, and such an institution, the Akiva School, was finally established in 1981.

Youth Leaders from Abroad (Kiryat Moriah), he transformed it from a social club into a Reform Zionist youth movement.

76   Ibid., 241. As Goldberg put it, 'Sunday morning religious instruction has reached the stage of bankruptcy. ... any further effort along these lines is sheer waste', quoted in Bardi, 'New', 83.

77   D. Marmur, *Living Judaism*, Autumn 1972, 45.

78   Marmur, *Reform*, 195.

Although it took another thirteen years before a second school was opened, the taboo had been broken. The existence of the Akiva School was a statement that some of those who had been staunchly opposed to Jewish day schools no longer saw such schools as a challenge to Reform's integrationist ideology, as they had just a few generations earlier. In 1981, Britain was a multicultural society within which the Jews' full civil emancipation had long since been a given; proponents of Jewish day schools were by this time a confident group. Who could have imagined, in the 1940s or 1950s, that within their lifetime a Reform rabbi would see fit to admonish Anglo-Jewry that 'reluctance to send children to Jewish schools has little to do with the desire to protect them from enemies and much [to do] with the wish to bar their access to Jewish commitment; it is an assimilationist ploy'.[79]

Conclusion

The number of children attending the LBJRE's Hebrew classes dropped significantly between 1958 and 1978. As we have seen, some of this decline is attributable to low birth rates among Anglo-Jewry. Another contributing factor was the denominational shift from membership in United Synagogue and Federation affiliated synagogues to membership in synagogues affiliated with the Progressive movements. But the most important cause was the increase in the number of children attending Jewish day schools: children withdrawn from local council to denominational day schools virtually always stopped attending Hebrew classes. Table 6 summarizes these developments as they played out in London, in many ways a microcosm of the country as a whole:

79   D. Marmur, *Beyond Survival* (London: Darton, Longman and Todd, 1982), 125.

Table 6   Day-school vs Hebrew classes/religion school enrolment in London, 1958–75

Day-school places	*1958*	*1975*	*Difference 1958–75*
Mainstream Orthodox	2,234	5,752	+3,518
Ultra-Orthodox	125	1,221	+1,096
Total	*2,359*	*6,973*	*+4,614*
Hebrew classes/religion school places			
LBJRE	11,618	6,901	-4,717
Reform/Liberal	1,000	3,870	+2,870
Total	*12,618*	*10,771*	*-1,847*

Sources: LBJRE Annual Reports for 1958 and 1975; 'Biennial Survey on Jewish Day Schools', *JC* 24 January 1958, 17; J. Braude, *Survey of Jewish Day Schools in the United Kingdom and Ireland* [unpublished report], London, Institute of Jewish Affairs, 1975, 12. CR C3 5 1976.

Particularly noteworthy is the drop in the number attending classes under the aegis of the LBJRE between 1965 and 1975, when the baby boom had ended and Anglo-Jewry's demographic profile had come to be characterized by late marriage, out-marriage, and small families. During the same period, the enrolment at day schools increased considerably.

The growth in day-school attendance, as we will see in the coming chapter, cannot be ascribed to dissatisfaction with the Hebrew classes, though such complaints were indeed commonplace. We have seen that increasingly vocal protests, particularly over plans to impose direct fees and make mid-week attendance compulsory, did not lead to mass desertion of the Hebrew classes framework. Granted, some, upon leaving the United or Federation synagogues, identified dissatisfaction with religion classes as a factor that entered into their decision. We are about to see, however, that the primary impetus for the jump in day-school attendance was not parental discontentment with the Hebrew classes. Rather, the rising interest in day-school education must be understood against the background of a number of other factors, including concerns about the comprehensive secondary schools, increased Jewish pride and identification in the wake of events in Israel and the struggle for Soviet Jewry, and greater cultural acceptance of ethnic self-identity within British society generally.

Nevertheless, it must be kept in mind that the majority of parents remained hostile to Jewish day schools. As late as 1978, when one in five London children attended these schools, opposition to them nonetheless remained high.[80] The Redbridge survey found that nearly two thirds of respondents rejected this day-school education, expressing the view that separating Jewish children from the wider community was harmful. Other respondents argued that mixing with children from all religions was important, and several used the term 'apartheid' to describe the day-school movement. A smaller number voiced concern that children who attended Jewish day schools might be 'brainwashed'.[81]

For the time being, for most parents, Hebrew classes, whether those offered by the LBJRE or those offered by the Reform and Liberal movements, remained the optimal framework for their children's Jewish education. A few hours on Sunday mornings, particularly prior to Bar/Bat-Mitzvah age, would, they felt, provide the children with the ability to read Hebrew and follow the synagogue service, as well as familiarity with festivals, ancient Jewish history, Bible stories and various rituals, and these competencies were, it seems, what mattered most to Anglo-Jewish parents. Although the different streams emphasized different elements of this general programme, the outcome was basically the same: children who were not able to speak or understand Hebrew fluently, who had little in-depth knowledge of Jewish history or culture, and who had little interest in increasing their knowledge.

In many ways, these attitudes paralleled those of the Christian majority in the middle-class neighbourhoods where most Jews resided. Religion generally played a secondary role in the identity of those in this demographic, and, judging on the basis of church attendance and observance of ritual at home, was on the decline.[82] The Anglican Sunday-school system was weakening, reflecting the more general decline in the importance of Christianity

---

80   In the provinces the figures were different: Manchester 27 per cent, Leeds 52 per cent, Liverpool 90 per cent, Glasgow 22 per cent, see *Securing*, 11.

81   Kosmin and Levy, *Jewish Identity*, 33–4.

82   Parsons, *Growth*, 1:312–14. Church membership declined from 8.42 to 6.44 million, that is, to about 15 per cent of the UK adult population, between 1970 and 1992, see Marwick, *British Society*, 461.

in British society. Regardless of the degree to which Jews perceived their Judaism as more than simply a religious identity, and as encompassing an ethnic sense of belonging – a question that will be discussed in the coming chapters – mainstream Christianity continued to serve as the paradigm for the appropriate expression of religious particularity. However, dramatic changes were taking place in Britain and beyond, changes that, over the 1960s, 1970s and 1980s, would have a marked impact on Jewish self-identity in general, and attitudes to Jewish day schools in particular. It is to these developments that we now turn.

CHAPTER 4

Reorganization of State Education and the Rise of the Day Schools

Anglo-Jewish education underwent a major transformation in the late 1960s and the 1970s. As we have seen, for most of the twentieth century, formal Jewish education took place chiefly within the framework of Sunday and/ or after-school classes – colloquially referred to as Talmud Torah, Hebrew, or *cheder* classes. These classes, attendance at which rarely extended beyond Bar/Bat-Mitzvah age, sought to instil the ability to read Hebrew and follow the synagogue service, familiarity with festivals, and a basic knowledge of Jewish history, Bible stories and religious rituals. Though complaints about the teachers, pedagogy and curriculum abounded, most parents showed little interest in giving their children a solid Jewish education. Yet as the 1960s came to a close, enrolment at supplementary schools was falling, while the demand for Jewish day-school education, both primary and secondary, had begun to rise.[1] By the late 1970s, the number of children enrolled in supplementary classes had dropped by almost a third, whereas Jewish day-school enrolment more than doubled.[2] Although Hebrew classes were still the dominant provider of Jewish education, their heyday had passed; within a decade, the day schools would overtake them.

In May 1965, the number of students attending Jewish day schools was just under 10,000; by January 1977, it had reached 12,790. The number of

---

[1]   The shrinking percentage of children attending supplementary schools also reflects the growth of the fervently Orthodox population within British Jewry.

[2]   Braude, 'Jewish Education', 121; Fishman and Levy, 'Jewish Education', 73; LBJRE Annual Reports, 1958, 1965, 1975. Attendance at the Reform movement schools, which were not under the aegis of the LBJRE, has also been factored in.

Jewish day schools increased from forty-nine to fifty-seven.[3] Most of the new schools were secondary schools in London.[4]

This chapter will explore the reasons for this rising demand for day-school education. The expansion of the day schools during this period appears remarkable considering that the community faced other needs perceived by many as more pressing. What contributed to the dramatic shift in the community's attitude to Jewish day-school education? Various factors have been suggested, including the permissive and unruly atmosphere reputedly pervasive at state schools, and an ethnic and religious revival in the wake of the Six-Day War.[5] As we will see, however, the greatest spur to Jewish day-school education was the reorganization of secondary education, particularly, the phasing out of grammar schools. Upon introduction of the non-selective comprehensive schools, parents fled the non-denominational state system, preferring voluntary-aided Jewish day schools, or, for those who could afford them, private schools.

3   Braude, 'Jewish Education', 124–5. Though it is tempting to note that in the preceding 10-year period, 1954–64, the number of schools had increased even more – from 23 to 48 – as had enrolment, the difference in availability of government funding during the two periods must be taken into account. In the earlier period the government granted state-aided status to 10 day schools, four of them secondary, whereas in the later period only five day schools were granted this status, all primary.

4   The schools in London that became state-aided during this period were Rosh Pinah, Menorah, and Simon Marks. In 1970, the Ilford Primary School was opened as a replacement for the state-aided Stepney School. In Manchester, the North Cheshire Jewish Primary School gained state-aided status, as did the Brodetsky and Silman schools in Leeds.

5   O. Valins et al., *The Future of Jewish Schooling in the United Kingdom* (London: Institute for Jewish Policy Research, 2001); H. Miller, 'Meeting the Challenge: the Jewish Schooling Phenomenon in the UK', *Oxford Review of Education* 27 (2001), 501–13; M. Davis, 'Resurgence', in *Let My People*; Bermant, *Lord Jakobovits*, 196.

The introduction of comprehensive secondary education

The attitude of Jewish parents to their children's schooling was strongly influenced by the Labour Party's 1964 election promise to eliminate the 11 plus examination and replace the tripartite secondary school system with a comprehensive, that is, non-selective, system. Labour's commitment to non-selective education arose from recognition of the social injustice inherent in the tripartite structure. The 11 plus examination was seen as handicapping working-class children, whose economic disadvantage was reinforced by a system that allowed little opportunity for remediation as the children grew older. Even in the late 1960s, most grammar school pupils were from the middle class; this disproportion was even higher among pupils of direct-grant grammar schools. In response to this de facto social streaming, educators, teachers, and Local Education Authorities (LEAs) increasingly favoured secondary school reorganization.[6]

Apart from the moral arguments for comprehensive education, various commissions of inquiry had established that reorganization of the education system was economically desirable. To compete in a technologically advanced world market, Britain required a well-educated workforce, and pupils from working-class backgrounds would have to acquire high-level secondary education. This could be achieved through large multi-tiered schools offering a broad range of courses, namely, comprehensive schools; grammar schools would be phased out.[7] Of the 1,300 grammar schools that existed in 1960, only 150 remained in 1990, while the number of comprehensive schools increased from 130 to about 3,000.[8]

Opponents of the comprehensive system feared that accommodating a spectrum of abilities in a single school would lead to a lowering of the academic level, to the detriment of the brighter students. Others feared

6　R. Pedley, *The Comprehensive School* (London: Penguin, 1969), 10–13.
7　Gordon et al., *Education*, 77.
8　B. Simon, *The State and Educational Policy* (London: Lawrence & Wishart, 1994), 164.

comprehensive schools would engender alienation. To fulfil their mandate
of offering a wide variety of courses, comprehensive schools had to be large
and, by implication, cold and impersonal. These critics claimed that smaller
schools, where teachers were familiar with their pupils' individual strengths
and needs, fostered community and social responsibility.[9]

Much of the hostility to the comprehensive system can be attributed
to affection for the grammar school experience on the part of those who
had been through it, many of whom were now implementing the transition to comprehensive education, and parents of children whose education
might be impacted by it. Grammar schools were generally characterized
by a high degree of solidarity: studies and memoirs reveal that graduates
often spoke fondly of their schools for the rest of their lives. Even graduates
whose recollections were less rosy viewed their grammar school education
as having afforded them upward social mobility.

From October 1964 to the end of the decade, though Labour was in
power, the government, aware that in some circles there was considerable
opposition to the comprehensive system, did not mandate that the LEAs
reorganize schools in accordance with it, but merely encouraged them
to do so. This generated uncertainty and vacillation on the part of educational institutions, apprehensiveness on the part of parents, and much
acrimony.[10]

After the Conservatives defeated Labour in the 1970 election, Margaret
Thatcher, a fierce opponent of reorganization, issued a directive permitting
LEAs that had opposed the comprehensive system to maintain selective
education. Yet the reorganization continued apace, and by 1974, 62 per
cent of maintained schools were comprehensive, twice as many as in 1970.[11]
Still, hundreds of grammar schools continued to exist.

9   Davis, *Grammar School*, 144–5.
10   For a more detailed account of the rocky path to comprehensive education, see D.
     Mendelsson, 'Embracing Jewish Day School Education in England 1965–79', *History
     of Education* 38 (2009), 545–63.
11   B. Simon, *Education and the Social Order, 1940–1990* (London: Lawrence & Wishart,
     1991), 586, table 6a.

The struggle between the two camps went on. Labour having returned to power in 1974, the Education Bill, mandating comprehensive education, became law in November 1976. But due to the grave economic crisis England was undergoing at the time, its implementation was stymied by budgetary constraints. And when a confidential document on the failure of secondary schools to produce enough engineers and scientists was leaked to the press, uproar ensued. Sensational articles and documentaries depicted the comprehensive schools as 'out of control, walled off from parental concerns and subject to the influence of Marxist ideology'.[12] Despite having passed the Education Bill, the Labour government faced an uphill battle on the education front. Hoping to harness the public's anger over a perceived decline in the secondary schools, both sides claimed to defend 'quality' and 'standards' in education, and the roller coaster ride continued. When the Labour party was defeated in 1979, the new Conservative government effectively repealed Labour's 1976 Education Bill, freezing reorganization.

Jewish parents and the comprehensive schools

The tug-of-war over the comprehensive system created anxiety among parents. Where the LEA had voted in favour of the non-selective system and submitted a plan for comprehensive education that was approved by the Department of Education and Science (DES), parents had to decide whether their children would attend the local comprehensive school or find an alternative. The dilemma was compounded by the fact that the LEA plan, though submitted, might be withdrawn following election of a new government or local council. The years of wrangling over comprehensive schooling thus had a profound impact on all parents, Jewish parents among

---

12   C. Chitty, *The Education System Transformed: A Guide to the School Reforms* (Manchester: Baseline, 1992), 63–6.

them. Anglo-Jews had high academic aspirations for their children.[13] The uncertainty regarding comprehensive schools was of great concern to Jewish parents, and influenced their decisions as to their children's schooling.

Jewish parents were keen supporters of grammar school education.[14] Many had attended grammar schools themselves, and doing so had served them well, especially as a stepping-stone to the professions.[15] For such parents, it was natural to hope their children would follow the same path. One historian explained that 'even those Jews who paid lip service to the idea of a classless society did not want it just yet ... they wished to enjoy the fruits of a middle-class existence, and the continued functioning of selective schools was perceived as an integral part of this inheritance'.[16]

Concern about academic achievement was a central factor in determining the esteem in which Jewish parents held an educational institution.[17] The widely accepted view – on the street and in the media – that comprehensive schools, by virtue of their size and non-selective intake, were unable to produce the O and A level results of the grammar schools, deterred many from sending their children to these schools.[18] However, it was not only the academic standards that concerned Jewish parents. Reports such

13 E. Krausz, 'The Edgware Survey: Occupation and Class', *Jewish Journal of Sociology* 11 (1969): 88; G. Cromer, 'An Inter-Generational Comparison of Educational and Occupational Aspirations in the Jewish and non-Jewish Family', *Research in Education* 15 (1976), 55.

14 See the section 'Parental Preference for Grammar Schools' in Chapter 1.

15 H. Miller, 'Meeting the Challenge', 505, 508; Waterman and Kosmin, *British Jewry*, 44.

16 Alderman, *London Jewry*, 104–5.

17 E.g., until the mid-1960s, the perception that the JFS did not produce first rate academic results deterred many parents from sending their children there, despite the school's new premises and state-aided status; see Black, *JFS*, 208. Surveyed as to their preference for a new school being planned for NW London, parents consistently preferred a 'selective, high achieving school over a comprehensive school'. S. Miller, 'A New Secondary School in NW London: A Feasibility Study'. CZA A434 Box 5. See too Valins et al., *Future*, ch. 9; S. Brook, *The Club* (London: Constable, 1989), 231.

18 E.g., at Christ's College Grammar School in Finchley, London, Jewish boys made up approximately 40 per cent of the enrolment during the 1960s. By 1980, after the school had 'gone comprehensive', Jewish enrolment was down to 10–15 per cent.

as the so-called Black Papers, five of which came out between 1969 and 1977, alleging that comprehensive schools had serious discipline problems and high rates of student promiscuity, discouraged parents from entrusting their children to such schools. Bermant probably spoke for many Jewish parents when he endorsed the criticisms voiced in the Black Papers.[19] In other words, though their paramount concern was academic achievement, parents also feared that comprehensive schools would adversely affect their children's behaviour and socialization. In 1975, Moshe Davis, director of the JEDT, claimed that anxieties over both the standards of education and the social implications of large state schools were an important factor in stimulating Jewish interest in denominational schools: 'There is a growing fear that children may be alienated from their homes and drawn into a lifestyle which is far removed from generally accepted standards and radically opposed to cherished Jewish attitudes'.[20]

But others interpreted these concerns as reflecting, not desire to preserve Jewish values and behaviour consonant with communal norms, but prejudice. In the past, those attending grammar schools had little contact with students from immigrant backgrounds; with the implementation of the comprehensive system, the likelihood of such encounters grew. Looking back, Bermant acknowledged that this was also a major concern of Jewish parents: 'With the growth of the coloured population, white children found themselves in a minority in some schools. This too encouraged many parents to opt for a Jewish school'.[21] In areas of Inner London, the boroughs of Brent, Ealing, and to a lesser extent Redbridge and Barnet, which had sizeable ethnic and Jewish populations, some Jewish parents were concerned that attending schools with a high percentage of pupils from populations allegedly to be scholastically weaker would be detrimental both to their children's academic achievement, and to their comportment. Such a sentiment is openly referred to – disapprovingly – in a letter to the *Jewish Chronicle*: 'As head of a primary school, I find it very disturbing to hear Jewish parents, who only a couple of generations ago were themselves immigrants, refusing to agree to send their children to this or that school simply on the grounds that they don't want their children to mix with those of coloured immigrants'.[22]

It is important to keep in mind that during the period in question, ongoing economic and political crisis coincided with dramatic demographic and sociocultural transformations in the country as a whole. High unemployment, strikes, recession, racial animosity on the part of the far Right, and growth of the radical Left, created an atmosphere of general nervousness. Anglo-Jewry was uncomfortable with the issues of immigration and race relations, and was not proactive in supporting the Black and Asian communities under attack by the xenophobic and racist National Front.[23] In part this can be attributed to a perception that these communities harboured antisemitic feelings and were anti-Israel. Politically, many of the ethnic minorities identified with the Palestinians, and aligned themselves with the radical elements in the Labour party – personified by Ken Livingstone, a vocal critic of Israel and supporter of the PLO – fuelling tension with London Jewry.[24] But quite apart from the question of antipathy to Israel, Anglo-Jewry was leery of being associated with groups still largely on the periphery of British society, viewing this association as a threat to its hard-won social acceptance, which was, at the time, of quite recent vintage.[25]

22   *JC* 3 March 1978, 18.
23   Alderman, *London Jewry*, 119–25. The Jewish Social Responsibility Council was a significant exception, see *JC* 18 June 1980, 20. And many individual Jews participated in the struggle against xenophobia, e.g., Maurice Ludmer, founder of *Searchlight*, and Aubrey Rose of the Reform Synagogues, who was proactive in fostering good relations with the ethnic minorities. But most of Anglo-Jewry stayed on the sidelines.
24   Ibid., 132–7. The tension between Anglo-Jewry and the ethnic minorities was exacerbated by the formation, in 1977, of the Anti-Nazi League (ANL), a broad coalition established to combat the National Front. The Anglo-Jewish establishment was unable to separate the fight against racial discrimination from the anti-Zionism of several key ANL figures, and declined to join the alliance. See Alderman, *Jewish Community*, 167–9.
25   Lipman, *History*, 235–8; Alderman, *Modern*, 331–9, 347–52.

   Parents whose children attended grammar schools had several options. They could acquiesce in a school's transformation into a comprehensive, relying on government promises that the best features of grammar school education would be preserved within the comprehensive framework. Another option was to become active in the 'Save Our School' committee that was invariably formed after the announcement of plans to reorganize a school. These groups lobbied the local council, the Minister of Education, and Parliament, in the hope of preventing the restructuring of 'their' school, a goal rarely achieved, though some SOS committees did succeed in delaying restructuring, enabling their own children to complete their secondary education under the selective system.[26] Yet another approach, one that entailed considerable expense, was to transfer children out of the local council school into a private fee-paying school. Such expense could be avoided by enrolling children in a direct-grant school, if there was such a possibility in the vicinity. Finally, there was the option of applying to a denominational state-aided school, as government assurances had been given that such schools would not be affected. Among parents, there was lively discussion as to the best course of action.

   There are no precise statistics on the response of Jewish parents to the comprehensive reorganization, as state schools did not record pupils' religious affiliation. Jewish educational agencies did attempt, for policy planning purposes, to collect this data, especially regarding schools believed to have a sizeable Jewish enrolment. From the information available, it is evident that Jewish parents increasingly sought a Jewish school, preferably a voluntary state-aided or a non-denominational independent ('public') school, for their children. The rising enrolment at Jewish day schools is evident from a comparison of the number of children at such schools before and after introduction of the comprehensive system. In London in 1965, 1,527 children attended secondary day schools; by 1981, the number

---

26   See D. Mendelsson, 'Between Integration and Separation: The History of Jewish Education in England 1944–1988', PhD dissertation, Hebrew University of Jerusalem, 2002, 271–4.

was 3,073, a 100 per cent increase over fifteen years.[27] Although some of this expansion can be explained by the growth of the ultra-Orthodox population, most of this new enrolment, at least until 1975, was at the JFS and the Hasmonean Grammar School for Boys, not institutions that attracted the ultra-Orthodox.[28] At the height of the effort to introduce comprehensive education, the JFS was reported to be turning away 100 applicants annually.[29]

Most parents who had previously sent their children to Jewish primary schools and then transferred them to non-denominational secondary schools stopped doing so. A good example is the North West London Jewish Primary School, where until 1968 about 30 per cent of the pupils transferred to Jewish secondary schools. After 1968, the figure reached 75 per cent, clear evidence that local comprehensive schools did not command parental confidence.[30]

In 1977, the headmaster of the Rosh Pinah primary school complained that although in the past many of his pupils had traditionally gone on to the JFS for secondary school, it was increasingly difficult for them to secure a place there. He does not ascribe this popularity to JFS's Jewish studies programme.

> It has to be admitted that the rush for the JFS in recent years has not been necessarily because parents are enamoured of the Jewish content of its education. Many children who applied this year would have, in years past, either gone to a state grammar school or opted for the private sector. Grammar schools today are fast disappearing, and the fees for private schools have become so astronomical that, for many families, educating children privately is simply unthinkable.[31]

27   A. Ziderman, 'Jewish Education in Great Britain', in H. Himmelfarb and S. Della-Pergola (eds), *Jewish Education Worldwide: Cross-Cultural Perspectives* (Lanham MD: University Press of America, 1989), 280; Braude, 'Biennial Survey', *JC* 6 August 1965, 12.

28   J. Braude, Survey of Jewish Day Schools in the United Kingdom and Ireland [unpublished report], Institute of Jewish Affairs, London, 1975. CR C3 5 1976.

29   *Hendon Times*, July 26, 1968, 26, quoting S. Levin, chair of the LBJRE; and see *JC* 12 September 1975, 7.

30   Headmaster's Report, October 1969. MS 183 395/1.

31   David Sassoon, interviewed in *JC* 12 August 12 1977, 16.

There is little doubt that the academic success of JFS and Hasmonean students contributed to these schools' ability to attract children with high academic potential. Pupils of the Hasmonean generally achieved a high rate of A-level passes: 80 per cent in 1966, and 86 per cent by 1969, almost half of these passes being with high grades (A or B).[32] Even the JFS, viewed as fit 'only for those children who had failed their eleven plus examination' when it opened in 1958, was, according to the author of a history of the school, by 1968 one of just a few comprehensive schools in the Inner London Education Authority (ILEA) able to attract their full quota of pupils with academic ability. Indeed, he asserts, the JFS was widely recognized as the equal of many grammar schools.[33] The achievements of these schools were regularly reported in the *Jewish Chronicle* and did not go unnoticed by parents. At the same time, it is clear that many parents who chose Jewish day education for their children did so because day schools were perceived, albeit naively, as impervious to the turbulence associated with the permissive society. Parents believed that in sending their children to Jewish schools, they were shielding them from the dangers of political radicalism, promiscuity, and drugs, which could impede their academic success and derail their future.

In response to the growing demand for Jewish day-school places, the Jewish community lobbied the local and national authorities for aided secondary schools. The focus of these efforts was on schools for the Northwest London and Redbridge communities. But in contrast to the 1950s and early 1960s, when the Ministry of Education and LEAs were able to provide fairly generous state aid to denominational schools, in the late 1960s the British economy was failing. Successive governments slashed public spending on education and social services, effectively freezing state aid to new educational projects, including denominational schools. Requests by the Hasmonean Grammar School for Girls for aided status were rejected, as were requests to establish new aided Jewish day schools in Northwest London and Redbridge.

---

32   Minutes, Governors of the Hasmonean Grammar School for Boys, September 18, 1969, MS 183 398/3. The Hasmonean Grammar School for Girls had similar pass rates.

33   Black, *JFS*, 209, 219–20.

Though disappointed, community leaders understood the budgetary constraints involved. Some members of the community, however, were less patient. Encouraged by the growing popularity of day schools, they decided to mount a campaign asserting a perceived entitlement to state funds. The tactic they adopted was to compare the provision made for state-aided Jewish denominational education with that made for Roman Catholic schools.

S. J. Prais, an economics professor, was the key figure behind this effort. Prais claimed that whereas 80 per cent of Catholic primary school children attended denominational state-aided schools, the comparable figure for Jewish children was a mere 20 per cent. He concluded that the Jewish community was being discriminated against.[34] Hoping for redress through an appeal to the European Court and its Commission on Human Rights, Prais sought the support of the Board of Deputies.[35] But Nathan Rubin condemned Prais's proposals, asserting that the Jewish community itself, and not the national or local authorities, was responsible for the paucity of Jewish state-aided schools. He warned that, in the event of an appeal to the European Court, he would defend the Department of Education and Science, adding that 'much of the evidence which would be produced would scarcely do credit to our community'.[36] The Chief Rabbi, too, strongly objected to the claim that discrimination was to blame for the discrepancy between Roman Catholic and Jewish denominational education, and deplored the idea of appealing to the European Court.[37] Though Prais had convinced a group of parents to join his campaign, he heeded the pleas that he leave negotiations with the national and local authorities to the Chief Rabbi and his advisers on education, Moshe Davis and Nathan Rubin.

Prais's allegations of discrimination completely overlooked the community's historic antipathy to day-school education. As we saw, a decade or two earlier, when state authorities had been prepared to fund development

---

34   Draft letter, Prais to Secretary of State for Education, 20 February 1977. CR C2 11.
35   F. Jacobs and V. Prais, 'Development in the law on state-aided schools for religious minorities', in Lipman and Lipman, *Jewish Life in Britain*, 130–41.
36   Rubin to Winston-Fox, 25 March 1977. CR C3 5 1977.
37   Davis to Prais, 22 February 22 1977. CR C3 5 1977.

of Jewish day schools, the community was decidedly uninterested, prefer-ring the local primary and grammar schools. To claim that discrimination was responsible for this situation and demand its reversal, particularly at a time of economic recession, was unmitigated chutzpah. But the efforts of Prais and his ad hoc committee of Jewish parents in the borough of Barnet did motivate the Chief Rabbi and his advisers to take a more proactive stance. They initiated a meeting with the Secretary of State for Educa-tion, who promised that her department would examine the possibility of selling surplus school premises in several London boroughs to the Jewish community.[38]

Naturally, when negotiating with the authorities for expanded denomi-national education, communal leaders were not inclined to explain the growth in Jewish demand as a response to the government's introduction of non-selective education. They cited other factors, such as a revival of Jewish consciousness, and the failure of the religion classes in state schools.[39] Fur-ther evidence of the preference for Jewish secondary schools among parents whose children had formerly attended state grammar schools is provided by the case of Liverpool. In 1964, the Liverpool city council ended selec-tive education, but permitted denominational schools to continue as in the past. Many Jewish parents had sent their children to nondenominational grammar schools, but, following the decision to end the tripartite system, sought to transfer their children to the local Jewish grammar school, the King David Grammar School.[40] Parents whose children were of grammar school ability could thus circumvent the comprehensive system. Clearly, parents responded to the reorganization of secondary schools by prefer-ring the King David Grammar School largely because of its impressive aca-demic record.[41] Competition for places at the King David School became

---

38   Williams to Jakobovits, 6 April 1977. CR C3 5 1977.

39   See, e.g., Memorandum submitted to Mrs Margaret Thatcher by Chief Rabbi Jakobovits [undated]. CR C2 11, 3.

40   M. Goodman, 'A Research Note on Jewish Education on Merseyside, 1962', *Jewish Journal of Sociology* 7 (1965), 43–4.

41   In 1965, 75 per cent of King David pupils secured A-level passes, whereas in the city grammar schools the figure was 69 per cent; see *JC* 29 January 1965, 20.

so intense that the school governors decided to give priority to children who had attended its junior division. When an expanded junior division opened, only 133 of its enrolment of 296 were pupils who had been enrolled at the original school, suggesting that the remainder were children whose parents enrolled them with a view to securing attendance at the secondary school.[42] By 1971, an unprecedented 95 per cent of Jewish children in Liverpool attended Jewish day schools![43]

Moreover, the gap between enrolment rates at primary Jewish day schools and secondary Jewish day schools was narrowing. Despite having lessened in the 1960s, the gap had still been pronounced in the 1970s, though by the end of the decade it was decidedly smaller.[44] This development cannot be explained solely by the decline in the Jewish birth rate. Rather, parents had gained confidence in the academic achievements and perceived social advantages of the Jewish day schools, and felt that enrolling their children in Jewish secondary institutions would, like a grammar school education a generation earlier, be beneficial.

Jews and the 'public' schools

Another response to concerns about the comprehensive schools on the part of Jewish parents was to endeavour to send their children to private and direct-grant schools. For the affluent, private education was the preferred option: the independent schools were perceived as the best means of ensuring academic achievement. In 1972, a survey of Jewish education in London found that, in addition to the 16 per cent of Jewish children attending Jewish secondary schools, thirty-one other schools were attended by at least 100 Jewish pupils each.[45] Ten of these were 'public' or direct-

42   JC 14 August 1964, 16.
43   Beele to Chief Rabbi 10 November 1971. CZA A434 Box 19.
44   Ziderman, 'Jewish Education', 281.
45   Prais, 'Sample', 147.

grant schools, including Haberdashers', Camden, and Latymer Upper, the remainder either not yet reorganized grammar schools or comprehensives. Seven years later, in 1979, a study found eighteen London schools with enrolments of between 100 and 300 Jewish pupils. Of these, ten schools, with a Jewish attendance of 1,830, were state schools. The remaining eight were 'public' or direct-grant, and had about 1,470 Jewish pupils. In other words, Jewish parents were sending their children to 'public' and direct-grant schools in unprecedented numbers.

The LBJRE, which was responsible for withdrawal classes – the alternative classes for children whose parents withdrew them from the state school religion classes (which were Christian in orientation) – was cognisant of these changes in enrolment patterns. Between 1962 and 1978 withdrawal classes ended in schools such as Hackney Downs and Paddington, and opened at Haberdashers' and City of London Girls.[46] Undoubtedly, such changes were also a function of the Jewish population's move to the suburbs.[47]

The growth in the number of Jewish parents who preferred to send their children to non-Jewish 'public' schools rather than Jewish day schools is significant. We can safely assume that had more parents been able to afford this type of education, an even higher percentage would have attended these schools. Of course, Jewish interest in the public schools was hardly new, as we saw in Chapter 1. Such schools, especially those with boarding facilities, were seen as the ticket into the English upper classes due to both their high academic level, and the social skills and ties they fostered. 'Not only were the Foreign Office, the Bar, the Army and the Navy largely manned, as by tradition, by public school men, but also business, the City, public relations ... in 1970, as in 1951, almost half of all MPs had been to public school'.[48]

---

46 LBJRE Annual Reports, 1962–78.
47 E.g., by 1989, two decades after Hackney Downs became comprehensive and the Jewish population had mostly left the area, there were just two Jewish pupils at the school, whose enrolment was increasingly Roman Catholic and Muslim; see Black, 'Jews of Hackney', 59–60.
48 F. Bedarida, *A Social History of England* (London: Routledge, 1990), 238, 285.

With the increased affluence of Anglo-Jewry, interest in the public schools grew. But ability to pay the fees did not suffice for a child to be accepted at a public school. Parents generally had to produce references attesting to their acceptability. At Harrow, parents provided what were called 'Harrow references and connections', membership in the Anglican Church being one such connection. According to John Rae, former headmaster of Westminster School, 'Roman Catholics, Christian Scientists and nonconformists were tolerated but not exactly welcomed; Jews were admitted on a quota basis'.[49] That many Jewish parents had been frustrated by their children's failed attempts to gain entrance to 'public' schools is evident from a *Jewish Chronicle* series on the quotas in 1961. It spelled out exactly what the quotas were: 'In most public schools in London the number of Jewish boys is not allowed to exceed 10 per cent of the total, in some schools the percentage is much lower, only at St Paul's is it higher, and there it is fixed at a maximum of 15 per cent'.[50] The justification generally offered for the *numerus clausus* was that almost all the schools in question were Church foundations, and their Christian character had to be sustained. This was manifest in demands made of pupils, such as attendance at Christian assemblies.[51] It is not surprising that the most popular 'public' schools among Jews were Haberdashers' and University College, neither of which was a church foundation.

In editorials, the *Jewish Chronicle* recognized these considerations, and while empathizing with parents whose children had not been admitted, noted that since Anglo-Jewry comprised under 1 per cent of Britain's population, '10 per cent entry might seem reasonable, even generous'.[52] It cautioned against an assertive stand on this issue, suggesting that Anglo-Jewry draw on the Roman Catholic experience. Anglo-Catholics had established their own 'public' schools 'to ensure their future elite ... without compromising their own distinctiveness'. According to the *Jewish Chronicle*, the success of this policy was manifest 'not only in the achievements of Catholics as

49   J. Rae, *The Public School Revolution* (London: Faber and Faber, 1981), 144.
50   *JC* 20 January 20 1961, 21, 28; see Brook, *The Club*, 388.
51   Some schools permitted Jewish children to organize their own services.
52   *JC* 3 February 1961, 20.

individuals, but in their religious cohesiveness'. It urged the community to follow the Catholic example and establish Jewish 'public' schools.

Clearly, however, Jewish parents sought 'public' school education for their children not to preserve Anglo-Jewish cohesiveness but to secure what they deemed to be the best available education for their children, and their integration into the upper classes. A letter from a teenager claiming that the 'public' schools obliterated individuality and were thus unfit for Jewish children, and that antisemitism was 'innate in the class of English people who send their children to public schools',[53] provoked spirited defence of the 'public' schools. Max Beloff, the eminent historian, for instance, claimed that his sons, then attending Eton, had not encountered 'the slightest trace of antisemitic prejudice', and had experienced 'nothing but kindness and consideration from their fellow schoolboys and masters alike'.[54]

The Liberal Party and National Council for Civil Liberties had a different response to disclosure of the quotas. They argued that the quotas unjustly denied a religious minority an important educational advantage, and called for steps to be taken.[55] Anglo-Jewry was uneasy with this response, and in an editorial entitled 'Misplaced Sympathies', the *Jewish Chronicle* suggested that it did not reflect Jewish communal opinion. There was concern that any challenge to the right of Christians to run schools in keeping with their faith would make it impossible for other religious groups to do the same. Since the Jewish community wished to reserve for itself precisely this right, it would 'categorically dissociate itself' from any demand that independent schools accept unlimited numbers of pupils of other faiths.[56] The Board of Deputies acknowledged the quotas, but denied that Jewish pupils were discriminated against in the 'public' or indeed any schools. It approached the Council of Christians and Jews, whose general secretary recommended quiet cooperation as the most effective way to tackle such a complex problem. As hoped, the issue soon disappeared from the communal discourse.

53　Ruth Frankel, Letter to the Editor, ibid.
54　*JC* 10 February 1961, 20.
55　*JC* 2 June 1961, 8; 16 June 1961, 9.
56　*JC* 9 June 1961, 22.

Over the 1960s and 1970s, the quotas faded away. Various factors brought about this change in the 'public' schools' attitude to Jewish applicants.[57] The financial crisis that beset these schools in the late 1960s compelled them to take their Christian foundations less literally, as a growing number of applicants came from homes that were 'not even nominally Christian'. Places not taken by British applicants went to overseas applicants. By 1979, there were 14,000 foreign nationals in Britain's independent schools, the majority from the Middle East, Asia, and Africa. The 'public' schools' Christian foundations, which had been adduced to limit the admission of Jews, proved no bar at all 'when it came to filling empty places with Moslems and members of other non-Christian faiths'.[58]

The number of Jewish children attending independent schools rose significantly between 1965 and 1979. The demise of the grammar schools was a critical factor in this process, exemplified by the case of Leeds. Jewish parents in the districts of Alwoodley and Moortown had traditionally sent their children in large numbers to the local Roundhay Grammar School. With its absorption into the comprehensive system, many of these pupils transferred to the fee-paying Leeds and Harrogate grammar schools.[59] Of course, this pattern was not limited to Jewish parents. As one observer put it, 'unfortunately, the middle classes, both Jewish and non-Jewish, have lost confidence in the comprehensive system in Leeds, and it is almost impossible to get a place in any of the private high schools'.[60]

The vicissitudes of the private school sector were closely linked to those of the direct-grant schools. Upon being appointed Secretary of State for Education in 1965, Anthony Crosland established a Public Schools Commission to advise him on integrating the public schools within the state system, and make recommendations on how best to handle the direct-grant grammar schools. At this point, LEAs controlled over 50 per cent of the places at only about half the 178 direct-grant grammar schools, a state of affairs

57   My account in this paragraph is based on Rae, *Public*, 148.
58   Ibid.
59   Jeff Barak (Black), pupil at Leeds Grammar School 1972–9, interview, May 5, 2001.
60   Alper, Memorandum, September 16 1986. CZA A434 Box 8.

inconsistent with Labour's goal of ending selective education completely. How could it abolish selection at fully maintained schools yet continue to finance selection at direct-grant schools? The Commission's second report, issued in 1970, recommended that direct-grant schools choose between becoming independent or integrating into the state system.

In October 1974, when Labour had a comfortable majority, legislation to end the direct-grant grammar schools was introduced. Over 100 schools chose independent status; the remainder were integrated into the state system as comprehensive schools.

Many Jewish parents sent their children to direct-grant schools. While most accepted the change, in some cases vigorous campaigns were fought to preserve direct-grant status. At the Henrietta Barnett School for Girls, for instance, Jewish parents took on key roles in attempting to fend off the proposed change. Although the campaign was unsuccessful, independence did not affect Jewish attendance: in 1978, Jewish girls were said to comprise upwards of 40 per cent of the enrolment at Henrietta Barnett and South Hampstead, former direct-grant grammar schools.[61]

Efforts to save grammar schools

Of the London boroughs, the two most densely populated by Jews have long been Barnet and Redbridge. In 1978 Jews made up 16.6 per cent of the population in Barnet and 8.6 per cent in Redbridge.[62] These boroughs, considered Conservative strongholds, can provide insight into the opposition to comprehensive education. While it is difficult to determine the degree of Jewish involvement – after all, Jews did not campaign as Jews but as 'concerned citizens' – a study of Barnet shows that Jews played a disproportionate role in lobbying to save the grammar schools.

61   Chief Rabbi to LBJRE 16 November 1978. CR C3 8 Speeches.
62   Waterman and Kosmin, *British Jewry*, 23, table 10; Kosmin et al., *Social Demography*, 9.

In 1968, the Barnet Council adopted a plan, popularly known as Plan C, whereby secondary modern schools would be paired with grammar schools to create comprehensive schools.[63] Local groups immediately began organizing against the plan. Parents at Hendon County Grammar School lobbied the borough's education officials, securing a promise that the school would not be integrated with St David's Secondary Modern School until 1971. The parents were supported by teachers, and one headmaster announced that he would resign if Plan C was implemented. At Christ's College Grammar School, the Parents' Association debated a proposal to sponsor candidates for the forthcoming local elections whose sole platform was opposition to comprehensive education. The Parents' Association also organized a petition opposing the amalgamation of their school with Alder County Secondary Modern School, and encouraged parents to write to the local press voicing opposition to the scheme. A group of Tory councillors threatened to rebel if the party pursued Plan C.

Opponents of comprehensive education drew encouragement from the Conservative Party's victory in the 1970 general election and Margaret Thatcher's appointment as Secretary of State for Education. Legislation was passed permitting Councils that so desired to withdraw plans for implementing non-selective education. A heated campaign for withdrawal ensued in the borough, much of which lay within the boundaries of Thatcher's own Finchley constituency, but ultimately, the Barnet Council voted in favour of continuing the reorganization.[64]

The precise involvement of Jewish parents in the debate over comprehensive education in the borough of Barnet is impossible to determine. Perusal of the local newspapers, the *Hendon Times* and *Finchley Press*, however, indicates that Jews were central players in the SOS campaign in Barnet. It appears that five of the six members of a deputation that met with Mrs Thatcher on behalf of Hendon County School were Jews.[65]

---

63   Much of the following account is based on stories in the *Hendon Times* and, to a lesser extent, the *Finchley Press*.

64   See Simon, *Education*, 411.

65   *Hendon Times* 24 July 1970, 1.

Leslie Burnham, secretary of the Christ's College Parents' Association at the time, confirmed that many office holders in the campaign against 'going comprehensive' were Jews.[66]

Explaining the day schools' newfound popularity

It is often claimed that a Jewish ethnic-religious revival rooted in Israel's Six-Day War spurred the demand for Jewish day schools. There is little doubt as to the immediate impact of the war on Anglo-Jewry. The Joint Palestine Appeal collected an unprecedented £60 million, and thousands sought to volunteer in Israel. Anglo-Jewry united in a major effort to lobby the British government to stand by Israel, and rallies were organized to express solidarity with the country and its people. For some, the events were an existential turning point. Before the Six-Day War, immigration to Israel from Britain had averaged just 220 immigrants annually, but in the fifteen years after 1967, the annual average was between 1,000 and 1,500.[67]

Rabbi Jonathan Sacks, who became Chief Rabbi in 1991, was an undergraduate at Cambridge during the Six-Day War. He relates that, until that time, 'many of the brilliant academics and research students already signalled for stardom were Jewish but nonetheless were conspicuous by their absence from involvement with the Jewish community'. Then came the Six-Day War and 'suddenly they appeared in the little *shul* [synagogue] in Thompson's Lane'. Others, he among them, resolved to attend a yeshiva upon graduation. 'Parents began to worry that their nice Jewish boys and girls would go to university and return, as they put it, religious fanatics'.[68]

---

66 Telephone interview, 24 April 2001.
67 Waterman and Kosmin, *British Jewry*, 17.
68 J. Sacks, 'Religious and National Identity: British Jewry and the State of Israel', in E. Don-Yehiya (ed.), *Israel and Diaspora Jewry: Ideological and Political Perspectives* (Ramat-Gan, Israel: Bar Ilan University Press, 1991), 5–34.

Both Sacks and his predecessor, Rabbi Immanuel Jakobovits, felt events in Israel had generated a resurgence in Jewish pride and self-confidence, which Jakobovits described as follows:

> Many of our parents, however willing they were, inside the synagogue, to demonstrate their Jewishness on Festivals or even on Sabbaths, outside in the street ... did not want to be seen as Jews ... Israel has helped to change all this. In my student days, it was simply not done – nor did I do it – to sit in the university with a yarmulke. Today this is taken for granted.[69]

Following the Six-Day War, Israel became the focus of communal activity. Fundraising events were popular, and visits by Israeli military and political figures drew crowds. Groups and individuals became involved in public relations. Despite its diverse opinions on so many other topics, the community rallied around Israel. One activist put it this way: 'There are few issues upon which there is one hundred per cent agreement among the Anglo-Jewish communal leadership. The one exception is Zionism.'[70] Travel to Israel, now affordable for most Anglo-Jews, increased. Tours, camps, working on a kibbutz, and studying at university there became popular. The *Jewish Chronicle* reflected these changes. After the Six-Day War, news from Israel began to dominate its content. 'Domestic news paled, while items from regional centres were reduced in size and scope. Communal institutions, such as the Board of Deputies, now received only a cursory degree of attention.'[71] Israel had become central to Jewish identity in Britain.

Moreover, Jewish voting patterns were influenced by the parties' and candidates' positions on issues related to Israel.[72] The policy of Foreign Minister Douglas-Home during the Yom Kippur War, for instance, caused a backlash against those who had supported it. By contrast, Conservative MPs who voted against the government's arms embargo were rewarded by Jewish support, even from those, such as Reverend Saul Amias of the Edgware Synagogue, who had traditionally supported Labour. In constitu-

---

69   Speech by Chief Rabbi to LBJRE, 16 November 1978. CR C3 8 Speeches.
70   Moonman, *Anglo-Jewry*, 24.
71   Cesarani, *Jewish Chronicle*, 231.
72   Alderman, *Jewish Community*, 143–4.

encies with significant Jewish populations, Israel was an important factor in the late 1960s and the 1970s.

Despite Israel's domination of the Anglo-Jewish agenda during this period, caution should be exercised in claiming that solidarity in the wake of the Six-Day and Yom Kippur wars was the principal factor impelling Jews to seek denominational education for their children. In fact, while undoubtedly contributing to increased Jewish awareness and pride, developments in Israel do not appear to have influenced parental decision-making vis-à-vis their children's schooling. On the contrary, the impact of Israel appears to have been temporary, reflecting perceived exigency – the immediate threat to Israel, its isolation and financial precariousness – and not a real shift in the community's self-identity. Although Anglo-Jewry remained very involved in Israel-oriented charitable causes, its financial contributions to Israel declined after the 1967 peak, largely because of what were perceived as more pressing needs at home, especially in the areas of education and welfare.

Events in Israel, particularly its struggle against Arab adversaries, heightened the sense of Jewish peoplehood not just in Britain but throughout the Diaspora.[73] In the Soviet Union, the re-emergence of Jewish national consciousness led to a growing desire, on the part of many Soviet Jews, to emigrate to Israel, despite the risks attendant upon requesting an exit visa. Their efforts attracted global sympathy, and British Jews joined in seeking to unfetter emigration from the Soviet Union. As in the case of support for Israel, the struggle for Soviet Jewry generally transcended communal differences and contributed to a deepening of ethnic solidarity within Anglo-Jewry.[74]

---

73 See E. Lederhendler, *The Six Day War and World Jewry* (Bethesda: University Press of Maryland, 2000).

74 This process was not occurring in a vacuum, of course. In the 1970s, the UK experienced a pervasive cultural shift characterized by the increasing respectability and even cachet of ethnic identification, exemplified by the rise of Welsh and Scottish nationalism, which sought inter alia to end English linguistic hegemony. What it meant to be British expanded and became more inclusive; 'hyphenated' identities,

Nevertheless, the Jewish ethnic identification that reflected this re-energized ethnic solidarity was not unequivocally embraced by Anglo-Jewry's representative bodies. It is significant in this context that whereas the Jewish community was, as we saw, reluctant to join the various ethnic groups engaged in actively opposing the Powellite agenda, the Anglo-Jewish establishment had no qualms about interfaith activities to combat religious and racial intolerance through the Council of Christians and Jews. Anglo-Jewry's willingness to cooperate with the traditional Christian churches while distancing itself from organizations associated with ethnic groups can be explained by its historical self-perception as a religious minority.[75] The United Synagogue, Anglo-Jewry's largest religious organization, had modelled itself on the Church of England, which greatly influenced the communal structure and public profile of Anglo-Jewry. In what was fast becoming a post-Christian society within which other religious and ethnic identities were establishing themselves, Anglo-Jewry struggled to find its way. Debate within the community as to its self-definition attests to anxiety about the community's identity, particularly among the highly acculturated, who were ill at ease with ethnic definitions of minorities in England.[76]

Attitudes to Jewish day-school education reflected this debate: those who confined their Judaism to the private realm tended to oppose day-school education, those comfortable with expressing their Jewish identity in public tended to support it. Despite the growing legitimacy of public expression of ethnic identity, most of the community, and certainly, its representative agencies, continued to prefer its traditional profile as a religious denomination rather than a self-avowed ethnic group.

---

such as 'Pakistani-British', were proudly embraced. See J. Paxman, *The English: A Portrait of a People* (London: Penguin, 1999), 734.

75   G. Alderman, 'British Jews or Britons of the Jewish Persuasion?', in S. Cohen and G. Horenczyk, eds, *National Variations in Jewish Identity: Implications for Jewish Education* (New York: SUNY Press, 1999), 125–36.

76   Englander, 'Integrated', 127–8; Brook, *The Club*, 412.

Day schools as a panacea for the 'Jewish continuity' crisis

Not all British Jews sought Jewish education for their children. Growing numbers saw Judaism as archaic and irrelevant. Anglo-Jewry gave increasing attention to this tendency, often viewing it as a crisis. Communal agencies typically addressed the issue by focusing on intermarriage statistics. The proliferation of research on this subject suggests a heightened concern about what would come to be known as the 'Jewish continuity' issue. A 1969 study of Wembley found that 56 per cent of the young people interviewed expressed willingness to marry a non-Jewish partner.[77] But in 1976, the Board of Deputies' research unit found the actual rate of intermarriage to be approximately 20 per cent.[78] Newspaper supplements discussed the issue, rabbis preached about it, and lay leaders worried about the survival of Anglo-Jewry. Even the national press, including the *Guardian*, *Sunday Times* and *Sunday Telegraph*, reported on the issue. Statistics on the shrinking Anglo-Jewish population were regularly updated and widely reported.[79]

Increasingly, the day-school movement was declared the solution to the intermarriage crisis. The LBJRE established a day-school committee. The Chief Rabbi, initially, and then other religious and lay leaders, rallied behind the day schools in the belief that they best ensured a child's lifelong Jewish identity. There was, however, little substantive discussion of the issue, and the idea that day schools would resolve the crisis remained but an assumption.

Proponents of the day-school 'solution' presented Jewish day schools as offering security in a turbulent environment. They would, it was suggested, provide attention to academic achievement, a caring community, and a haven from the permissive and possibly dangerous atmosphere of the state schools.

77   G. Cromer, 'Intermarriage and Communal Survival in a London Suburb', *Jewish Journal of Sociology* 16 (1974), 162.
78   Kosmin, Structure and Demography, 5.
79   Prais and Schmool, 'Size and Structure', 34; Waterman and Kosmin, *British Jewry*, 6–7.

It is doubtful whether the continuity issue was a major factor in parental decisions regarding their children's education. Though concerned, to varying degrees, about intermarriage, parents viewed schools as institutions that revolved around study-related activities, not socializing. The appropriate context for addressing non-academic concerns, they thus felt, was not the schools, but youth groups and Hebrew classes. This attitude was not shared by communal leaders, a growing number of whom, conscious of the community's decline in numbers, believed that Jewish day schools would, at the very least, hold the trend at bay.

Nevertheless, no research was carried out to credibly assess the relationship between Jewish day-school education and Jewish commitment. Such a study was undertaken for the first time only in 1978.[80]

Conclusion

The growing Jewish consciousness sparked by, on the one hand, fear of intermarriage and, on the other, solidarity aroused by the Six-Day War and campaign for Soviet Jewry, created fertile soil for the Chief Rabbi's plan to expand the day-school movement. But ultimately, it was not interest in providing their children with a rigorous Jewish education, nor the desire to encourage their socializing within the community, that impelled Jewish parents to embrace Jewish day schools. Indeed, despite the communal – rabbinical concerns about intermarriage, parents generally favoured giving their children the opportunity to interact with non-Jewish peers. Rather, parental acceptance of day schools reflected dissatisfaction with the education provided by local council schools, and the conviction that the Jewish day schools offered a better quality secular education than did the comprehensive schools. Parents were concerned about declining academic standards in schools whose values, ethos, and atmosphere had changed

80   Kosmin and Levy, *Jewish Identity*, 22–3.

dramatically, so much so that they perceived these schools as detrimental to their children's best interests and, in particular, their academic success. Their chief priority remained academic success and the upward mobility it made possible. Hence when comprehensive education was introduced, they did not accept it, but sought ways to preserve selective high-level secular education, even if that meant embracing denominational education, or paying for independent schools. The same parents who, in the pre-comprehensive era, had been content to give their children a minimal Jewish education, now sent them to schools with a sizeable religious studies component.

CHAPTER 5

Communal Support for Day-School Education

Armed with an understanding of the growing parental acceptance of day-school education, let us now take a closer look at the concomitant communal dynamics. Which groups and individuals in the community promoted the day schools, and which opposed them? Where was day-school education situated in terms of the broader Anglo-Jewish agenda? Was the day-school movement's growth planned, or spontaneous and ad hoc? And how were communal resources marshalled to build and maintain these expensive institutions? This chapter will explore the community's response to the increased demand for day-school education.

The Chief Rabbi's educational programme

Immanuel Jakobovits was elected Chief Rabbi of the United Hebrew Congregations of the British Commonwealth[1] in 1966 following the retirement of Rabbi Israel Brodie.

Jakobovits was born in Koenigsberg in 1921, and brought to London by Rabbi Solomon Schonfeld some fifteen years later. After graduating from one of Schonfeld's day schools in Stamford Hill, Jakobovits entered Queen Mary's College, London to read science. At his father's behest, Jakobovits left the university to study at Jews' College and Etz Chaim Yeshiva. After

---

1   This is the official title. The Chief Rabbi is not formally the head of the Reform, Liberal or haredi communities, though informally, he is often perceived as religious spokesperson for Anglo-Jewry in its entirety.

receiving rabbinical ordination, he served as minister at the Brondesbury Synagogue in NW London and then at New Cross Synagogue, also in London. In 1946, he was offered a position at the Great Synagogue in London's East End, and about eighteen months later became Chief Rabbi of Ireland. Beginning in 1956, he served as rabbi of New York's prestigious Fifth Avenue Synagogue.

In April 1967 Immanuel Jakobovits became Chief Rabbi of the United Kingdom and the Commonwealth. At his inauguration, he promised to make Jewish education his top domestic priority:

> Wherein lies the glory of beautiful synagogues if tomorrow they will be empty monuments to our neglect? In this emergency of appalling defections among our youth, our expenditure in money and energy in Jewish education represents our defence budget in the communal economy, and it must be given the highest priority over every other Jewish effort.[2]

During his term in the United States, Rabbi Jakobovits had become acquainted with developments in American Jewish education, particularly in New York, where the public school sector had experienced a major crisis due to financial pressure on the city budget and worsening inter-ethnic relations. Increasing numbers of New York Jews were choosing to enrol their children in private Jewish day schools, a development made possible by the community's growing economic prosperity. But the increased US day-school enrolment also reflected concerns about Jewish survival – the declining birth rate, increasing intermarriage, and alienation of the younger generation – in short, the much-agonized-over 'Jewish continuity crisis'.

Mindful that these trends were also affecting Anglo-Jewry, Rabbi Jakobovits sought to expand the Jewish day schools in Britain, and turned to American educators for help in assessing the state of Jewish education in Britain, and planning its expansion. In May 1968, he invited Dr Joseph Kaminetsky, head of the New York-based Torah Umesorah movement, and Rabbi Simcha Teitelbaum, dean of the Yeshiva High School of Queens, to visit Britain, 'to help in the preparation of a comprehensive Jewish educational reconstruction plan, designed to modernize, intensify and expand

2   *JC* 14 April 1967, 1, 11; Bermant *Lord Jakobovits*, 192.

our educational services.'[3] Rabbi Jakobovits reiterated his commitment to making education the primary communal concern, asserting that he hoped to shift the emphasis of Jewish educational activity from Hebrew classes to day schools. He also proposed that Hebrew be the sole language of instruction in these institutions. To make these goals achievable, he called for a major fund-raising effort.

The American experts arrived in November 1968. Over a ten day period, they visited Jewish educational institutions in London, meeting with professional and lay leaders, sitting in on classes, and discussing statistical data with community officials. They then returned home to reflect on their findings and draw up recommendations. About a year later, their report was published. Though commending the dedication of those working in the field, it was critical of all aspects of Jewish education in England, from the classroom facilities to the pedagogic methods and curriculum. It found fault with the supplementary school (i.e., Sunday and afternoon 'Hebrew classes') teachers, specifically, their youth and lack of training. It called for a cadre of dynamic educators who, with greater knowledge and more in-service training, could inspire their pupils. Acknowledging that teaching was 'the Cinderella of the professions', they nonetheless asserted that change was imperative, describing this as 'the most crucial of your problems'.[4]

The experts endorsed the Chief Rabbi's proposed grand strategy for Anglo-Jewish education, and recommended that it be directed from his office. A vibrant educator – perhaps someone brought over from the United States, they suggested – should head up the initiative. The most far-reaching proposal called for establishment of five new Jewish day schools as soon as possible: two primary schools for the approximately 4,000 families in Ilford; one for South London; and two new secondary schools for Greater London. The report also recommended researching the need for a secondary school in Leeds and a primary school in South Manchester.

---

3   J. Kaminetsky and S. Teitelbaum, Report on Educational Mission to England, November 24-December 4, 1968, Survey and Recommendations, 1. CZA A434 Box 19.

4   Ibid., 9.

The experts supported the Chief Rabbi's call for a major fundraising campaign, recommending a target of £3,000,000, to be collected over five years. The funds would be distributed through the Chief Rabbi's new educational office, and allocated only to projects that improved or expanded educational facilities, or increased the time devoted to Jewish learning. Mindful of the Anglo-Jewish context, in which schooling was mainly free, the experts called for a concurrent public relations campaign to explain the importance of education for the future of the Jewish community. Comparing the importance of Jewish education to that of the State of Israel, they suggested that the community ought to habituate itself to raising for Jewish education an amount equalling 10–15 per cent of the sum raised in the annual JPA (Joint Palestine Appeal) campaign for Israel. 'The community must be made to understand that Jewish education is as crucial to Jewish survival as the prosperity of the Jewish State'.[5] It would take many years before the Jewish community, and in particular, the major donors, accepted this formula. In the interim, the ongoing tension between Israel and its neighbours, underscored by the War of Attrition (1968–70) and Yom Kippur War (1973), continued to be perceived by Anglo-Jewry as a greater threat to the Jewish people than the lack of quality Jewish education.

The suggestion that a fee-paying day school be founded was an important departure from the community's traditional approach. Up to this point, the LBJRE, the JSSM and the ZF had focused their efforts on attaining state-aided status either prior to establishing a new school, or soon after it was established. The American experts were proposing creation of an independent school that would constitute a new paradigm for Jewish education in England, educate the community 'to take responsibility themselves', and have a major impact on day-school education.[6]

Like the JSSM schools, the schools of the Torah Umesorah movement were premised on the 'Torah im Derech Eretz' philosophy. Not surprisingly, the experts recommended that the model school take this approach and,

5   Ibid., 14.
6   Ibid., 7. The proposal was finally implemented in 1990 with the opening of the Immanuel School.

by dividing the available hours equally between secular and religious subjects, provide both an intensive religious education, and a first-rate secular education. The experts acknowledged that Carmel College and the JSSM were already pursuing this goal, but sought to expand this mandate.

On one crucial issue, the American experts felt that they could not endorse the Chief Rabbi's plan. They stated that their professional experience had taught them that it was impossible to adopt Hebrew as the language of instruction, and declared that precedence should be given to teaching Torah and religion rather than Hebrew language.[7] They gave no further explanation for this recommendation, but clearly, it reflected their ideological premises. Their priority was *limudei kodesh* (religious studies), and given the difficulty of second-language studies in English-speaking countries, they felt the time and effort that would have to be expended to teach in Hebrew would be prohibitive.

The report met with a mixed response. In an editorial, the *Jewish Chronicle* argued that the experts had contributed 'little that is not painfully familiar to our readers'. The newspaper criticized the authors for failing to fully appreciate the British context, a feeling shared by local educators. The ambitiousness of the plan to establish new private or voluntary-aided schools was questioned, especially the feasibility of raising funds for the endeavour. Serious reservations were voiced about the wisdom of bringing education under the control of the Chief Rabbi's 'already busy' office.[8] But it is unlikely the Chief Rabbi was deterred by the views expressed in the *Jewish Chronicle*. He believed its editor, William Frankel, to be running a personal vendetta against him in the wake of the Jacobs affair, and felt that the newspaper would find fault with his plans in any event.[9]

The harsh attack by Israel Feldman, a member of the Chief Rabbinate Council, however, was something else. He accused Rabbi Jakobovits of trying to build up an empire, and bemoaned what he saw as the eclipse of the admirable Anglo-Jewish tradition of a division of labour between the

---

7   Ibid., 8.
8   *JC* 11 April 1969, 6.
9   Bermant, *Lord Jakobovits*, 90.

rabbinical and lay leadership. He voiced apprehension that in addition to being the spiritual and religious leader of the community, Jakobovits was seeking to become its 'executive director'.[10] Columnist Chaim Bermant rushed to defend the Chief Rabbi, accusing the United Synagogue, of which Feldman was a senior member, of acting as if Anglo-Jewry was its private fiefdom. The Chief Rabbi, he said, had not 'usurped territories held by others' but was 'working land that had been left derelict'.[11]

Despite the criticism, the Chief Rabbi remained committed to his programme. Two months later, his vision for Jewish education got an important boost when Sir Isaac Wolfson, president of the United Synagogue, pledged £1,000,000. With this capital in hand – an indisputable endorsement of his project – the Chief Rabbi announced the establishment of the Jewish Educational Development Trust (JEDT) in November 1969. Rabbi Jakobovits then circulated a formal five-year Jewish education plan among the communal institutions. It retained most of the American experts' major recommendations, adding the establishment of a student residence at an existing teachers' college. Establishment of a fee-paying day school, however, was rejected: the vociferous opposition to the idea had convinced the Chief Rabbi that Anglo-Jewry's non-haredi elements were not supportive of fee-paying Jewish day schools. The plan called for three rather than five new schools. The Ilford Jewish community would get a new secondary school, but not a primary school. North West London would get a new primary and a new secondary school, but the proposals for South London were shelved. Funding was allocated for helping several schools attain state-aided status. And Jakobovits heeded the recommendation not to introduce Hebrew as the language of instruction for Jewish studies: the plan instead stipulated that where possible, Hebrew was to be taught 'as a living language'.[12]

---

10   *JC* 11 April 1969, 8.
11   *JC* 18 April 1969, 6.
12   Summary of Five-Year Plan for Jewish Education, July 1969. CZA A434 Box 19. Unless otherwise specified, correspondence and archival material in this Chapter pertaining to the JEDT is from CZA A434 Box 19.

His next step was to appoint an executive director for his new educational development programme. In the fall of 1970, Yaacov (formerly Jack) Lehman was brought over from Israel to fill this position. Originally from England, he had studied at the Gateshead Yeshiva before immigrating to Israel, where he did graduate studies at the Hebrew University and became a senior official in the Ministry of Education. His mandate was to advise, assist, and represent the Chief Rabbi on educational matters generally, but above all, prepare and implement a programme of educational expansion.[13]

A number of the JEDT's founding trustees were major donors to the JPA. The Sacher and Sieff families became founding patrons, each pledging £100,000 to the education appeal. But some philanthropists were unconvinced of the value of day-school education, and patrons of other causes – particularly those associated with Israel and the existing Jewish day schools – feared that the Chief Rabbi's venture might undermine the causes they held dear. To circumvent these opponents, Jakobovits sought the support of world Jewry's preeminent figures, in the hope that their association with his project would win over the leaders of the JPA. These heavyweights included Yigal Allon, Israel's Deputy Prime Minister and Minister of Education, Louis Pincus, the chairman of the WZO and Jewish Agency, and Yaacov Herzog, the Irish-born Israeli diplomat who had been the preferred candidate for Jakobovits's own position just a few years earlier. The Chief Rabbi offered Herzog a place on the board of the JEDT.[14]

Herzog's role was critical to countering the argument that the senior leadership of the JPA objected to the Chief Rabbi's plan and viewed it as competing with fundraising efforts on behalf of Israel. Jakobovits had already secured the backing of other, second-tier leaders of the JPA, adducing these names (Cyril Stein, Rosser and Trevor Chinn, and Conrad Morris) to convince Louis Pincus of the Jewish Agency that most of the JPA supported his activities.[15] Pincus, having been informed of the opposition to

---

13 Chief Rabbi to Fox, 23 September 1970.
14 Chief Rabbi to Yaacov Herzog, 8 July 1971. CR C5 6, Pledges 1972.
15 Chief Rabbi to Louis Pincus, 14 July 1971.

the Chief Rabbi's plans, was not taken in. He congratulated the Chief Rabbi on his educational initiative, but reminded him of the need to coordinate his activities with the JPA and the educational leadership of the ZF.[16]

Late in 1971, the Chief Rabbi published a White Paper on education, entitled *Let My People Know*. In essence, it was a restatement of his previously-announced plans. The author was actually Moshe Davis, who would soon become the first Executive Director of the JEDT. *Let My People Know* was a polemic aimed at convincing the community of the importance of Jewish education for Jewish survival in the contemporary world. It opened with an impassioned plea for more comprehensive Jewish education, and particularly, new day schools.

Jakobovits saw the sorry state of Anglo-Jewish education as responsible for alienating Jews from Judaism:

> The defection of our young people, a growing rate of intermarriage and the dropout rate of our uncommitted threaten an unprecedented crisis. Inadequate Jewish education clearly lies at the root of the problem, and only a thorough and mature understanding of Judaism, through a greatly improved Jewish education, can provide a solution.[17]

He lamented the fact that only one in six Anglo-Jewish children attended a Jewish primary school, and just one in twelve a Jewish secondary school. In other English-speaking countries, he claimed, notably Canada, South Africa, and Australia, the proportion of Jewish children in Jewish day schools was one in three. These communities, he admonished, 'unlike our own, maintain their schools entirely out of their own resources without any State aid'.[18] No attempt was made to explain this disparity, as the aim was not to present an objective examination of the state of Anglo-Jewish education, but to highlight the inadequacy of the current situation and rally the community to change it. Jakobovits envisioned doubling the number of Jewish children in day schools within fifteen years.

16   Pincus to Chief Rabbi 30 September 1971 (Hebrew).
17   *Let My People*, 15.
18   Ibid., 3.

The greatest opposition to the Chief Rabbi's plan came from the honorary officers of the Zionist Federation Education Trust (ZFET), especially Levi Gertner, its founder, and Ernest Frankel, the treasurer, who was most apprehensive about the day-school campaign. Were the Chief Rabbi's plan to succeed, the ZFET's leading donors would inevitably be asked to support it. Frankel anticipated an unpleasant rivalry between the ZFET and the Chief Rabbi, and worried that the stature of the Chief Rabbi's office and the support of eminent Jewish leaders would prove alluring to his donors. He expressed these concerns at a meeting with the Chief Rabbi, arguing that the plan threatened to jeopardize ZFET fundraising.[19]

As we saw in Chapter 2, with the establishment of the state of Israel in 1948, the ZF had sought a new role for itself. During the five years that followed, the notion that its mission ought to embrace promotion of Zionist day schools gradually crystallized. The ZF had been active in the field of formal Jewish education since 1953, when it signed a cooperation agreement with the Hillel House Primary School in Willesden, London. Since then, its activities had expanded considerably. The ZFET was founded in 1955, and by 1971, was directly responsible, in London and the provinces, for eight schools, and a partner in running four others. These activities were costly. For example, state-aided status had recently been secured for the ZFET day school in Clapton, but the authorities had stipulated that the premises had to be upgraded to meet the building code, mandating improvements amounting to £250–300,000. Similar demands were being made regarding the ZFET's Rosh Pinah School in Edgware, and two other schools needed major renovations. The ZFET was thus facing substantial capital costs.[20] Frankel feared that the Chief Rabbi's campaign would divert limited resources from established schools to projects whose feasibility was as yet unproven.

The Chief Rabbi's tactic of appealing to leading figures in world Jewry and then publishing their letters of support ignited a deep resentment

19   Minutes, Meeting between Chief Rabbi, Abe Kramer and Ernest Frankel, 25 October 1971.
20   'ZFET: Present Position and Future Plans', 1971.

among the ZFET leadership. Indeed, the Chief Rabbi appeared to have won over one of the ZFET's principal contributors, Michael Sacher. This was critical, since the Sacher family was one of two families, the other being the Sieffs, who were the financial backbone of both the JPA and the ZFET. Each year the Trust ran a dinner appeal addressed by a distinguished guest, often a member of the government, and attended by many Marks and Spencer suppliers. The evening generated some £100,000, which was used to cover maintenance costs of the ZFET schools. Frankel and Gertner worried that if these funds were henceforth diverted to the Chief Rabbi's education fund, the schools would have to accept the Chief Rabbi's sponsorship, and lose their independence. This was an important point, since the ZFET's autonomy meant that while the schools were nominally Orthodox, they did not have to require that their teachers maintain an Orthodox lifestyle at home. Gertner expressed this concern directly:

> The Chief Rabbi is given to influences from the far right. When he works in edu-
> cational matters within the Zionist movement, he has done so through the Torah
> Department [of the WZO]. Our movement aims at the middle of the road, and we
> do not have it in mind to let anyone determine for us who we can appoint as teach-
> ers, principals or *shlichim* [emissaries].[21]

The honorary officers of the ZFET were placated by reassurance from Sacher and Sieff that if, as a result of the Chief Rabbi's appeal, ZFET fund-raising suffered, the Sacher-Sieff family would make up the difference.[22]

Despite the fact that the Chief Rabbi's JEDT had been launched with £1,000,000 already pledged, the fundraising target was three times this figure. Would the Jewish community rise to the challenge, or would the Chief Rabbi's plans remain no more than a testament to his naiveté?

---

21   Gertner to Ravid 8 November 1971.
22   Summary, conversation between Sacher, Scheinwald (Treasurer, Jewish Agency,
      London) and E. Frankel, 4 November 1971.

The philanthropists' role

The White Paper on Jewish education was greeted with scepticism by the *Jewish Chronicle*. While praising the Chief Rabbi for putting the subject on the communal agenda and enlisting such an impressive roster of benefactors, the newspaper doubted he had really done his homework. Rabbi Jakobovits had stated that he had no intention of proposing a detailed curriculum, and would confine his efforts to building up the infrastructure for Jewish education. The *Jewish Chronicle* saw this as putting the cart before the horse. What was needed was not a discussion of building plans, but an investigation into the fundamental question of what Jewish education ought to be. If at present Jewish education was having little positive influence on the Jewish commitment of those who received it, then a review of its substance and principles was surely in order.[23]

The newspaper criticized the Chief Rabbi for taking on such a serious financial commitment at a time when the LBJRE and its main sponsor, the United Synagogue, were experiencing serious financial difficulties. It attacked the 'facile assertion' in *Let My People Know* that 'thousands of children would be clambering for places at Jewish day schools'. Granting that there were indeed certain factors that had of late increased these schools' popularity, it pointed out that statistics recently published by the Board of Deputies had demonstrated a contraction in the numbers of Jewish school-age children. Moreover, interest in careers in Jewish education was not rising, as evidenced by the poor enrolment at Jews' College and other teacher training institutions. After admonishing against empire building and 'the taking over of what is already being done by existing bodies', the *Jewish Chronicle* recommended that 'every encouragement be given ... to the initiative',[24] a contradiction that can perhaps be explained as endorsement of the need to buttress Anglo-Jewish education.

23   *JC* 5 November 1971, 20.
24   Ibid.

The Zionist-sponsored *Jewish Observer and Middle East Review* was far more enthusiastic about the Chief Rabbi's initiative, describing it as 'long-needed', and noting that Anglo-Jewry's major donors to Israeli causes, such as Michael Sacher, had expressed support for the new communal body. It praised the Chief Rabbi for bringing together representatives of the United Synagogue and the Reform movement; there was also a representative of the Masorti (Conservative) movement on the JEDT board, further reflecting this policy of inclusiveness. Such solidarity had traditionally been reserved for matters related to Israel and Soviet Jewry, hence, given the growing opposition of the 'right-wing' Orthodox elements in the community to any cooperation with the non-Orthodox movements, this was a courageous move.[25]

Jakobovits's approach here was in line with his general policy of avoiding schism, which he feared might ensue if the non-Orthodox elements in the community were ostracized. His flexible attitude to these movements had become apparent shortly after his induction as Chief Rabbi, when without undue publicity he had authorized the Board of Deputies to allow the Conservative New London Synagogue to employ a marriage registrar. Although this policy had been pursued quietly, it soon led to a major row within the Board of Deputies. In October 1971, the Liberal and Reform synagogues requested that their rabbinical councils be recognized as bodies the Board of Deputies would consult with on religious matters. Despite vehement opposition from the Union of Orthodox Hebrew Congregations (UOHC), Jakobovits assented to the proposal and the Board of Deputies' constitution was duly amended. The UOHC promptly left the Board of Deputies, never to return. A cynical assessment of the Chief Rabbi's educational initiative might conclude that his policy of inclusiveness reflected a 'desperate search for ways of underpinning and bolstering his presumed authority to speak for the whole of an increasingly fragmented Anglo-Jewry'.[26] A more generous reading might be that in his view a united front best served negotiations with governmental agencies, and was thus in the best interest of the entire Jewish community, to all elements of which he was sincerely devoted.

25   *Jewish Observer and Middle East Review*, 5 November 1971.
26   Alderman, *Modern*, 370–5.

It was also claimed that the Chief Rabbi's educational programme neglected the communities outside London. This complaint was well-founded. *Let My People Know* proposed a two-stage development plan: in the first phase, five new day schools were to be built, all in London; in the second phase, to commence five years after completion of the first, nine new schools would be established in the provinces, but this was less a firm commitment than a vague suggestion.

When the plan was launched, the Chief Rabbi had secured pledges totalling over a million pounds from a number of wealthy families, including the Wolfsons, Rothschilds, Sachers and Sieffs. However, the broader philanthropic sector remained unconvinced of the project's worthiness. A confidential report distributed to the founding patrons and trustees of the JEDT at the end of 1972 gave the total sum raised in the form of pledges as little more than £1,250,000.[27] Another concern was the slow pace at which the building plans were being implemented. True, the JEDT had acquired land in Ilford for construction of a comprehensive school, but it was still in the early stages of receiving approval from the LEA. The Chief Rabbi began to interest himself in short-term projects that would demonstrate the effectiveness of his programme. One such project, not originally envisaged in *Let My People Know*, was a proposal to expand the sixth form intake at the JFS. This project was ideal for bolstering the JEDT's credibility, as it could be approved and implemented quickly, allowing the Chief Rabbi to declare that his fund had created 150 day-school places.

The short term projects continued throughout 1972 and 1973, and served to demonstrate that funds were being allocated across the spectrum of Jewish educational organizations. Beneficiaries included the Lubavitch movement, the Hasmonean Grammar Schools, and the ZFET's Mathilda Marks School, though the large sums did go to LBJRE schools.[28] For the Chief Rabbi, then, inability to implement the building plans had a silver lining, enabling him to counter allegations that the funds were going to just one segment of the community.

27 Confidential Progress Report of JEDT, November 1972.
28 JEDT Commitments and Projects, May 1973.

Finances remained the chief problem for both the JEDT and the ZFET. Both bodies were well aware that the most effective fundraising operation in Anglo-Jewry was run by the Joint Palestine Appeal. It had enjoyed a special status within the community since the Six-Day War, when it had raised unprecedented sums. Unlike other Anglo-Jewish institutions, which were accountable to the local community, and subject to its scrutiny, the JPA's operations, unconstrained by transparency requirements, were particularly adroit. Its long-time leaders were Edward Sieff and Michael Sacher, chair and vice-chair of Marks and Spencer, whose influence on community affairs was far-reaching. Connected by family and business ties, they tended to function as a kind of mini-Cousinhood.

However, a new generation of wealthy contributors had emerged within the JPA, and would soon have considerable impact on its workings and direction. This new generation of JPA activists included Trevor Chinn of Lex Garages, Cyril Stein of Ladbrokes, the betting firm, Stanley Kalms of Dixons, the electronics magnates, Gerald Ronson, industrialist and property developer (the Heron group), and Fred Worms, accountant and entrepreneur. Moshe Davis, who became Director of the JEDT in January 1973, courted these donors. He believed that a closer association with these entrepreneurs, and utilization of their skills, could make full implementation of the Chief Rabbi's programme possible. Over the following years this policy paid off, and Davis has been credited with finally getting the Chief Rabbi's day-school programme off the ground.[29]

Davis had been involved in communal affairs since 1960 when, following a stint as Chaplain to the Armed Forces, he was appointed Director of the Jewish National Fund's Youth and Education Department. In 1967 he combined this with a central role in the ZF's Information Department. His commitment, enthusiasm, and industriousness made Davis an excellent choice for JEDT director.

Davis's background in the Zionist movement came in handy in tackling one of his first tasks at the JEDT: negotiating an agreement with the ZFET. These talks, which opened in the spring of 1973 chaired by Sieff and Sacher, were described as an attempt to find a formula for cooperation between the organizations, but the real intention was for the JEDT to

29   Bermant, *Lord Jakobovits*, 194.

bring the ZFET under its control. The JEDT proposed that under the new regime, funds would be available to support existing and proposed ZFET schools. It also promised to consult and cooperate with the ZFET on its own future building projects, which it had not done previously, generating much tension between the two bodies. In July 1973 the ZFET and the JEDT reached an agreement whereby in return for the ZFET's cooperation with the JEDT, the JPA promised the ZFET 1 per cent of its gross income annually. Though this sum was modest, the decision to allocate funds for local needs was unprecedented.[30]

Financial crisis besets the day schools

The renewal of hostilities in the Middle East in October 1973 stalled further discussions between the JEDT and the ZFET. This time there was to be no dramatic Israeli victory as there had been in 1967. British Jewry was shocked at the Israeli forces' initial setbacks and the many deaths incurred. Solidarity with Israel immediately became the paramount communal concern. Anglo-Jewry rallied to Israel's support on three fronts: pledging money, lobbying, and volunteering. As to the first, the Joint Palestine Appeal (JPA) set an initial target of £30,000,000, reached within the first few days of the war. A new target of £70,000,000 was set and almost reached. In fact, Anglo-Jewry contributed the highest per capita sum of any Diaspora community, with the possible exception of Switzerland. With regard to lobbying, this was deemed necessary due to the community's disappointment with the government's 'even-handedness' policy, which included a boycott on arms shipments to the antagonists. When the Foreign Minister announced that American planes being sent to replace those Israel had lost in battle would not be permitted to land at British airfields, the major Jewish organizations lobbied MPs and protested with mass demonstrations. And as had been the case during the 1967 war, thousands sought to volunteer, and tons of medical supplies were immediately dispatched to Israel.

---

30   CZA A434 Box 19; CR C5 5.

With the signing of the cease-fire accords, the Jewish community sought to return to its previous agenda. However, the impact of the war still reverberated not only in the Middle East and in the corridors of international diplomacy, but globally. Britain, like other industrial nations, was suddenly threatened with the possibility of rampant inflation as oil prices quadrupled following a massive cut in energy supplies, and retail prices soared. Matters deteriorated further when, following a dispute with the National Union of Mineworkers, the Prime Minister called for imposition of a three-day work-week.

By February 1974, the British economy was under siege. The trade deficit had reached £1.5 billion, and the annual inflation rate was almost 20 per cent. Oil supplies from the Middle East were drying up, and the miners were on strike. Edward Heath, the Conservative Prime Minister, called a general election, but the result was essentially a stalemate. Labour won just a slight majority, and the ensuing political instability made another round of elections virtually inevitable. In the interim, inflation climbed to almost 30 per cent, with unemployment at a post-war high. In an effort to secure wage increases that kept pace with inflation, the trade unions battled the government and employers. The government slashed public spending and raised income and value added taxes. The cost of borrowing became prohibitive.

Charities and non-profit organizations soon felt the impact of these problems, and Anglo-Jewish causes were no exception. The Chief Rabbi's education plan, launched with great hopes for communal generosity and government sympathy, now faced much-changed circumstances. The government was seeking to cut £200 million from the education budget, including a freeze on new primary and secondary school building plans.[31] This was a severe blow to Jewish educational organizations that had building projects on the drawing board, as there now seemed to be no hope of winning state-aided status for new or existing denominational schools.[32]

---

31   Simon, *Education*, 428.
32   E.g., the Jewish primary school that had been on the borough of Brent's 1973–4 design list and 1975–6 building list was postponed due to the funding freeze.

In light of the economic crisis, voices within Anglo-Jewry increasingly called for the restructuring of communal fundraising. In particular, the Chief Rabbi, having received dire reports about the finances of communal educational and welfare organizations, appealed to the Joint Palestine Appeal – renamed the Joint Israel Appeal (JIA) in 1973 – to assume responsibility for domestic needs as well.[33] The JPA had already established a precedent for assisting Jewish education when, as we saw, it approved a 1 per cent allocation to cover the ZFET's maintenance costs. But at a meeting of the JIA, it was unanimously agreed that a 'combined' appeal to raise funds for both Israel and Anglo-Jewish needs was unwise.[34] The JIA feared that a joint appeal would result in an overall decrease in the funds collected, and that a reduction in the number of those involved in fundraising would diminish the incentive to contribute. Some worried that legal problems might ensue if a combined appeal formally stated that it was raising funds for Israel but intended to make allocations to domestic charities as well.

The Chief Rabbi reiterated his concerns to key JIA leaders, stressing his fears that schools not immediately rescued would face imminent collapse. Moshe Davis wrote to Michael Sacher outlining the specific problems faced by a long list of small, independent Jewish day schools, e.g., Yesodey Hatorah, many affiliated with non-Zionist groups. He stressed how hard it was for these schools to service their debt, mentioning the figure of £600,000 as the sum needed to alleviate their immediate distress.[35]

In October 1974 the Chief Rabbi returned to his efforts to unify all the educational frameworks that accepted his religious authority. He appealed to the ZFET to put an end to the waste that resulted from maintaining separate educational frameworks, namely, the LBJRE and the ZFET. There was further redundancy, as the World Zionist Organization (WZO) had two educational bureaus in London, one 'general' (formally called the

---

33   JEDT, Memorandum on Allocation from JIA, May 1974. CR C5 4.
34   *JC* 19 July 1974, 1.
35   Chief Rabbi to Sacher 8 July 1974. CR C3 3; to Young 23 July 1974. CR C3 3; Davis to Sacher, Memorandum on Jewish Education in Great Britain, August 1974. CR C3 4 LBJRE 1975; Chief Rabbi to Young 23 July 1974. CR C3 3.

Education and Culture Department), and one 'religious' (Torah Education Department). The ZFET's chairman was pessimistic about the idea of a single organizational framework for Anglo-Jewish education, arguing that there were substantive differences between the orientations of the ZFET and the LBJRE. He cited the poor working relations between the two as evidence of the incompatibility, detailing specific problems he had encountered. It was clear that for the time being, a merger was untenable.[36] What was possible, though, was cooperation in seeking financial support.

To this end, the two organizations composed a joint memorandum to be presented to the JIA. Reminiscent of the July 1973 agreement on securing funds from the JIA, it proposed that 2 per cent of the JIA's annual income be set aside for Jewish education. Half of this sum would go to the ZFET, the remainder to schools with a Zionist orientation. While Davis expressed agreement with this proposal, behind the scenes he worked to expand the criterion for eligibility to include all Jewish day schools. He knew that if he could convince Michael Sacher to accept this position, then Frankel would reluctantly go along. Davis organized a tour of three Jewish day schools; one under the auspices of the ZFET, one a Lubavitch school, and the third from Yesodey Hatorah. As anticipated, Sacher concurred that the distinction between Zionist and non-Zionist schools was untenable.[37] Indeed, when the final version of the memorandum was submitted to the JIA's campaign committee, eligibility for funding was not restricted to schools with a Zionist orientation.[38]

The most striking feature of the memorandum was the effort to convince the JIA that supporting Jewish education in Britain in no way worked against Israel's interests. Reference was made to a recent gathering of world Jewish leaders in Jerusalem (known as the Solidarity Conference), where it had been resolved that 'the educational needs of Diaspora communities would rank on par with the needs of Israel'. The memorandum went on to

---

36   Minutes, Meeting between Kramer, Chief Rabbi, and Davis, October 1974. CZA
      A434 Box 19.
37   Davis to Chinn 25 November 1975. CR C3 4.
38   Memorandum to Campaign Committee of the JIA, 28 May 1976. CR C6 8.

explain the short-sightedness of jeopardizing vital domestic institutions in order to support Israel. Without intensive Jewish education in the Diaspora, it asserted, there would be no future generation of Jews, Zionists, supporters of or immigrants to Israel. The authors melodramatically claimed that whereas an injection of even a million pounds would make but a fractional difference to Israel's security, for Anglo-Jewry it might mean the difference between survival and disintegration.

The final version of the memorandum on Jewish education was submitted to the JIA's campaign committee in May 1976. It was soon clear that some committee members were not sympathetic to the educational allocation, being opposed to siphoning off, so to speak, money that had been raised in the name of Israel. Others argued that if the committee was going to allocate funds for educational needs, it should also consider the requirements of the various welfare organizations.[39] In July, the Chief Rabbi received the news that the JIA had voted against the memorandum. Rabbi Jakobovits was bitterly dismayed by the decision, writing to Trevor Chinn that he had backed the JIA in all its endeavours, signing manifestos and sponsoring the Kol Nidre appeal, and thought he had the right to expect that the JIA leaders would reciprocate by sharing his concerns. He promised that he would not make his opposition public, but cautioned that he would exercise this restraint only if reassured that 'a similar sense of responsibility' would prevail among JIA leaders.[40]

Unlike the Chief Rabbi, Fred Worms, a member of the JIA Campaign committee, had publicly – that is, by way of an article written for the *Jewish Chronicle* – announced his disapproval of the decision. He had been an advocate of streamlining Anglo-Jewish fundraising for some time, and in a short booklet entitled 'Facing Facts', had outlined several ways in which this restructuring could occur. On the American Federation model, a single super-appeal, as it were, raised funds that were then allocated to Israel, internal communal needs, and global Jewish needs. Worms felt this model was not suitable for British Jewry. Another option, which he

39 Davis to Frankel 17 June 1976. CZA A434 Box 19.
40 Chief Rabbi to Chinn 23 July 1976. CR C6.

endorsed, was to broaden the scope of the JIA to encompass the work of the Chief Rabbi's educational trust.[41] Worms unsuccessfully sought support for this idea from Yehuda Avner, the British-born Diaspora Affairs advisor to Israel's Prime Minister.[42]

Aware that the leading JIA contributors tended to defer to the Israeli leadership, Jakobovits and Davis were now convinced that they would have to appeal to Jerusalem for support if they were to sway the JIA. Only if the Israeli leadership endorsed the diversion of funds for local needs would it be accepted by the JIA. In August 1976 Davis and Avner began to correspond.[43] Avner sympathized with the plight of Anglo-Jewish educational institutions, and conveyed to Davis some of the Israeli cabinet's deliberations on the issue, informing him that the Prime Minister and heads of the WZO and the Jewish Agency were adamant that all funds from Israel appeals in established communities such as the UK be earmarked for Israel and Israel alone. When Prime Minister Rabin composed his Rosh Hashanah greetings to the Anglo-Jewish community for 5736 (1975/6), he stated this position in no uncertain terms:

> The expansion and deepening of Jewish education must be pursued in every community. ... In all conscience, however, this effort must never be at the cost of Jewry's material assistance in helping Israel resolve the acute and even agonizing educational, human and social problems which face us daily.[44]

Although a compromise formula, on which funds would arrive in Israel and then be sent back to cover Anglo-Jewish educational needs, was put forward, distrust of Jewish Agency machinations made it impossible for the JIA to accept. Its leaders had to come up with a new formula that would enable them to endorse the Chief Rabbi's plans for Jewish education without incurring the wrath of the Israeli government. By the end of

---

41 'Facing Facts', March 1976. CR C3 4.
42 See F. Worms, *A Life in Three Cities* (London: Halban, 1996), 226–45.
43 Correspondence between Davis and Avner 11 August, 31 August, 25 October 1976. CR C3 5 (2).
44 'Greetings from Prime Minister Yitshak Rabin', Rosh Hashanah September 1976. CR C3 5 (2).

the year, key JIA activists had approved a proposal for a special appeal to their top 200 donors for an additional 10 per cent of their regular donation, which would be earmarked for Anglo-Jewish education. Five years after launching his *Let My People Know* initiative, the Chief Rabbi had finally secured the funding necessary to implement his plan.

The saga of the protracted negotiations between the Chief Rabbi and Davis, on the one hand, and the leaders of the JIA, on the other, highlights the primacy of Israel in Anglo-Jewish philanthropy at the time. Israel's needs, particularly in the areas of immigrant absorption and social services, took precedence over Jewish education at home. It had taken years to convince the JIA leaders that Jewish education was deserving of at least a small percentage of the proceeds from the community's major fundraising appeal. The change of heart occurred primarily as a result of the day-school funding crisis, but also reflected growing acceptance of the idea that without serious support for Jewish education, it was unlikely that the coming generations would be devoted to Jewish life and to Israel. Commenting on the funding agreement, the *Jewish Chronicle* declared that 'after Israel, education is now the primary concern of the community'.[45]

Broadening the JEDT's mandate

Given that the JEDT's key players were now drawn from the JIA, and their largesse had to be recognized in the JEDT's organizational structure, the parties involved had to reconstitute the JEDT. It is intriguing to compare the trustees of the reconstituted JEDT in 1977 with the founding trustees back in 1971. Whereas the early list was dominated by figures drawn mainly from the United Synagogue, along with a few academics and an Israeli diplomat, the appointees listed in the new prospectus issued in 1977 represent

45 *JC* 18 March 1977, 24.

the major JIA fundraisers and entrepreneurs in the Jewish community.[46] While the original list drew on the established, wealthy, and Orthodox elite, the balance had now shifted toward a younger and more business-oriented cohort, reflecting the changed complexion of Anglo-Jewish life.

The prospectus outlined the JEDT's plans for the next twelve years. It focused on the changed realities of Jewish education in Britain, particularly the difficulty of securing government assistance for building new schools. The JEDT recognized that if it wished to establish day schools, it would only be able to do so after covering the building costs itself. State-aided status would be requested only later, and could not be counted on. The decision to re-situate the Solomon Wolfson School from Bayswater to North West London at the community's expense exemplifies this awareness. As we saw, the economic situation had adversely impacted not only plans for expanding day-school education, but even plans for existing schools. In the aftermath of the oil crisis of 1973, the financial resources of many private Jewish day schools had been stretched to – or beyond – the limit. The JEDT prospectus promised to examine the financial situation of all schools requesting help, and provide assistance where possible. Although it had originally emphasized day schools, the prospectus listed other areas where it was willing to offer support. One such area was the teaching profession. The JEDT now proposed to assist in improving teacher training facilities, attracting higher calibre teachers, and upgrading the remuneration of those in senior positions. A commitment was made to reduce the dependence of Anglo-Jewry on Israeli teachers, who often had little training in Jewish religious education and little knowledge of Anglo-Jewish life. This dependence had been an ongoing community concern.

Although the prospectus does not outline a systematic pedagogic philosophy, there is evidence the issue had received some thought. The JEDT's goal is defined as producing young Jews who are committed to and personally involved with the Jewish people, and want to understand their Jewishness. Emphasis is placed on knowledge and appreciation of Jewish history,

---

46   JEDT Admin. Committee, Initial List of Trustees, 19 July 1971. CR C5 4; Revised
      Prospectus of the JEDT, May 1977. CZA A434 Box 19. The trustees are listed in a
      JEDT letter dated April 1979. CR C4 10 1979.

culture, and values; familiarity with spoken Hebrew; awareness of contemporary Jewish communities; and fostering personal links with Israel. The prospectus clearly reflects a broader understanding of Jewish identity than was traditionally the case. Moreover, the various drafts of the prospectus, as well as the final version, all reject a monolithic model of Jewish education, and instead 'encourage creativity and diversity of approaches'.[47]

As the JEDT did not actually run the schools in question, it could not implement this philosophy directly. But its commitment to it could be manifested in, say, distribution of funds to schools that embraced this pluralism, or appointment of committees whose composition was representative of all sectors of the community. The discussion as to who might be an appropriate candidate for the JEDT's panel of education specialists is therefore a good test of the commitment to the new outlook. Davis recommended that the education specialists be selected, not on the basis of the relative strengths of the different Jewish educational agencies within the community, but rather, with a view to ensuring representation of the full spectrum of religious orientations within Judaism. He reluctantly accepted that representatives from the Education and Culture and Torah Education departments of the WZO, who were considered functionaries rather than real educators, would have to be included. Initially he proposed four candidates. The first was Dennis Felsenstein, who had been deputy principal at the JFS, and was currently a schools inspector for the ILEA. Davis argued that Felsenstein was recognized as an expert by all groups within Anglo-Jewry. A second candidate, whom he later described as 'reasonable and impartial', was Dr Edward Conway, who had served as the head teacher at the JFS from 1958 to 1976. Conway was liberal-Orthodox in outlook, and connected to the ZFET. The other two were academics: David Patterson, a professor of modern Hebrew literature at Oxford, and Cyril Domb, a professor of theoretical physics whose presence Davis believed would satisfy 'the right wing'.[48] While Patterson was not Orthodox, none of the suggested candidates were associated with the Progressive or Masorti streams.

---

47   See, e.g., Memorandum on Jewish Education in Great Britain, final draft submitted to Campaign Committee, 19 January 1977. CR C6 8.
48   Davis, Memorandum on Education, 4 November 1976, 7. CR C6 8 1976.

The third draft list mentioned some other possible candidates, among them Rabbi Sidney Brichto, a leading figure in the Reform movement. However, Brichto's name was not on the final list presented to Trevor Chinn in May 1977. Nor was Patterson's. Felsenstein and Conway were still on the list, but Dr Jacob Braude, a lay statistician of Jewish education, whose orientation was strictly Orthodox (UOHC), had replaced Domb, while names of several other Orthodox educators were now listed.[49] No attempt to 'encourage creativity and diversity of approaches' can be detected in the suggested members of the JEDT panel of educators. This is all the more striking in view of the fact that Trevor Chinn, the JEDT trustee charged with approving the list, was a senior figure in the Reform movement. It would seem that this situation can be attributed to the Chief Rabbi's fear of alienating the 'right-wing' Orthodox elements within the community.

Israel in the Jewish day schools

Although the community's major organizations and philanthropists were highly committed to the Jewish state, the Jewish day schools, in general, took a rather limited interest in teaching about Israel. Obviously, the space accorded Israel in the curriculum of any particular school was a function of its ideology. For example, the Yesodey Hatorah and Lubavitch schools, being non-Zionist, devoted little attention to developments in Israel. The principal of the Hasmonean Schools, Rabbi Solomon Schonfeld, was hostile to Zionism, though many parents and some of the teachers were enthusiastic supporters of Israel, as reflected in their membership in Mizrachi, the religious Zionist organization.[50] The principal's influence was nonethe-

49   Davis to Chinn, 27 May 1977. CR C4 6.
50   Bermant attacked the school's governors and parents alike for hypocrisy in this regard, claiming that Zionism in the school had become 'an underground activity'. *JC* 6 February 1976, 18.

less considerable, and from time to time he demonstrated his opposition to Zionism by ignoring Yom Haatzmaut, Israel's independence day. On Yom Haatzmaut in 1975, for instance, the deputy headmaster attempted – albeit unsuccessfully – to stop pupils from singing Hatikvah, Israel's national anthem, at the end of an assembly.[51] In 1976, Rabbi Schonfeld pre-emptively closed the school, preventing the Chief Rabbi from attending a student-sponsored celebration. Yet such incidents did not keep the Hasmonean Schools from using pedagogic materials put out by the Torah Department of the WZO. Over the years, the antagonism diminished. In 1980, Rabbi Roberg, acting headmaster of the school, thanked the Chief Rabbi for visiting the school on Yom Yerushalayim (an Israeli national holiday honouring the reunification of Jerusalem) and the following year the school organized its first study tour of Israel.[52]

Naturally, schools under the aegis of the ZFET were more profoundly involved with Israel. Schools such as the Mathilda Marks, Clapton Jewish, and Rosh Pinah not only employed Israeli teachers supplied by the WZO's general education department, but also included study of Israel in the curriculum. Hebrew, taught as a living language, was a core feature of the Jewish studies curriculum. In the ZFET schools, Israel was increasingly invoked as a pedagogic resource for a wide spectrum of subjects, such as biblical history, geography, Jewish law, and the contemporary Jewish experience. The ZFET also sponsored visits to Israel for teachers, and many of its schools arranged trips to Israel for their pupils. Increasingly, other schools did so as well. Pupils at the JFS and the King David School in Manchester had participated in trips to Israel since 1961.[53] Visits to Israel were typically structured so as to intensify Jewish identity by presenting Judaism and Hebrew in a vibrant and engaging context. Judging by the enthusiastic articles recounting the participants' experiences that invariably appeared in community newspapers at the end of the summer, the goal of strengthening Jewish identity was indeed achieved by the trips. In the words of

---

51 *JC* 30 April 1976, 12.
52 Rabbi Roberg to Chief Rabbi Jakobovits 16 May 1980. CR C3 6 1979–80.
53 Black, *JFS*, 211.

Edward Conway, JFS head teacher, 'Teaching about religion and about Israel in a Diaspora classroom tends to become an isolated experience, remote from the actual experiences of pupils outside school hours. To make Jewish education meaningful and attractive one had to take the classroom to Israel'.[54] Conway noted that after the Six-Day War, the pupils' interest in Israel increased markedly, including their motivation to learn Hebrew. They petitioned, and the school agreed, to replace classical (i.e., biblical) Hebrew with modern Hebrew as the first compulsory foreign language on the curriculum.[55]

The idea of studying in Israel, and not just touring, took root gradually. In 1971, the WZO had developed a plan whereby children could spend one school year in Israel, but nothing substantial came of the idea. Yet by 1974, Conway was concluding an agreement for the establishment of what became known as the Givat Washington programme. A group of seventeen pupils in their third year at JFS left England for five months to attend the religiously-observant Givat Washington residential high school near Ashdod, Israel. The programme was the first of its kind to receive the approval of the state education authorities: the ILEA gave its blessing to the scheme, and paid the salary and accommodation costs for an accompanying teacher. The ZF and JIA also assisted with the costs.[56]

Another important means by which Israel had pedagogic impact on Jewish day schools was the employment of Israeli teacher – emissaries hired for a maximum of three years. Although initially only a few Israeli teachers taught in Jewish schools – in 1961, the ZFET reported a dozen teachers employed in its schools – by 1977, Braude put the number at 40. This dependence on Israeli teachers was due to the scarcity of qualified local personnel, a situation frequently bemoaned by educators. Recourse to Israeli teachers was, however, fraught with problems. The temporary nature of their employment created a sense of flux and transience that some considered detrimental. The English skills of many such emissaries were inadequate, often leading to classroom discipline issues that garnered

54   *JC* 20 February 1987, 27.
55   Edward Conway, 'Israel Study Tours', 4. CZA A434 Box 27.
56   Conway to Shmueli 19 September 1974. CZA A434 Box 27.

many complaints. In some cases the teachers from Israel, while competent as instructors of Hebrew language and literature, were by no means truly engaged with the religious material that constituted a significant part of the Jewish studies curriculum.

A further source of tension between Israeli educational agencies and the Anglo-Jewish community was the perception that the various organizations overlapped, causing redundancy and waste. The WZO's Education and Culture Department had been the first to become involved in formal education in England. Associated with Israel's secular political parties, it had been invited by the ZF to help with its efforts to establish a day-school system by providing teaching personnel and pedagogic resources. Shortly thereafter, the Torah Education Department, aligned with the religious Zionist movement, arrived as well, to work with the schools deemed Orthodox, namely, the schools associated with the LBJRE and the JSSM.[57] Naturally, tensions arose between the two WZO departments, which in many cases sought to provide their services to the same schools. The Jewish National Fund's education department complicated matters further, although unlike the other two bodies, it did not supply teachers, but just pedagogic materials.

In the 1970s, as the financial situation of Anglo-Jewish educational institutions became more precarious, and the JIA was asked to allocate money for them, there had been calls to rationalize the activities of these three agencies. A committee was set up under the chairmanship of Michael Sacher to study the matter and make recommendations. In its report, Sacher declared:

> My personal conclusion is that no case can effectively be made for the maintenance of three separate and distinct education bodies under the general Zionist framework. ... I personally would have liked to recommend an early and full amalgamation of these separate entities. But it is clear to me that political problems both here and in Israel, and probably elsewhere in the Jewish world ... prevent in the immediate future any change in this unsatisfactory situation.

57 'Report on the Function and Activities of the Torah Education and Culture Departments of the WZO in Great Britain 1982'. CZA A434 Box 7.

Instead, the report recommended trying to achieve the maximum cooperation and coordination possible, while at the same time seeking to improve
the quality of the education that could be provided with the available money
and personnel.[58] This illustrates the attitude of Anglo-Jewry's philanthropic
leadership toward Israeli agencies in general and the WZO in particular.
They were considered unnecessarily ideological, and insufficiently conscious
of the need for efficiency and budgetary restraint. But out of deference to
Israel, Anglo-Jewish leaders did not act on this sentiment.

Despite the multiplicity of Zionist organizations offering pedagogic
services to Anglo-Jewish educational institutions, with the exception of
the ZFET day schools and the JFS, which were committed to integrating
the Israeli experience into the curriculum, the impact of Israeli culture on
the day schools' curricula was limited.

58   Sacher Committee, Third Report, 'Education and Torah Departments', 6 March
      1976. CR C3 5 Box 2.

CHAPTER 6

Jewish Education in Multicultural England

This chapter will explore how socio-cultural developments in British society in the 1970s and 1980s impacted Anglo-Jewish education. England was becoming a multicultural, multi-ethnic society. This was not simply a matter of its changing demographic profile. Indeed, at the beginning of the 1990s, 'visible ethnic minorities' made up little more than 6 per cent of the overall population, though the concentration of ethnic populations in specific areas was far higher. For example, in Greater London, Leicester, and Wolverhampton, ethnic minorities comprised 20 per cent of the population, whereas in East Anglia, and the north and south west, they constituted less than 4 per cent.[1] Perhaps more importantly, multiculturalism also entailed a weakening of the hitherto quite monolithic cultural system, and its replacement by a plurality of identities and cultures. These changes were in turn reflected in Britain's state educational system, and affected Anglo-Jewish education as well.

Legislation

Through the first half of the 1980s, the Department of Education and Science (DES) was badly managed, under-funded and dispute-ridden. Kenneth Baker, a new minister brought to the helm of the DES in the hope that

---

1   Census 1991, quoted in C. Cook and J. Stevenson, *British History from 1945* (London: Longman, 1996), 160; Social Trends 1994 [Central Statistical Office], quoted in Marwick, *British Society*, 458.

he might turn the tide, implemented a series of education reforms that, taken together, comprised the most serious body of educational legislation since 1944.[2] The 1986 Education Act dealt with school governing bodies, curriculum, sex education, school terms and holidays, discipline, and appointment and dismissal of staff. The Teachers' Pay and Conditions Act was added in 1987. But the most comprehensive piece of legislation was the Education Reform Act of 1988, widely held to be as important as the milestone acts of 1870, 1902, 1918 and 1944.[3]

The 1988 Education Reform Act sought to redress the balance of power between central and local government. In particular, the Act reduced the role of LEAs: they lost control of local colleges and polytechnics, and had their authority over schools trimmed. Governors were now granted control of school budgets, and the power to hire and fire principals and teachers. Some schools, it was predicted, would opt out of LEA control altogether in favour of receiving funding directly from Whitehall. The threat of 'opting out' served to further weaken the LEAs, which would endeavour to forestall opting-out by avoiding conflict with school heads and governors. Indeed, although, as we will see, the Labour-controlled and left-of-centre ILEA played a significant role in developments in Jewish education in London in the 1970s and 1980s, ultimately it too went the way of other bureaucracies streamlined or eliminated by the Conservatives during the Thatcher years, and was abolished in 1990.

The new legislation greatly increased the Secretary of State for Education's authority vis-à-vis curriculum and the number of grant-maintained schools. This concentration of power in the hands of the Secretary of State for Education would in the future 'permit rapid and fundamental changes of educational policy.'[4] Other sections of the Act introduced a national school curriculum and regular examinations. The former identified the core subjects as English, mathematics, and science; and made history,

2   R. Aldrich, 'Educational Legislation of the 1980s in England: An Historical Analysis', *History of Education* 21 (1992), 57.
3   Gordon et al., *Education*, 315.
4   Ibid., 320.

geography, technology, music, art, physical education – and for secondary
pupils, a modern language – 'foundation subjects'. School pupils were to
be examined at regular intervals, at ages 7, 11, 14 and 16.[5] These innovations
followed much agonizing over educational standards, and the belief that
Britain's poor economic performance was linked to low levels of scholastic
achievement.

Although no legislation directly relating to multiculturalism in education was introduced, educators were anxious to influence ongoing educational policies and heatedly debated the issue. Broadly speaking, there were
three camps: assimilationists, multiculturalists, and radicals. The assimilationists saw the role of education as narrowing the differences between
immigrants and old timers so that the former would adapt to the mores
of the latter. Newcomers were expected to participate in what was viewed
as a meritocratic educational system that provided equal opportunity for
all. The multiculturalists perceived the new mosaic of ethnic and religious
diversity as a positive addition to British society and did not see cultural
differences as problematic. They called on pedagogues to develop teaching
methods that embraced 'the Other'. The radicals argued that the multicultural approach did not go far enough in countering disadvantage and
discrimination. This camp believed that schools should develop anti-racist
policies to 'confront and counter all manifestations of racism, whether they
take the form of individual prejudices or structural disadvantage rooted in
the organization and practices of the school or wider society'.[6]

5   Marwick, *British Society*, 361.
6   D. Mason, *Race and Ethnicity in Modern Britain* (Oxford: OUP, 1995), 75.

The Swann Report

The Rampton (later Swann) Commission provided an important opportunity to discuss education in the multicultural context. In 1979, the government established a committee of inquiry into the education of ethnic minorities. The committee's report – published in 1985 as the Swann Report – stated that schools had a significant contribution to make toward 'preparing all pupils for life in a society which is both multiracial and culturally diverse'. Although the committee was to give 'particular attention to the educational needs and attainment of pupils of West Indian origin', it was also instructed to assess the 'needs and attainments of children from the whole range of ethnic and minority groups'.[7]

Concern over the underachievement of Afro-Caribbean pupils was not new. However, though by the late 1970s most of these children had been brought up in England, they remained in the lower streams of the secondary schools, achieving weaker results than white or Asian children. Many Afro-Caribbean parents and community workers believed that the explanation for underachievement lay in the state school system, which 'routinely and systematically miseducated their children'.[8] There was increasing demand for black supplementary schools. The goal of these schools was not principally to develop cultural identity, but rather to improve academic achievement. Supporters of the 'Black education' movement believed that 'schools designed for white majority children cannot offer equal opportunities to black children'.[9]

In 1981, after resignations and intrigue, Lord Swann, former head of the BBC, took over as chair of the Rampton Commission. Though the

---

7   Swann Report, 'Education for All. Report of the Committee of Enquiry into the Education of Children from Ethnic Minority Groups', London, HMSO 1985. See B. Troyna, *Racism and Education: Research Perspectives* (Buckingham, UK: Open University Press: 1993), 63–79.

8   Troyna, *Racism*, 63.

9   S. Tomlinson, *Home and School in Multicultural Britain* (London: Batsford Academic and Educational, 1984), 70.

inquiry had focused mainly on the Afro-Caribbean community, its mandate had been universal, and it also examined the experiences of other ethnic minorities, including Asians, Chinese, Italians, Greek and Turkish Cypriots, Vietnamese, Travellers, and Liverpool Blacks. Evidence was submitted by 358 individuals and 247 organizations.

The committee's report was submitted to the DES only in 1985. It recommended a fundamental change in attitude, asserting that the problem was not how to educate children of ethnic minorities, but how to bring out the full potential of all pupils. The committee rejected the idea of giving greater status in the curriculum to mother tongues, maintaining that learning English was the priority. This was, it argued, in the best interests of the ethnic minorities, enabling their members to secure 'equality of opportunity, academic success and participation on equal terms as a full member of society'. The committee preferred that mother-tongue skills be acquired in supplementary schools. As for religious education, a compulsory subject in primary and secondary schools, the committee recommended a 'non-denominational, non-dogmatic' syllabus, which would enable 'all pupils, from whatever religious background, to understand the nature of religious belief, the religious dimension of human experience, and the plurality of faiths in contemporary Britain'.[10] In keeping with this non-confessional, secular approach, the report rejected daily worship, though recommending that this be investigated further.[11] Although the committee acknowledged the legal right of denominations to establish voluntary-aided schools, it deemed this strategy contrary to the long-term interests of the ethnic minorities: separate schools might 'exacerbate the very feelings of rejection which they are seeking to overcome'.[12] Nonetheless, many submissions to the committee, particularly those representing Muslim groups, supported denominational schools. Attempting to appease them, the Swann Commission recommended that LEAs be more understanding of Muslim wishes. A key interest of the Muslim community was gender separation during school

10   Swann Report, 518.
11   Ibid., 497.
12   *Times Educational Supplement (TES)* 15 March 1985, 12–13.

time, and Swann suggested that LEAs might establish single-gender schools. The committee also proposed various measures intended to ameliorate racial tension, for instance, that teacher training include study of Britain's pluralistic society and exposure to multiracial schools.[13]

Response to the Swann Report was mixed. *The Times*, in a cynical article entitled, 'Long voyage, light cargo', congratulated the 'survivors' of the committee for 'coming home to port after so many agonizing trials, mutinies and desertions', but expressed serious reservations as to whether 'the voyage was worth it'.[14] The *Times Educational Supplement* did concur with the findings regarding separate schools:

> Swann, is however, absolutely right in arguing that unless we want to see education fragmented with yet more separate denominational (and in this case black, non Christian) schools with all that this might imply for institutionalized social and ethnic divisions, the very least we need to do is to create genuinely multicultural schools which value and respect all the cultural components of modern, multi-ethnic Britain.[15]

The right-wing Monday Club condemned the Swann report, criticizing it for 'fostering ethnic minority culture' and 'denigration of Britain's history, heritage and institutions'.[16] In the House of Commons, the Secretary of State for Education Sir Keith Joseph acknowledged the Swann Commission's findings, but a week later announced that he had no intention of implementing its recommendations. Instead, he affirmed a commitment to the daily act of worship, religious education, and state support for denominational schools.[17]

Some of the most determined opposition to the Swann Report came from the Muslim community. A joint statement by the Islamic Academy in Cambridge and the Islamic Cultural Centre in London attacked the 'extremely secular philosophical basis' of its findings. These organizations

13   Ibid.
14   *The Times* 15 March 1985, 19.
15   *TES* 15 March 1985, 2.
16   *TES* 17 May 1985, 7.
17   *TES* 22 March 1985, 6.

warned that implementation of the recommendations would exacerbate the existing conflict that Muslim children experienced between the ethos of their schools and 'the religious approach to life and events which they learn at home'.[18]

There was also criticism of Swann's rejection of instruction in mother tongues during school hours. It was claimed that by denying ethnic groups language development, Swann's recommendations would engender alienation and frustration, the very outcomes the report sought to forestall.[19] Several members of the Swann Commission signed a note of dissent concerning the rejection of separate schools, and predicted that the demand for separate schools would grow because integrated schools were failing black children.[20] Indeed, many educators contended that black children were the victims of institutionalized racism. They alleged that teachers in state schools internalized popular stereotypes concerning non-white pupils, assuming that Afro-Caribbean boys were 'disruptive' and Asian girls 'submissive'. They also deemed the state school curriculum Anglo-centric, particularly in history and English.[21] Separate schools were thought to provide better opportunities for black children, as teachers from the same backgrounds were believed to have greater empathy with their pupils.[22]

18   *News of Muslims in Europe*, 36, 1986, quoted in *TES* 9 May 1986. The *TES* report noted that other signatories to the statement included the Muslim World League, the Islamic Circle Organization and the Muslim Educational Trust.

19   Troyna, *Racism*, 69. And see M. Khan-Cheema, 'British Muslims and the Maintained Schools', in S. Ali Ashraf and P. Hirst (eds), *Religion and Education: Islamic and Christian Perspectives* (Cambridge: Islamic Academy, 1986), 194.

20   *TES* 24 May 1985, 6.

21   Mason, *Race*, 72.

22   Tomlinson, *Home*, 77–8.

The Jewish community and the Swann Report

The establishment of the Rampton Commission and publication of its interim report in 1981 drew no public response from the Jewish community.[23] Of Britain's many diverse ethnic communities, all had made submissions save one – the Jewish community. More precisely, only a single organization, a virtually unknown haredi school, the United Jewish School, submitted evidence (well after the deadline) to the committee.[24] Edward Conway, former JFS headmaster and JEDT consultant, had difficulty identifying this organization, which apparently had 'little association with the organized Jewish community'.[25]

Not only did the organized Jewish community fail to submit evidence to the Swann Commission, it also went without representation on the committee. This was in marked contrast to representatives from the Afro-Caribbean and Asian communities, who stressed their participation. Following publication of the recommendations, a number of letters to the *Jewish Chronicle* criticized the Board of Deputies' Education Committee and its chairperson, Clive Lawton, for not participating in the committee's work. They were written by members of the haredi communities who felt there was much to be gained from identifying as an ethnic minority.[26]

Lawton saw things differently. He argued that the Jewish community had little to offer the Swann Commission. 'Manifestly, Jews do not collectively suffer the levels of failure and discrimination that black and brown children experience daily'. Nevertheless, Lawton recognized that, given the committee's recommendations, particularly its criticism of confessional religious education and worship, and its challenge to voluntary-aided denominational schools, 'we have much to say in response'.[27]

---

23   The *Jewish Chronicle*, e.g., gives no indication of any Jewish communal response to the Swann Report.

24   O. Baddiel, 'Submission to the Committee of Enquiry into Education and the Ethnic Minorities on behalf of the United Jewish School' 26 October 1984. CR C3 10.

25   E. Conway, 'Educating for a Multicultural Society', *L'Eylah* 22, 1986, 64–5.

26   See Alderman, *London Jewry*.

27   *JC* 26 April 1985, 25.

Anglo-Jewry's conduct vis-à-vis the Swann Commission clearly shows that it did not see itself as an ethnic minority, and wished to distance itself from Britain's ethnic minorities. Though the committee took no steps to involve the Jewish community, it is likely that had the Jewish community made representations, the committee would have willingly learned from the Jewish experience. To be sure, the Commission perceived the Jews as a white religious denomination like the Anglicans and Catholics. And anti-racist activists saw Jews as a sub-group of the dominant white society who, despite having suffered prejudice in the past, were now powerful, whereas ethnic minorities suffered racism in the present, and lacked power.

Though the leadership of Anglo-Jewry rejected this analysis, it was comfortable being classed with the traditional Christian denominations. The latter had rejected Swann's recommendations concerning religious education and worship, and his opposition to denominational schools. When the Secretary of State for Education announced that these clauses of the 1944 Education Act would not be changed, they were very relieved.

Teaching religion in multi-faith England

Under the 1944 Education Act, schools were to begin the day with a collective act of worship, and all children were to receive religious instruction regularly. The nature of the religious education was to be determined by a conference composed of representatives of the following bodies: the Church of England; other religious denominations deemed appropriate by the LEA; the LEA; and the teachers' association. The Act did not specify which religions were to be taught, but it was understood that the instruction would be generically Christian. Indeed, the various 'Agreed Syllabuses' did seek to inculcate Christian teachings. Schools were assumed to be 'Christian communities preparing children for Christian living in the wider society'.[28] Similarly, the collective worship was broadly Christian in nature.

---

28   G. Parsons, 'There and Back Again? Religion and the 1944 and 1988 Education Acts', in Parsons, *Growth*, 2:167.

By the late 1950s, pupils were complaining that the religious education imparted to them was dry and irrelevant. Religious education specialists suggested refocusing the aims, methods, and content of the classes to render them directly relevant to the pupils' lives. In 1966, the West Riding EA presented a new set of Agreed Syllabuses, which took the child's psychological development into account, mandating that the material must relate to life as experienced. Other LEAs followed suit. Many introduced units on world religions and philosophies. Yet despite the putative commitment to openness, the new approach to religious education basically remained Christian in orientation.

By the 1970s, declining church attendance and observance of religious rituals, on the one hand, and the rise of the multi-ethnic, multi-faith society, on the other, engendered a new approach to religious education. Mainline Christianity no longer monopolized religious life, and other religions and sects had many adherents. In areas where the population was highly diverse, presenting religion in purely Christian terms clashed with the assumptions of the 1944 Education Act. Religious education syllabuses were therefore revised so as to reflect these societal changes, in the hope that this would foster mutual understanding and tolerance. The teacher, it was now argued, was 'to portray a variety of religious positions and religious beliefs sympathetically, displaying an imaginative grasp of their significance, content and claims while not advocating one religious tradition rather than another'.[29] Religious education was conceived as a school subject like any other, and the cultivation of Christian values was replaced by commitment to pluralism.

The 1944 Education Act allowed parents to withdraw their children from religious education classes to receive instruction in their own faith. Secondary schools were to provide space for this instruction if the transfer of pupils to an outside venue was impractical. By the early 1950s, the LBJRE had established 'withdrawal classes' in twenty-five schools, serving over 3,000 children. But by 1975, only eight centres, serving 680 pupils,

29   Ibid., 174.

remained operative.[30] The LBJRE ascribed the decline to the new religious education syllabus, since its neutral and pluralistic nature appeared to render withdrawal unnecessary.[31] Clearly, though, much of the decline arose from the fact that many Jewish parents were now sending their children to independent schools or day schools.

Some considered the new approach an improvement. Several Jewish state school teachers spoke out in favour of the change, asserting that the new religious education presented all faiths in a positive light, and was conducive to empathy and tolerance. Parents were more comfortable with the non-dogmatic, values-free approach to religious education. And some Jewish educators preferred the new approach. Clive Lawton, chairperson of the Board of Deputies' Education Committee, and former principal of the Liverpool Jewish high school, felt that the positive presentation of Judaism 'in a non-Jewish environment', would serve to validate it for some children. The academic-objective – as opposed to confessional-doctrinal – nature of the syllabus, gave these children an opportunity to appreciate their heritage without feeling it was being forcibly imposed on them.[32]

Other educators regretted the new regime, arguing that withdrawal classes had been an opportunity to provide some Jewish education to children who would otherwise receive none.[33] Fred Worms, a governor of the North London Collegiate School for Girls, was pleased when the principal announced that she intended to impart a more Christian focus to the religious education classes there, as this enabled him to organize parallel classes, similarly committed to inculcating religious principles, for Jewish children.[34] Indeed, the LBJRE sought to open new withdrawal-type classes in independent schools with high Jewish enrolment, suggesting that it was aware that many such schools continued to teach old-style religious education as a means of imparting Christianity.

30   Ziderman, 'Jewish Education', 279.
31   LBJRE Biennial Report, 1977–8, 4.
32   C. Lawton and S. Sless, Provision of Jewish Education in Non-Jewish Schools. Unpublished report, 1982. CR C3 7.
33   Ingram and Manasseh to *Jewish Chronicle*, 12 March 1982, 23.
34   Worms, *Life*, 35–6.

The 1988 Education Act stimulated discussion of religious education in state schools. Rabbi Jonathan Sacks, then principal of Jews' College, addressed the issue on BBC Radio's 'Thought for the Day'; his remarks were quoted by Chief Rabbi Jakobovits during a debate in the House of Lords. Rabbi Sacks deemed the new syllabus superficial, arguing that its smorgasbord approach to religion failed to recognize 'that only one faith resonates with personal meaning: the faith of our community, our culture, our family, our past.'[35] Sacks recalled his childhood experience at a state primary school where the religious education had been Christian: 'The effect of this schooling on our Jewish identity was curious. It made us, of course, acutely aware that we were different. But because those around us were taking their religion seriously, it made us consider Judaism seriously too'. Jakobovits, like Sacks, preferred the old model of religious education to the neutral-pluralistic approach. Indeed, he conceived of religious education as doctrinal instruction: 'Effective religious instruction can no more be administered by and to persons of a different faith than can a blood transfusion be safely given without first ensuring blood-group compatibility. Indiscriminate mixing of blood can prove dangerous and so can the mixing of faiths in education.'[36]

Inspired by the new model's openness and theoretical approach, an interested and wealthy member of the community, Robin Spiro, became involved in seeking to introduce modern Jewish history courses into the curriculum. Principals of several secondary schools, mainly independent, welcomed these courses, which were academically recognized at the 'O' and later 'O/A' levels. Spiro's motivation was to foster awareness of Jewish history and culture, not religion. But when he appealed to the Chief Rabbi, the JEDT, and the LBJRE for support, he emphasized the assumption that studying history strengthens religious/ethnic identity.[37] Spiro's initiative was successful, and in the 1983/84 school year, the Spiro Institute offered courses in fifteen schools, teaching some 550 pupils, two thirds of whom were Jewish.[38]

35 *L'Eylah* 26, 1988, 4.
36 Ibid.
37 See Robin Spiro to Tony Brown, 6 December 1978. CR C3 6 1978–9; Moshe Davis to Robin Spiro 6 October 1981. CR C2 9.
38 Spiro Institute for the Study of Jewish History and Culture, 'Analysis of Students Studying Modern Jewish History: 1978–84', June 1983. CR C6 9; 'Programme of Courses', CR C3 7.

Other religions demand state-aided schools

Though the Swann Commission had rejected separate state-funded day schools for religious/ethnic minorities, the debate continued. In particular, the Bradford Muslim community, where Muslim pupils constituted over a fifth of the school population in 1985, lobbied for the establishment of its own voluntary-aided schools. Anglicans, Catholics, and Jews, it argued, had state-funded denominational schools, why, then, should Muslims be denied this right?

Scholars have claimed that the source of Muslim dissatisfaction with the state school system was the differing values underlying Islamic and English education.[39] Some saw the materialistic and competitive nature of English education, the individualistic style of learning, and the manner in which girls were taught, as well as the separation of schooling from other aspects of life, as contrasting markedly with the Muslim educational ethos.[40] In language reminiscent of that voiced by their Jewish counterparts, Muslim organizations expressed concern about their British-born children drifting away from the community's faith and culture:

> A major worry for Muslim parents is that their children soon begin to adopt English standards and ideas. They start to question not only traditional customs, but religious ideas which seem strangely alien to life in a Western materialistic society. Islam is not something which can be learnt and adhered to overnight, it must be lived, breathed and fostered.[41]

Yet reconciling Muslim values with the ethos of the English education system was not a simple matter. Local schools seemed unreceptive to the religious needs of Muslims vis-à-vis dietary requirements, dress, swimming, dance, sex education, and the education of girls. Moreover, global events such as the Iranian Revolution (1978–9), the Rushdie Affair (1989) and the Gulf War (1991) had engendered an assertive attitude within the Muslim communities, contributing to the increased demand for denominational schools.

---

39 J. Nielsen, 'Islamic Communities in Britain', in P. Badham (ed.) *Religion, State and Society in Modern Britain* (Lampeter UK: Edwin Mellen, 1989), 225–41.

40 Tomlinson, *Home*, 78.

41 Union of Muslim Organizations 1975, quoted ibid., 79.

The National Muslim Educational Council had lobbied unsuccessfully for separate Muslim schools since 1978. The turning point came in the 1982/3 school year, when the Bradford-based Muslim Parents Association formally requested that five county schools be reclassified as voluntary-aided and that the heads and school governors be replaced by Muslims. The LEA rejected the application, claiming it had not been shown that the city's Muslim population supported the idea, and the Association's ability to maintain the schools had not been established. Opponents argued that the scheme would exacerbate existing social tensions. 'White' teachers threatened to leave the schools if they became Muslim controlled.[42]

To counter the demand for separate Muslim schools, the Bradford EA implemented a policy aimed at placating its ethnic minorities. Various concessions were made: Muslim parents could withdraw children from non-secular assemblies, music, dance, sex education and any other activity deemed not in conformity with Islamic requirements; recognition of Islamic festivals as days off for Muslim children; permission for Muslim children to attend Friday prayers either at a local mosque or within the school building with an imam; provisions for separate gender swimming; Muslim girls could wear trousers and a headscarf.[43] The Bradford EA became the first to provide *halal* meals for interested Muslim pupils.

The demand for voluntary-aided schools was also voiced elsewhere, particularly in the London Borough of Brent, which had a large Muslim community. In 1985, Yusuf Islam, the former pop-star Cat Stevens, led the campaign to achieve state-aided status for the local Islamia School. The school's Islamic nature was reflected in its curriculum, 20 per cent of which was devoted to religious studies, with Arabic the only foreign language taught. Sex education and evolution were not taught; history was given an Islamic slant. Boys and girls were educated separately at the secondary level.[44] In March 1986, despite opposition, the Brent LEA agreed in prin-

42   Khan-Cheema, 'British', 189–90.
43   Ibid., 191.
44   *TES* 30 August 1985, 5.

ciple to support Islamia's bid for voluntary-aided status. (It later mandated building improvements, impeding implementation of the agreement.)

There was much public debate over the idea of state-aided Muslim schools. In September 1985, Lord Swann reiterated his committee's opposition to the establishment of new denominational Muslim schools. He maintained that Muslim schools would be tantamount to educational ghetto-ization. He also objected to gender separation, an opinion shared by many, who deemed it incompatible with the role of women in contemporary society. A further concern was that Muslim schools would in fact have been totally Asian, since most Muslims at the time were from Pakistan and Bangladesh, and this de facto *ethnic* separation, it was claimed, would have adverse consequences for both the pupils' academic success and their community's integration.[45]

Muslims were not alone in seeking denominational state-aided schools. Various Christian groups, mainly evangelical, made similar demands. Here too, the desire for separate schools reflected discomfort with the secular ethos of the state system, and the conviction that Christian values should be imparted to their children.[46] The Sikhs, experiencing discrimination in the state system, and anxious about maintaining their children's religious identity, also sought to develop day schools.[47]

A new situation had, then, emerged in England by the 1980s. Whereas the dominant secular and humanist approach of the English education system called for an inclusive and multicultural approach to education, many religious groups preferred to establish state-aided denominational schools for their communities. Yet ironically, though Britain was now more accommodating of pluralism, its attitude to separate religious – and even more so, ethnic – education became more guarded.

45   *TES* 20 September 1985, 15.
46   Parsons, 'There and Back', 182.
47   Tomlinson, *Home*, 81–3.

The haredi schools and multicultural Britain

Although, in the main, Jews did not identify themselves as an ethnic minority, the multiculturalist ethos created a congenial environment for the expression of minority identity. In particular, the haredi sector took advantage of changing attitudes to lobby for state support of its schools. In 1978, Joe Lobenstein, a leading member of the Union of Orthodox Hebrew Congregations and Agudas Yisrael, ran as a Conservative and was elected to the Hackney Council in the heavily haredi New River ward. In 1982, Rabbi Avraham Pinter, principal of the Yesodey Hatorah Schools, joined him, standing for the Labour Party. Political alliances of this nature offered the haredi community a chance to influence council policies and secure much-needed funding.

Let us describe the development of the haredi schools up at this point. The first Yesodey Hatorah School opened in a classroom in Stamford Hill, North London in 1942. Its mandate was to offer more intensive Jewish education than that offered by existing schools, such as those of the JSSM. The arrival of haredi Holocaust survivors brought new pupils, and by 1946, it had an enrolment of 300, who were housed in a converted residence in Amhurst Park. Following the 1956 Hungarian uprising, the enrolment rose to 470 primary school and 240 secondary school pupils.[48]

The Lubavitch schools developed similarly. The first opened in 1958, and by 1969 there were two primary schools – one for each gender – with a total enrolment of 208, and two secondary schools, with a total enrolment of 97.[49] Growth occurred during the 1970s and 1980s due to natural expansion, immigration of Jews from Aden and Iraq, and the newly religious. By 1988, the Lubavitch schools had 641 pupils; the Yesodey Hatorah schools 1,000.[50] Other, smaller Chassidic groups (Satmar, Bobov, Belz, Ger, and Vishnitz) had also established their own *cheders*. A 1984 JEDT report on

48   Supplement on Yesodey Hatorah Schools, *JC* 20 December 1957.
49   Bermant, *Troubled Eden*, 130.
50   *Securing*, 62–3; Brook, *The Club*, 78.

the 'Expansion of the Far Right' put the number of children attending haredi schools throughout England at 3,300, double the number listed in the Chief Rabbi's *Let My People Know* thirteen years earlier.[51]

Numerically, the fervently Orthodox had become a sizeable segment of Anglo-Jewry: in 1970 they made up just 2.6 per cent of London Jewry; by 1990, they were 8.8 per cent.[52] In 1976, 29 per cent of all pupils in Jewish kindergartens and schools in the UK were haredi; by 1991, about 43 per cent were haredi.[53] Thus a significant segment of the Jewish day schools were ultra-Orthodox in orientation, and not only in London. In Manchester, where about a quarter of the Jewish community was haredi, over half of the Jewish children attended Jewish day schools. In Leeds, where the ultra-Orthodox comprised about 10 per cent of the Jewish population, just under 30 per cent of Jewish children attended Jewish day school.[54] Given the declining birth-rates among mainstream Anglo-Jewry (due to late marriage, small families and out-marriage), the share of haredi-run schools within the Jewish day-school sector continues to rise.

The haredi schools devoted at least half the school day to Jewish subjects. Most of these classes were conducted in Yiddish, the first language of most pupils. In kindergarten pupils learned to read Hebrew and English, and in primary school, they began by studying *Chumash* (Pentateuch); by 8, the boys were already studying the Talmud and commentaries. The mode of instruction was almost always the traditional method of oral repetition of the text being studied, often accompanied by vigorous *shuckeling* (swaying). Secular studies, taught in the afternoon, were limited, especially for boys. At the age of fifteen, most of the boys transferred to *yeshivot* (religious seminaries) where there were no secular studies at all.[55]

For girls, Jewish studies were more limited. Sections of the Bible, typically translated into Yiddish, were studied, but not Talmud. Many girls,

51 M. Davis, Memorandum, 'Expansion (No. 2) The Far Right', 4 February 1983. CR C5 1.
52 Alderman, *Modern*, 366.
53 *Securing*, 9.
54 Ibid., 11.
55 *Securing*, 2–3.

especially at the Yesodey Hatorah and Lubavitch schools, pursued secular studies up to 'O' level. They studied the standard subjects, but certain texts, such as works by Dickens and Shakespeare, were censored to avoid clashes with religious teachings.

The haredi population was not affluent, and only the Lubavitch and Satmar had school buildings that had been expressly designed to serve as schools. Most buildings were poorly equipped. The United Jewish School's submission to the Swann Commission stated:

> Schools lack furniture; books; teaching aids even of the most primitive type; playground equipment ... lighting should be better, the buildings are in need of redecorating; in summer ventilation is wanting and the managers struggle ... to provide heating in winter.[56]

The Lubavitch schools were assisted by the magnate Cyril Stein, owner of Ladbrokes, and by the Wolfson Foundation, but other groups lacked similar support. Moreover, few parents – 10 to 15 per cent at best – paid full school fees, with similar numbers receiving a complete subsidy.[57] Not surprisingly, therefore, these schools turned to both the Jewish community – the Yesodey Hatorah and Lubavitch foundations, for instance, received funds from the JEDT[58] – and the state for assistance.[59]

As we saw in Chapter 1, the local and national authorities only funded schools that met strict criteria governing the school premises, teaching staff, curriculum content and delivery, and the sponsoring organization's

---

56   Baddiel, 'Submission to the Committee of Enquiry', n 24 above, 4.
57   Davis, Memorandum, n 51 above, 4.
58   In 1976–7, the JEDT gave Yesodey Hatorah £50,000 to help fund a new girls' primary school, and in 1978, transferred another £250,000 for debt-eradication. It also awarded the Lubavitch movement £45,000 for Sixth Form facilities. See Davis to Pinter 27 April 1978. CR C6; 'Reconstruction of the JEDT' 18 February 1977, Draft 3. CR C2 11.
59   In 1969, Bermant wrote that 'Yesodei Hatorah is not interested in state-aid because it would mean interference in the curriculum', *Troubled Eden*, 132. Yet in 1968, the Yesodey Hatorah movement had quietly requested state-aided status for its girls' division.

wherewithal to maintain the school. The Yesodey Hatorah girls' primary school had submitted an application for state-aided status as early as 1968. In 1971 the school was told of a decision, in principle, to award it voluntary-aided status, provided the school improved its premises, teaching, and curriculum. The improvements were made, but in 1975, the DES, acting on the ILEA's recommendation, informed the school that because of an anticipated surplus of maintained places in the Hackney area, its application was being suspended. Two years later, supporters of the school, among them David Weitzman, Labour MP for Hackney North and Stoke Newington, lodged a complaint with the Parliamentary Commissioner for Administration, charging that the DES had reneged on its promise. Although the Ombudsman censured the DES for creating expectations by not fully apprising Yesodey Hatorah of the contingent factors impacting conferral of state-aided status, no redress was awarded.[60]

The Yesodey Hatorah organization resubmitted its application for state-aided status in 1980. Though the general attitude toward minorities was now more favourable, this was not the case with regard to denominational state-aided education. The same year, the Greater London Labour Party published a manifesto stating that no child should be educationally segregated on the grounds of sex, religion, ethnic or socioeconomic status. Though Labour was no longer in power, it continued to control many local authorities, including the Greater London Council, where the 'anti-segregation' policy could have had a dramatic effect on Jewish day-school education. The Board of Deputies, attempting to allay communal fears, requested a meeting with Ashley Bramall, Labour leader of the ILEA, who promised that existing voluntary-aided schools would not be affected.[61] But fear persisted that schools that had applied for state-aided status would now be rejected due to policy considerations.

A further complication emerged for the Yesodey Hatorah Primary School for Girls when it was discovered that the Lubavitch Foundation

---

60 Report by the Parliamentary Commissioner for Administration to David Weitzman Q. C., M. P., 17 November 1977. CR C3 8.
61 Alderman, *London*, 127.

had submitted a parallel application for state support for its own girls' school. Nat Rubin, the community's senior educational affairs officer, was convinced that the ILEA would reject both applications because of surplus places at existing state-aided Jewish schools.[62] He warned that 'until such time as the Jewish Community as a whole will accept the authority of a central body in submitting applications for aided status, these problems are likely to recur to the detriment of our community'.[63] The ILEA did express concern about vacant places at Jewish state-aided schools in the area, as well as declining rolls in maintained (i.e., state) schools, a trend expected to continue. But it also criticized the schools' premises, teaching staffs, and teaching methods.[64]

The schools resubmitted their applications for state-aided status in June 1981 and were again rejected. Nine months later, the DES informed both organizations that the Secretary of State for Education had reached the same conclusion. A further appeal in the spring of 1984 was denied.[65]

Nonetheless, in 1985 the Lubavitch Foundation and the Yesodey Hatorah Primary School for Girls came one step closer to achieving state-aided status when Hackney Council passed a motion in sympathy with their cause. By 1987, Rabbi Pinter and Joe Lobenstein, leaders of the campaign, had rallied considerable support for the schools. As it was to be a general election year, they enlisted the backing of both major parliamentary candidates for Hackney North and Stoke Newington. Diane Abbot, the Labour incumbent, was well aware of the haredi influence in the constituency – about 30 per cent of the borough's population was haredi – as were the Conservatives, who had selected a Jewish candidate. Statements

---

62   These were the Avigdor and Simon Marks primary schools; the former affiliated with the JSSM and the latter with the ZFET.

63   Rubin to Davis 31 March 1980. CR C3 6 1979–80.

64   Extract from Report of the School Sub-Committee to Meeting of the ILEA Education Committee to be held 1 April 1980 (Yesodey Hatorah and Lubavitch Foundation applications for state-aided status). CR C3 6 1979–80.

65   *The Times* 21 October 1981, 2; Barwick to Rabbi Pinter, Yesodey Hatorah, Rev. A. Sufrin, Lubavitch Foundation, 18 March 1982. CR C3 7 and 8; *JC* London Extra 30 March 1984, 1.

in support of the schools were made by eminent political figures and race relations activists, and the national press also gave the schools a sympathetic hearing.[66] In February 1987, Hackney Council approved the applications, recommending that the ILEA grant its approval as well. When members of ILEA's Labour majority met to consider state-aided status for the schools, a fairly strong body of public opinion appeared sympathetic to the haredi cause. But the National Secular Society, which opposed state funding for denominational schools, called on Labour to 'remain firm' and reject the schools' applications, as it had twice before. The opposition was not to the haredi schools per se, but arose from concern that funding them would encourage proliferation of other separate state-funded school systems, Jewish, Muslim, and Sikh. The Society's president attacked the haredi community for failing to integrate into British society. 'Having been here for half a century, they could reasonably be expected to have integrated by now with the host community – at least to the extent of speaking English and sending their children to English state schools'. She deemed the fact that the children spoke Yiddish, wore 'strange clothing' and were deliberately separated from non-Jewish children, similarly objectionable. Warning that segregation would exacerbate existing prejudice, she recommended an integrated approach to education, with all children attending a single school system, devoid of religious education.[67]

Despite optimism among the ultra-Orthodox and their allies, ILEA rejected the application again, on the grounds that the premises, curriculum, teachers, and methods were inadequate. Arguably, however, the major reason for its refusal to confer state-aided status was ideological. The ILEA opposed single-gender schools, which they perceived as counter to their 'equal opportunities' policy. But like the National Secular Society, the ILEA opposed educational sectarianism, and was apprehensive that if it recommended state-aided status for the Yesodey and Lubavitch groups, this might

---

66   *JC* London Extra 4 September 1987, 3; *The Times* 31 October 1983, 12; M. Trend, 'No Justice for Jewish Children', *The Spectator* 15 August 1987, 16–17.

67   Barbara Smoker, Memorandum of National Secular Society to Members of the Labour Group of the ILEA, 23 March 1987. CR C3 10 1987.

'open the floodgates' not only for haredi groups but also for other religious groups, particularly those associated with ethnic minorities.[68]

The Yesodey Hatorah Schools embarked on a campaign to further pressure the ILEA. They utilized the lexicon of the Left to argue against integration of their children into the broader community. In a widely-distributed pamphlet entitled 'Equal Opportunity to a State Education', the ultra-Orthodox asked how their children, who were predominantly working class, would have equal opportunities if their schools were denied the resources available to other children. Surely, they claimed, the ILEA's refusal to fund their schools meant that haredi children would not have access to the laboratories, workshops, and computers available to state school pupils. Similarly, without adequate resources, they could not be expected to recruit or retain qualified teachers. Thus, if the authorities wished to raise the standards of haredi schools, it was incumbent on them to supply funding. Seeking to expose internal contradictions in the ILEA position, Yesodey Hatorah argued that the ILEA's policy was itself discriminatory. It adduced evidence that per capita, other religious groups had more state-funded denominational schools than the Jews. 'Every child wishing to be educated in a Roman Catholic state-aided school who lives in the ILEA area has that opportunity'. Why, then, should the haredi children in Hackney be denied this, asked the pamphlet. In language departing from the low-key diffidence with which the Anglo-Jewish establishment preferred to express its concerns, but in tune with the assertiveness associated with ethnic minorities, the haredi community claimed 'discrimination', 'arrogance', and 'hypocrisy'.[69]

How did the Anglo-Jewish establishment respond to haredi demands for government funding? As early as 1980, the Chief Rabbi had written to Sir Ashley Bramall in support of the Yesodey Hatorah Primary School

---

68   Ruth Gee, Deputy ILEA Leader, interviewed in *The Times* 31 October 1983; *JC* 10 April 1987, 48.

69   H. Berger, Equal Opportunity to a State Education, London, 1987. This pamphlet was published by an ad hoc committee representing the Stamford Hill fervently-Orthodox community. CR C3 11.

for Girls.[70] Three years later, Moshe Davis wrote to members of the JEDT about expansion of the 'far right' schools in London. He expressed no opinion as to whether the JEDT should support the schools' applications for aided status, but said he believed the girls' and possibly the boys' primary school might be able to meet the authorities' criteria.[71] By 1986 the *Jewish Chronicle* had declared its support for the Yesodey Hatorah girls' primary school. The ILEA's 'chicken and egg' arguments over premises and resources were, it asserted, poor grounds for denying the school state-aided status. After all, the newspaper commented, 'it is improbable that either Roman Catholic or Church of England schools could themselves sustain ILEA standards without voluntary-aided status'. The newspaper proposed that ILEA allegations that the school devoted insufficient time to educating haredi children to respect other ethnic groups be investigated. 'ILEA should be able to come up with a formula which would enable the Yesodey Hatorah not merely to state its case, but to prove it'.[72] The Board of Deputies came out in support of the Yesodey Hatorah application, and Michael Cohen, LBJRE Director, advised the school in its negotiations with the ILEA and the DES.[73]

The rationale for this broad communal support was articulated in a memorandum written by Simon Caplan, JEDT director, in 1986, after Yesodey Hatorah had requested additional financial assistance. Caplan visited the school to get a first-hand impression. He expressed reservations–'it is part *cheder*, part childminding service – not a school'–but concluded that the JEDT should nonetheless encourage the Yesodey Hatorah organization to seek state-aided status for the girls' primary school because it seemed the most likely of the haredi institutions to secure state support. Its curriculum included more secular studies than did the boys' school, the girls took 'O' levels at age sixteen, and the school was relatively efficiently organized. He doubted the schools could meet the LEA's criteria, but 'whatever the stand-

70   Chief Rabbi to Sir Ashley Bramall (ILEA) 17 January 1980 CR C3 6 1979–80.
71   Davis, Memorandum, n 51 above.
72   *JC* 20 March 1987, 24.
73   Michael Cohen to Rabbi Pinter, 11 March 1987. CR C3 10.

ards of the schools ... the alternative must be worse'. Caplan's perspective
– and presumably this opinion was shared by Anglo-Jewry's leadership –
was that it was preferable for haredi children to attend 'quasi schools' with
a 50 per cent secular curriculum than study in the numerous *cheder*s that
would emerge if the Yesodey Hatorah Schools collapsed.[74]

During the same period in which the haredi communities repeatedly sought and failed to attain state-aided status for their schools, several
modern-Orthodox day schools were successful. These included the Michael
Sobell Sinai, the Hasmonean Grammar for Girls, and the Independent
Jewish Day School. Two schools with aided status were given permission
to expand. The cost of this expansion would be born by the community,
but thereafter, the enlarged schools would be maintained by the state.
Presumably, the successful requests for aided status reflected compliance
with the strict criteria governing premises, teachers, and pedagogic methods. And whereas the syllabuses of the haredi schools, and those of other
ethnic minorities, often downplayed secular studies, modern-Orthodox
schools related to general studies in a manner that reflected commitment
to integration into British society.

The 'ethnic minority' rubric

The London Jewish community experienced deepening estrangement from
the Labour leadership of the Greater London Council (GLC) and the
ILEA. The Labour Party was increasingly viewed as hostile to Anglo-Jewish
interests. In London, tensions focused on Ken Livingstone, who following
Labour's GLC victory in 1981 became leader at County Hall. His antipathy
to Zionism and Israel was notorious. During the first days of Israel's Leba-
non War, a cartoon entitled 'The Final Solution' appeared in the *Labour
Herald*, a party magazine edited by Livingstone, depicting Israel's Prime

74   S. Caplan, Memorandum: Yesodey Hatorah Schools, 3 November 1986. CR C6 10.

Minister in Gestapo uniform astride the corpses of Palestinian Arabs.[75] The following year the GLC permitted the pro-PLO Labour Committee on Palestine to use County Hall as its base. A year later, the ILEA initiated a schools essay competition on 'The Palestinians – A People without their Land'. In 1984, the city council gave funds to the Palestine Solidarity Campaign. In an interview with the Israeli newspaper *Davar*, Livingstone contended that the Board of Deputies had been 'taken over by Jews who held extreme right wing views' and that Jews had been 'organising here in London, and throughout Britain, into paramilitary groups which resemble fascist organisations'.[76] Although the GLC Labour Group succeeded in getting Livingstone to retract his accusations, Livingstone remained head of the GLC and chair of its Ethnic Minorities Committee.[77]

The GLC realized that the damage being done to its public image by the radical left was in need of repair. Labour members were sensitive to the charge that Livingstone's anti-Zionist orientation smacked of antisemitism. In October 1982, the GLC, attempting to improve relations with the Jewish community, offered funds to Jewish groups and organizations from its 'ethnic minorities' budget. (As part of a commitment to affirmative action, Labour Councils had established 'Ethnic Minorities Units', whose mandate was to assist in meeting their minorities' housing, employment, educational, and leisure needs). An advertisement was placed in the *Jewish Chronicle* announcing a meeting at the West London Reform Synagogue, where Ethnic Minorities Unit representatives would explain how Jewish groups could apply for financial aid. Despite criticism of the venue – in Anglo-Jewish circles, Orthodox groups and individuals rarely attended activities at Reform and Liberal Synagogues – the meeting went ahead. Many of the participants warned the organizers that their efforts would require the support of the Board of Deputies. Although some progress was made, the GLC was not prepared to accede to the Board's demand that it receive the right

75   Alderman, *London*, 125.
76   Translated in *JC* 14 December 1984, 6.
77   Alderman, *London*, 135.

to veto grant allocations. Nonetheless, to the delight of the GLC's Labour leadership, a number of haredi groups, led by Agudas Yisrael, applied for Ethnic Minorities Unit funds. They had not attended the gathering at the Reform synagogue, but proposed a meeting in Stamford Hill.[78]

Unlike most Anglo-Jewish organizations, Agudas Yisrael had no qualms about accepting funds from critics of Zionism. Nor did they view the Board of Deputies as representative of their interests, since it included non-Orthodox organizations. Furthermore, the 'ethnic minority' rubric that so discomfited much of Anglo-Jewry was of no consequence to the haredi groups, particularly when funding was at stake. A coalition of interests therefore emerged between the ultra-Orthodox and the Labour-led GLC headed by Livingstone. For the latter, distribution of funds to the haredi community could be adduced to counter accusations of antisemitism.

Hence despite the haredi bodies' ongoing failure to win state-aided status for their schools, the GLC and Hackney Council began awarding them grants. In 1984 the Yesodey Hatorah Schools received a grant of £60,000 for its nursery facility so that it could undertake the improvements necessary for DES recognition. The following year, under the same programme, Hackney Council announced a grant of £100,000 toward leisure activities for the haredi communities, of which £25,000 went to the Lubavitch Women's Group, £15,000 to the Vishnitz Centre, and £50,000 to Lubavitch and Aguda library projects. The Hackney Council also announced a grant of £139,000 to be shared by the Lubavitch and Yesodey Hatorah nursery schools.[79]

Although the haredi organizations saw the benefit of embracing the 'ethnic minority' rubric, the Anglo-Jewish establishment did not. Anglo-Jewry saw itself as integrated into British society, identified with British norms and values, and rejected the suggestion that Jews were an ethnic minority. The general feeling was that this categorization lumped the Jews together with ethnic minorities such as Bangladeshis and Pakistanis, considered by many to be on the periphery of British society.

---

78   According to Mr Wong, Hackney's Senior Race Relations Adviser, the meeting was
     'fruitful'. *Jewish Tribune* 10 December 1982, 3.
79   *JC* London Extra 22 and 27 November 1985, 1.

This attitude is well illustrated by the Chief Rabbi's response to the Archbishop of Canterbury's 1985 'Faith in the City' report, issued following race riots the previous year. The report attacked the Conservative Party's approach to inner city problems, and proposed a more Christian approach of intervention by the authorities to alleviate the plight of ethnic minority populations. The Chief Rabbi was invited to make his own observations on the subject.[80]

> We never demanded that, ourselves being heirs to a distinct culture and tradition, British society at large ought to change its character and assume a new multi-ethnic form. ... We were quite content for Britain to remain 'ethnocentrically' British.

Drawing on the immigrant experience of Jews in the East End, he proclaimed that despite not speaking English and having to endure antisemitic hostility, Jews had secured their place in Britain through hard work and self-help. Jakobovits quoted from his farewell address to his New York congregation, and suggested that his comments then – during the civic unrest of the 1960s – remained relevant:

> How did *we* break out of our ghettos and enter the mainstream of society and its privileges? How did *we* secure emancipation and civil rights? Certainly not by riots and demonstrations, by violence and protest marches, or by preaching 'Jewish power' or even non-violence. Above all we worked on ourselves, not on others. We gave a better education to our children than anybody else had. We hallowed our home life. We channelled the ambition of our youngsters to academic excellence, not flashy cars.[81]

Jakobovits's tract elicited heated responses. Many letters published in the *Jewish Chronicle* criticized his 'smug', 'complacent', and 'condescending' attitude to those in the inner cities, particularly the ethnic minorities. Others were opposed to his identification of Anglo-Jewry with the values of

---

80 'Chief Rabbi Replies to his Critics', *JC* 14 March 1986, 27.
81 Jakobovits, 'From Doom to Hope: Jewish Reflections on Britain's Social Malaise'. *JC* 24 January 1986, 26.

the Conservative Party.[82] Rabbi Michael Rosen expressed the opinion that 'when it comes to social issues, I feel solitary in the rabbinate. The United Synagogue has become the Tory Party at prayer'.[83] In a lecture presented to the Institute of Jewish Affairs in London, Greville Janner, former president of the Board of Deputies and Labour MP for Leicester West, attacked as 'untenable' and 'unreal' the Chief Rabbi's comparison of the turn-of-the-century Jewish immigrant experience with the present-day Afro-Caribbean experience. Janner was cautious, not wishing to offend the Chief Rabbi, yet committed to an empathetic approach toward the ethnic minorities. Janner was uncomfortable that the spiritual leader of the Jewish community seemed insensitive to the needs of other communities, and espoused values in line with those of the Conservative Party.[84]

The Reform and Liberal Synagogues distanced themselves from the Chief Rabbi's comments, deeming them unacceptable, and harmful to relations between Jews and the ethnic minorities.[85] Yet there is little doubt that the sentiments expressed by the Chief Rabbi were widely shared by Anglo-Jewry.[86]

With respect to working with other denominational groups, the conduct of Anglo-Jewry's educational agencies had long paralleled that of its religious and lay leadership: there was collaboration with the mainstream

82   See the letters from Rabbi Sidney Brichto, Rabbi Julia Neuberger, Martin Vegoda in *JC* 31 January 1986, 22; from Alter Goldstein, Louise Ellman (Leader, Lancashire County Council), *JC* 7 February 1986, 22.

83   As quoted in Brook, *The Club*, 349.

84   See G. Janner, 'Black-Jewish Controversies in Britain', *Patterns of Prejudice* 20 (1986), 4–11. Over 150 Conservative MPs signed a motion congratulating the Chief Rabbi on 'From Doom to Hope'. Janner recalls that 'out of respect for the office and person of the Chief Rabbi' he lobbied his Labour Party colleagues to keep them from proposing amendments attacking Jakobovits's view.

85   Brichto and Neuberger, *JC* 7 February 1986, 22.

86   See letters from Ernest Golman and Ben Miller, *JC* 7 February 1986, 22. Similar sentiments were expressed in a survey of Hackney Jews. A typical comment was 'Who helped the Jews? They helped themselves. Why can't they [the Blacks] do the same?' See Y. Ginsberg, 'Jewish Attitudes toward Black Neighbors in Boston and London', *Ethnicity* 8 (1981), 212.

denominations, but little or none with other minorities. As early as 1962, Nat Rubin was making common cause with his Anglican and Catholic counterparts to try and influence proposed legislation and overturn adverse decisions. Commenting on such a joint effort in 1962, when Rubin had worked with his counterparts in the Church of England and Roman Catholic Church to ensure that following the Government's decision to establish the ILEA, children from the Greater London area could continue their studies within the newly established district, Rubin had declared:

> It is heartening to be able to report on the effective liaison machinery now established between the three denominational bodies for purposes of approach to Government departments on educational matters. ... In no circumstances should the Jewish authorities take unilateral action.[87]

The denominations coordinated their efforts regarding the 1967 Education Bill, which included a clause increasing the funding for voluntary-aided schools' building and maintenance costs.[88] By 1973, following establishment of the Consultative Council of Voluntary Schools, cooperation had reached a point where the three denominations gathered at Catholic House to coordinate strategy before meetings with representatives of the LCC and ILEA.[89] In 1980, a deputation from the Anglican, Catholic, and Jewish communities addressed a Brent Council meeting to protest a decision ending free travel passes for pupils travelling beyond the three-mile zone to denominational schools. Their efforts proved successful.[90]

Only once, in 1987, did Jewish educational agencies make common cause with their Muslim counterparts. Yusuf Islam, working with several Muslim organizations, organized opposition to the sex education in

---

87 Meeting with the Churches 30 October 1962 and related correspondence between Rubin, Bishop Beck and Sir David Eccles (Minister of Education) February–October 1962; Rubin to Chief Rabbi 26 October 1962. ACC 2805/112.

88 See P. Chadwick, *Shifting Alliances: Church and State in English Education* (London: Cassell, 1997), 33.

89 Interview with Nat Rubin at his home in London. 3 February 1993.

90 See Rubin's correspondence with Shirley Williams and Rhodes Boyson, and a press release issued 17 July 1980. CR C3 6.

Brent's maintained schools, especially the 'positive' attitude to gay sex.[91] Apart from this occasion, Jewish educational interests did not join forces with Muslim, Sikh, or Black groups. For example, Jewish groups took no position regarding the Islamia School's campaign to achieve state-aided status, even though in the same borough only several years earlier, Jewish denominational authorities encountered their own difficulties in securing state-aided status for the Michael Sobell Sinai School. Mutual suspicion and even antagonism prevailed, preventing formation of a joint front to promote shared interests.[92]

The Anglo-Jewish educational leadership did not join discussions held by ethnic minorities with local and national bodies. Anglo-Jewry preferred to act on its own and seek the assistance of sympathetic politicians, increasingly from the Conservative Party. In particular, Dr Rhodes Boyson, the Brent North MP, was considered a friend of the community because of assistance rendered regarding the Michael Sobell Sinai School. When it finally opened after fifteen years of negotiations with the authorities, the Chief Rabbi thanked him, declaring: 'If I had to award an honorary membership of our people, Dr Boyson would be one of the first candidates.'[93] Norman St John Stevas, a former Conservative spokesperson on education, also helped address concerns of Anglo-Jewish denominational education.[94] Joining forces with ethnic minority groups could not, many felt, engender such effective assistance.

91   See Yusuf Islam (Islamic Circle Organization) to Nat Rubin 9 July 1987, and related correspondence. CR C3 11.
92   See Alderman, *London*, 125–6.
93   *JC* 4 July 1980, 8.
94   See correspondence between Davis and St John Stevas. CR C3 4 LBJRE 1975 and CR C3 8.

Growing demand for Jewish day schools

Both Anglo-Jewry's affluence and its ongoing commitment to high academic achievement ensured that independent schools continued to be much in demand. A record number of Jewish children now attended these schools, though there are no precise statistics. In 'public' schools situated near suburbs with large Jewish populations, Jewish children constituted a significant portion of the enrolment.[95] A 1991 study found that almost all children who left the Jewish day-school system at ages 5 and 11 transferred to non-Jewish selective schools.[96] For many parents, in choosing the type of schooling their children received, a school's academic level and prestige remained the decisive factor.

Nevertheless, quite a few parents, and a growing number of those affiliated with the United Synagogue, were keen to send their children to Jewish day schools, particularly at the primary level.[97] As we saw, their preference for Jewish day schools over state schools was based on several factors: the belief that the state schools were not achieving acceptable academic standards, the high proportion of ethnic minority pupils in state schools, concerns over social norms in comprehensive secondary schools, and intensified Jewish ethnic self-identification.

Some day schools were founded through grass-roots community initiatives. One such initiative was establishment of the Independent Jewish

95　*JC* 7 October 1983, 20. Among these were Haberdashers', the North London Collegiate School, South Hampstead and University College School.
96　*Securing*, 8.
97　In 1991, a United Synagogue survey found that 41 per cent of respondents supported Jewish schooling at the primary level, but only 26 per cent at the secondary level. They explained that at the secondary level, children ought to be exposed to non-Jewish peers so that they would mix with greater ease later on, and that educational standards could not be compromised at the secondary level of studies. Clearly, parents felt that Jewish day schools were not of the same academic standard as the 'public' schools; see S. Kalms, A Time for Change: United Synagogue Review, London, 1992, 257–8.

Day School in 1979[98]; it gained voluntary-aided status in 1986. Funding for the school came mainly from parents, though the JEDT also provided generous grants. A similar project in the planning stages by the late 1980s was a primary school in Southgate, later named the Wolfson Hillel School. Yet another initiative was taking shape in the expanding communities of Borehamwood and Elstree, where parents had already opened a nursery school.[99]

Yet it would be incorrect to conclude that responsibility for planning and funding new Jewish educational institutions had been privatized, and had devolved on local groups, as opposed to the centralized, community-wide agencies – the ZFET, the JSSM, and the LBJRE – that had formerly been solely responsible for planning and running these facilities. This was by no means the case, and the central agencies continued to be accused of operating in a paternalistic fashion, reflected in the absence of parents on school governing boards.

The ZFET expanded its activities in a number of provincial centres, particularly Leeds, where it funded a middle school and coordinated communal efforts to establish a secondary school. The ZFET was also involved in the North Cheshire Jewish Day School, which though state-aided, depended on ZFET and parental contributions for its Jewish studies programme. In London, after considerable effort, the ZFET's state-aided Rosh Pinah School received permission from the borough of Barnet to substantially enlarge its capacity. By 1985 the school had moved to new premises and had 420 pupils. But this increased activity put serious financial pressure on the ZFET, which reached a crisis point when the lease on its Mathilda Marks Kennedy Primary School ended. Ernest Frankel, the ZFET's stalwart treasurer, predicted that between £600,000 and £800,000 would have to be raised for capital expenditure in the 1984 fiscal year.[100]

---

98   The 'guiding principle' for the Independent Jewish Day School was to be 'promulgation of traditional Orthodox Jewish values'. At the same time, the rubric 'tolerant Orthodoxy' is mentioned in the school's policy statements. The school also sought to provide excellent secular education, to facilitate entry to the better secondary schools. J. Kornbluth, 'Some of the Torah and General Educational Aims of the Independent Jewish Day School', June 1979. CR C3 6 1979–80.

99   JC London Extra 13 November 1987, 1.

100   Frankel to T. Chinn (JEDT) 7 November 1983. CR C2 8.

The JSSM was bedevilled by financial difficulties, mainly due to continued financial mismanagement by Rabbi Schonfeld and his compliant board of trustees.[101] In 1979, the courts ordered that a receiver take charge, appointing Bernard Garbacz to this position. Garbacz was a JSSM supporter – his son had attended the Hasmonean Grammar School – and a respected chartered accountant. Appeals for financial assistance were made to the JEDT, in the hope that it would rescue the school yet again (see Chapter 2), but the JEDT conditioned any assistance on removal of Rabbi Schonfeld and his trustees.[102] Schonfeld responded by publishing allegations that funds intended for the Hasmonean Grammar School for Girls had been banked by the JEDT; he then proceeded to lodge complaints with the local police and later, Scotland Yard. The charges proved baseless. This weakened his position, impelling him to resign.[103] Five trustees took control of JSSM affairs. These efforts paved the way for the borough of Barnet to award state-aided status to the Hasmonean Grammar School for Girls in 1983. By this time, the JSSM had 1,500 pupils enrolled in five schools.[104]

During the 1970s, the LBJRE extended its activities in the day-school sphere, assuming responsibility for the Ilford Jewish Primary School and the Kingsbury project, later named the Michael Sobell Sinai Primary School. These schools were transferred from Bayswater and Stepney, where they had previously existed under the auspices of the Cousinhood.[105] Within a short time, the growing demand for primary school places in Ilford created a dilemma: should the community purchase an old school from council stock or build onto the existing school? As the latter was more economical, that option was chosen. Once enlarged, enrolment doubled.[106]

101 See B. Garbacz, Letter to the Creditors, 8 January 1980. CR C3 8 JSSM.
102 Davis to Ronson, 22 January 1980. CR C3 8 JSSM; Myer Robinson to Davis 21 December 1976. CR C3 5 1976 (2).
103 See Davis, Memorandum to JEDT trustees. CR C3 8 JSSM; Minutes, JSSM Governors 22 April 1979. MS 183 595/2.
104 B. Ferber (trustee) to Dr J. Black (Wolfson Foundation) 8 December 1983. CR C3 8 JSSM.
105 The Michael Sobell Sinai School replaced the Jews' Infants' School and the Solomon Wolfson School that had operated in Bayswater. The Ilford Jewish Primary School replaced the Stepney Jewish Primary School.
106 Minutes, Meeting of JEDT Extended Executive Committee 22 March 1983. CR C5 1.

As to the Kingsbury project in NW London, as far back as 1966, Nat Rubin had approached the Brent Education Committee about building a one-form entry Jewish voluntary-aided school in the borough. Although an agreement in principle had been reached, obstacles emerged, including the council's opposition to a request by the school planners to double the intake, legal objections to development of the proposed site, and government cuts in education funding. These problems continued into the 1980s, and the LBJRE, with JEDT assistance, decided there was little to be gained by waiting. It expressed readiness to assume the costs of building the school, on condition that it would thereafter be awarded state-aided status. This allowed the LBJRE to satisfy parental demand for day-school places in the Kingsbury–Kenton–Wembley area, despite the authorities' 'inability' to foot the building costs.[107]

The strategy of negotiating agreements with LEAs whereby the initial building costs would be covered by the community, provided that once built, the school would be granted state-aided status, was an effective, if expensive, way of coping with the procedural constraints imposed by the local and national authorities. The combination of parental initiatives and strategic efforts by educational agencies increased enrolment rates. In London in 1991, about 28 per cent of Jewish children attended day schools, an increase of over 20 per cent from 1975.[108] But only slightly over half (4,461) of the London Jewish day-school places were aided.[109] In 1991 some 12,785 Jewish children were enrolled in UK Jewish day schools, as compared with 11,590 in 1981, 10,293 in 1971 and 6,726 in 1961.[110] We saw in Chapter 3 that a milestone was reached in 1987, when for the first time more children attended day schools than Hebrew classes. And an increasing percentage of Jewish children were attending haredi day schools, few of which were, at this point, state-aided.

---

107   N. Rubin, The Brent Jewish Primary School: A Record of 15 Years of Negotiations for the Establishment of the School. LBJRE Biennial Report, 1977–8, 11.

108   *Securing*, 7–11.

109   Ziderman, 'Jewish Education', 280.

110   Ibid.; *Securing*, 7–11.

Day schools and Jewish identity

Given the dramatic increase in Jewish day-school enrolment, it might be assumed that it had been empirically established that day-school education intensified Jewish commitment. In fact, the push for day-school education had been based on an assumption, namely, that given their Jewish environment and extensive Jewish studies curriculum, day schools would inculcate greater devotion to Judaism and the Jewish people than Hebrew classes. This assumption was manifest in the Chief Rabbi's 1971 White Paper on Jewish education, *Let My People Know*, discussed above in Chapter 5. In his introductory remarks, Jakobovits wrote:

> With tens of thousands of Jewish children receiving no Jewish instruction at all, and 80 per cent of the remainder forsaking their meagre studies at an age when they cannot but remain juvenile Jews for the rest of their lives, it is no wonder that so many of our young people find their Jewishness too crippled and underdeveloped to sustain their loyalty to our faith, to our community, to Israel and indeed to the moral values of our society. ... Every year our schools are turning away hundreds of applicants, for whom they have no places, simply because the community defaults on its duty to provide full time Jewish education for all those who seek it. To ensure Anglo-Jewry's continuity and growth, we must double our present capacity in the next ten to fifteen years.[111]

But research into the impact of day-school education on Jewish affiliation in Britain was first undertaken only in 1978. A study by Kosmin and Levy caused consternation among proponents of day-school education: it argued that both synagogue classes for teenagers and adult evening classes were 'at least as effective' as Jewish day schools. More specifically, while enrolment at a Jewish primary school was found to have had a positive impact on synagogue attendance later on, the secondary day schools were found to have had negative impact.[112]

---

111 *Let My People*, 2.
112 Kosmin and Levy, *Jewish Identity*, 22–3.

A decade later, a more comprehensive assessment of the impact of secondary day schools found that:

> Positive impact of Jewish secondary schooling is only in evidence at the level of practical observance. It has no connection with attitudes to observance or desire to remain Jewish, and there is actually a negative association between Jewish schooling and the ideological factors (belief in God, ethical concern). A harsh conclusion would be that Jewish schooling reinforces the mechanical aspects of Judaism at the expense of the intellectual and spiritual dimensions. ...
>
> Whether one analyses immediate outcomes, as in our study; or long term outcomes, as in the Redbridge study; or outcomes in particular groups such as university students, the message is always the same. Jewish secondary schools have at best no impact, and at worst a negative impact, on religious behaviour, attitudes and motivation.[113]

And a United Synagogue survey in the early 1990s found that 66 per cent of respondents who had attended a Jewish primary school recommended such schooling, whereas only 45 per cent of respondents who had been to a Jewish secondary school recommended the experience.[114]

Indeed, these findings were corroborated by HM Inspectors' reports.[115] Clearly, Jewish day schools, especially at the secondary level, were not achieving their goals. The boredom and apathy that plagued part-time Jewish educational frameworks were equally characteristic of day schools.

It has been argued that the main reason for the pupils' alienation was the gap between their home environments and that of the school. Though the families of most JFS pupils, and about half of the Hasmonean pupils, were affiliated with the United Synagogue, their religious observance was generally far less stringent than the Orthodox standard. Jewish studies were often taught by yeshiva graduates whose outlook was rigorously Orthodox.

---

113 Miller, 'Impact', 161–2.
114 M. Schmool and S. Miller, 'Jewish Education and Identity among London Synagogue Members', in S. DellaPergola and J. Even (eds), *Papers in Jewish Demography 1993* (Jerusalem: Institute of Contemporary Jewry, 1997), 353.
115 E.g., at the JFS, Inspectors found that Hebrew and Religious Studies departments were 'producing negative results' and the 'staff had not been integrated into the life of the School', Black, *JFS*, 222.

Although the Israeli teachers often presented an alternative model, this did not alleviate the dissonance, as they too were perceived as culturally and religiously 'foreign'. Not surprisingly, many pupils found Jewish studies an alienating experience irrelevant to their future.[116]

Some schools chose to address this by selecting pupils whose religious experience at home matched the ethos of the sponsoring organization. At the primary level, this trend was evident in the Independent Jewish Day School and the Reform movement's Akiva School. But at the secondary level, London remained without a religiously-selective school until the 1990 opening of the Immanuel School in Bushey.

The question remained: could better teachers and teaching, and a more relevant curriculum, enhance the Jewish studies experience in non-religiously-selective schools? Some, such as Michael Cohen, LBJRE director of education, argued that more intense Jewish studies would achieve the desired results; others feared that this approach would isolate children whose homes were less Orthodox. The dilemma is well-illustrated by a long-running dispute at the JFS's Goldbloom Department of Jewish Studies, jointly administered by the LBJRE and ZFET.[117]

Cohen had attended the JSSM's Avigdor Primary School and then William Ellis, a non-denominational grammar school. After reading law at King's College, Newcastle, he had studied at Jews' College and Etz Chaim Yeshiva. He had served as headmaster of the Mount Scopus Primary School in Melbourne, Australia.[118] This balanced secular and Jewish academic background endeared him to the LBJRE's honorary officers. One of Cohen's responsibilities was the standard of Jewish education at the JFS, which he found far from satisfactory. He criticized the Hebrew teachers provided by the ZFET, through the WZO's General Education Department, as insufficiently religious, and called on the LBJRE to have

116 N. Ben-Bassat, 'The Jewish School and the Community – a Look at their Inter-relationship in Great Britain', *Journal of Jewish Education* 55 (1987), 24–9.
117 A similar dispute erupted in 1982 over the Jewish studies department at the King David Primary School in Liverpool. See Minutes, Modern Hebrew and Jewish Studies Sub-Committee – King David Foundation, 11 January 1982. CZA A434 Box 31.
118 *JC* 30 November 1979, 6.

the WZO's Torah Education Department supply its teachers.[119] Cohen submitted several proposals for altering the school's direction, the most comprehensive being his 1985 *The JFS – Towards a 'Jewish' Future*, which sketched a blueprint for transforming the JFS from 'the School for Jews' to 'the Jewish School'.[120]

Cohen alleged that despite the institution's secular academic achievements, the school remained 'Jewishly close to bankruptcy'. Jewish learning, he argued, was confined to the troubled Goldbloom Department, which was perceived by teachers and pupils alike as simply one of the school's many units. Cohen recommended a Jewish ethos that would not be relegated to just the classroom, but would permeate all school activities, from assemblies to events such as the annual swimming gala. He recommended building a synagogue, study hall (*beit midrash*) and Jewish library. How was it possible, he asked, that the school had laboratories and musical facilities but no 'Jewish home?' He suggested devoting more curriculum hours to Jewish studies, creation of a yeshiva stream for capable students, entrance requirements for Hebrew and religious knowledge, compulsory wearing of yarmulkas and ritual fringes (*kipot* and *tzitzit*) during school hours, blessings before and after school meals, compulsory attendance at prayers, and gender separation for Jewish subjects. In sum, Cohen proposed an explicitly Orthodox ethos that would put the JFS to the 'right' of mainstream Anglo-Jewish Orthodoxy.

The report specifically attacked the ZFET's input, recommending that the joint administration of the Goldbloom Department, and its commitment to *Ivrit b'Ivrit*, be reconsidered. It also claimed that the Givat Washington scheme was not in keeping with the proposed religious standards.

Ernest Frankel and Abe Kramer, the key honorary officers of the ZFET, had from the outset objected to Cohen's proposals as an attempt to move the JFS in the direction of the strictly Orthodox Hasmonean

---

119   Notes on a Meeting of the Honorary Officers of the LBJRE and Representatives of the ZFET, held 12 November 1981 at Woburn House, London. CZA A434 Box 27.

120   M. Cohen, 'The JFS–Towards a "Jewish" Future'. LBJRE, London, 1985, 2. CR C3 1985.

schools. This would, they believed, cause many parents to withdraw their children. Frankel warned that 'the disastrous result of this [Cohen's] type of intolerance' would yield the same outcome as prevailed at the Hasmonean schools, where 'half of the children join the *yeshivot* and the other half become *apicorsim* [free-thinkers]'.[121] Most parents preferred a less rigid interpretation of Judaism, and Frankel warned Moshe Davis and the Chief Rabbi that the ZFET would go public about Cohen's plans.[122] For a year or two, they were able to restrain Cohen, though he succeeded in imposing a full-time JFS 'school rabbi'. JFS biographer Gerry Black said little about the controversy surrounding the Goldbloom Department, but his remark about outside interference in running the school suggests that neither the staff nor the headmaster sympathized with the approach favoured by Cohen and the LBJRE.[123]

Interestingly, the Jewish studies programme at the Hasmonean School for Boys was also criticized for failing to engender commitment to Judaism, but here the proposed solution went in the opposite direction. A group of parents led by Harvey Chesterman distributed an alternative syllabus, in which the focus on Talmud and ritual was replaced by study of spoken Hebrew, contemporary history, and Jewish values. The parents sought to end the streaming of Jewish studies according to ability.[124]

Another area of contention was the requirements made of Jewish teachers. The JFS's traditional policy was that all Jewish teachers, whether they taught Jewish or general studies, had to be committed to Orthodox Judaism. This policy was based on the premise that teachers not only impart knowledge but also act as role models, hence the employment of Reform or unobservant Jews would be counterproductive. The directive had no bearing on non-Jews whose religious behaviour was of no concern to the school authorities. The outcome was paradoxical: the governors sought to create a Jewish atmosphere in the school, yet by rejecting non-Ortho-

---

121 Frankel to Shoshana Eytan 13 November 1981. CZA A434 Box 27.
122 Frankel to Abe Kramer, 19 November 1981. CZA A434 Box 27.
123 Black, *JFS*, 222.
124 Chesterman to group of Hasmonean boys' school parents 17 May 1976. CR C3 5 1976 (2).

dox candidates, the pool of applicants was so limited that the majority of teachers were not Jewish.[125] The policy was applied quite severely during Michael Cohen's tenure: he rejected the appointment of a replacement teacher because, despite being a member of an Orthodox synagogue, she taught at a Reform Hebrew class on Sunday mornings.[126]

In December 1986 a Jewish physics teacher who had failed to gain employment at the JFS appealed to an employment tribunal to overturn the school's decision.[127] The tribunal found against the plaintiff, arguing that although ethnically Jewish, the petitioner was an acknowledged atheist. It agreed with Nat Rubin that the school would be acting against the purposes for which it was founded – as a denominational school of the Orthodox Jewish faith – if it employed the teacher.[128] The *Jewish Chronicle* took a different view:

> It is entirely intolerable ... that Jewish teachers otherwise qualified are rejected by the School on a creedal test. The teaching of religion, of course, demands special criteria, but in general subjects this discriminatory practice, by exacerbating an already serious dearth of teachers, conflicts with the School's first duty, which is to provide the best possible education for the children in its charge.[129]

The policy of hiring observant teachers remained contentious. The JEDT invested enormous effort in trying to attract excellent teachers. Yet as had been the case in earlier decades, teachers in the Jewish schools were poorly paid and had few options for advancement. This led many Jewish teachers to prefer employment in non-Jewish schools.[130] As we have seen,

---

125   Woolf Abrahams to Honorary Officers and Members of the Executive, Finance, Education, and Staffing Committees of the LBJRE, January 1976. CR C3 4 LBJRE.

126   Notes from Meeting of the Honorary Officers of the LBJRE and the ZFET concerning the Goldbloom Department of the JFS, 14 July 1981. CZA A434 Box 27.

127   See Rubin to Chief Rabbi. CR C3 10.

128   *JC* 12 December 1986, 44.

129   Quoted in Black, *JFS*, 217. The school has since changed its policy and accepts non-Orthodox teachers for general subjects.

130   E. Conway, Report on Survey of Teachers in Jewish Schools – March 1985, 5. CZA A434 Box 34.

the Jewish schools usually had no choice but to rely on Israeli teachers, often not religious at all, on the one hand, and yeshiva students, on the other. To change the situation, the JEDT provided financial incentives, staff development programmes – including in-service training in Israel – and created a career structure for those entering the field.[131] These efforts bore fruit, and by the late 1980s a record number of candidates were attending community-sponsored teacher-training institutes.

Another issue on the schools' agenda was their policy vis-à-vis applicants who were not halakhically Jewish, that is to say, children not born of a Jewish mother or who had not had an Orthodox conversion. The haredi and Orthodox schools required parents of prospective pupils to indicate their synagogue affiliation on the application form; the ZFET schools were inclined to be laxer. Parents seeking to transfer a child from a ZFET primary school to the JFS were informed that their child, not being halakhically Jewish, was ineligible.[132] As the ZFET schools formally accepted the Chief Rabbi's authority, they could not ignore complaints about their policy of accepting non-halakhically-Jewish applicants. Indeed, when Levin, the United Synagogue president, obtained evidence that 'non-Jewish children' had been admitted to the Rosh Pinah School, whose premises belonged to the United Synagogue, he threatened to have the school closed.[133] The perceived inflexibility of the religious authorities created a quandary as to whether to go public about this sensitive issue.[134]

131 See M. Cohen and S. Caplan, 'Personnel Development in Anglo-Jewish Education', October, 1985. CZA A434 Box 9.

132 In 1986, Rubin wrote to Shimon Cohen (Office of the Chief Rabbi) that the problem of non-halakhically-Jewish applicants arose mainly with regard to the ZFET schools. 'The JFS is then left in a most difficult situation in having to refuse such children admission should they wish to transfer to us'. Rubin to Cohen 13 May 1986 CR C3 10.

133 Levin to A. Kramer 27 September 1978. CR C2 8.

134 In a letter to the JFS headmaster, Rabbi Kokotek of the Belsize Square Liberal Synagogue expressed reluctance to make public – or take up with the ILEA – the JFS's refusal to accept children whose mothers he had converted. 'I hope that we may be able to resolve this problem in amity and preserve the image of unity in our Jewish community'. Kokotek to Gatoff 10 May 1978. CR C3 6 1978–9.

The conflict over the JFS's Goldbloom Department, and the problems of non-observant teachers and non-halakhically Jewish pupils, attested to the educational establishment's ongoing formal commitment to Orthodoxy, a shift to the right among the 'actually' Orthodox, and increasing incongruity between the schools' regulations and ethos, and the views and practices of a good portion of their constituencies.

The Bushey School and the modern-Orthodox agenda

The saga of the JFS's Goldbloom Department is a good example of how ideology and turf wars hindered efforts to improve the schools. Thus when discussions opened as to the nature and ethos of a new secondary day school for North West London, there was strong resolve not to repeat the failures of the past. In particular, the founders sought to avoid the compartmentalization of Jewish and general studies that was so entrenched in other Jewish secondary schools. Implicit in this goal was a broader critique of Anglo-Jewish modern-Orthodoxy. British modern-Orthodox day schools put most of their resources into the general studies programme. Those planning the new school intended to show that a school could achieve excellence in both the Jewish and the general realms.

The model for excellence in secular subjects was Haberdashers' Aske's Boys' and Girls' Schools in Elstree, to which many Jewish parents aspired to send their children due to these schools' outstanding academic achievements, as reflected in 'A' level results and university admissions. Supporters of the new school believed that in this regard, the JFS and Hasmonean were far from satisfactory.

When the Chief Rabbi had proposed establishing an independent, fee-paying Jewish day school in 1968, there had been considerable opposition, mainly on the grounds that such a school would not attract sufficient parental or philanthropic support.[135] Some rejected as unethical the idea of the community's establishing a school for its wealthier members. But by the mid-1980s, support for such a project had grown, as approval of denominational schooling had increased, and the community had become more conservative. It was not envisioned as a school for children of the poor, children of immigrants, or those lacking scholastic aptitude. Rather, it was expressly conceived as a school for those able to provide their children with the finest education available. Because the new school was planned by a coalition of lay and religious leaders, educators, and parents, it illustrates how the various sectors' sometimes divergent visions, which for the first time in the history of Anglo-Jewish education were well documented, came into play.

The JEDT and the WZO's Torah Education Department had commissioned Stephen Miller to study the feasibility of opening of a new Jewish secondary school in North West London; its findings, published in March 1985, demonstrated that parental demand for a selective school was more compelling than demand for another voluntary-aided comprehensive. Miller determined that the area between Edgware and Borehamwood would be the ideal location.[136] He identified two groups of parents who might be interested in the school: those who were committed to sending their children to a Jewish secondary school, but had reservations about the existing options, and those who intended to send their children to a fee-paying, non-Jewish independent school, but expressed interest in a Jewish selective school. For the latter, 'there was more to be gained academically than would be lost Jewishly' at a non-Jewish independent school.[137]

---

135 See Chapter 5.
136 Miller's study showed that Jews were moving to the suburbs of Hertfordshire and Harrow, whose Jewish population had risen by over 24 per cent from 1977 to 1983. See S. Miller, A New Secondary School in NW London: A Feasibility Study [undertaken for JEDT and the WZO Torah Education Department], 7. CZA A434.
137 Ibid., 15.

Miller interviewed both groups of parents about their expectations for the school.[138] These were prospective clients, and failure to satisfy their expectations would jeopardize the project. Their responses made clear that they expected academic standards comparable to those of the best non-Jewish independents; rigorous selectiveness, and an environment geared toward intellectual achievement, entry to top universities, and professional careers. They expected department heads experienced in teaching up to university scholarship level, well-equipped school premises, and a curriculum offering extensive artistic, musical, and sporting activities.

Regarding the school's religious orientation, many interviewees expressed anxiety about adoption of a 'rigid Orthodoxy', defined as a regime that devoted over 20 per cent of the timetable to Jewish studies, with gender separation beyond some religious subjects and physical education.[139] Most supported a modern-Orthodox outlook, that would be 'open to inquiry', 'sensitive to ethical and moral issues', and willing to admit halakhically-Jewish children from 'a wide range of religious backgrounds'. Two factors would determine their final decision: the division of time between general and Jewish studies, and the gender-separation policy. All parents were interested in a strong emphasis on modern Hebrew; those whose children had experienced the *Ivrit b'Ivrit* method at primary school expected it to continue. Parents felt that a broad-based governing body would be preferable to governance by a community educational agency. They suggested that the governors be drawn from different schools, communal institutions, higher education, parents, and teachers.

The feasibility study also investigated the attitudes of four head teachers whose primary schools were expected to 'feed' the proposed independent Jewish secondary school. All felt the new school would have trouble securing high calibre Jewish teachers for both general and even Jewish subjects; two predicted that this problem would prove insurmountable.[140]

---

138 He conducted small-group interviews of 64 parents whose children were attending one of the following primary schools: the Independent Jewish Day (NW4), Kerem (NW11), Rosh Pinah (Edgware), Mathilda Marks Kennedy (NW11) and the Michael Sobell Sinai (NW8).

139 Ibid., 14.

140 Memorandum from Shimon Cohen (Office of the Chief Rabbi) to Stanley Kalms, Ronny Metzger and Simon Caplan (JEDT) 2 October 1985. CR C3 9.

Six months later, the Chief Rabbi and Stanley Kalms, JEDT chairman, identified the founders of the Independent Jewish Day School as potential founders of the new independent secondary school. Their review of the parental focus groups' input had given them the impression that both groups – the parents and the IJDS founders – shared a similar vision for the school.

Funding was clearly an issue, necessitating involvement of benefactors and communal agencies. In 1985, Stephen Miller had estimated the cost of the project at the unprecedented sum of £4 million; by the time the school opened in 1990, it had cost three times that.[141] The bulk of the funding came from two founding sponsors, Stanley Kalms and Gerald Ronson, who along with the retiring Chief Rabbi, gave the school its cumbersome name: The Charles Kalms/Henry Ronson Immanuel College.

It was thus the JEDT, led by Chief Rabbi Jakobovits, and chaired by Stanley Kalms, that formulated the school's goals. Also involved in shaping the school's identity were Rabbi Jonathan Sacks, the principal of Jews College, Simon Caplan, JEDT director, and Gaby Goldstein, the preferred candidate for school head.[142] All five were modern-Orthodox and personally committed to Zionism; all five sat on the school's Professional Advisory Committee, which was responsible for setting the school ethos and syllabus, and hiring staff.[143]

A comparison of the Professional Advisory Committee's goals for the new school with those articulated by the parents reveals intriguing differences. The parents made no mention of the school's responsibility for developing a cadre of communal leaders. By contrast, the advisory committee saw this as a central goal. Caplan put leadership at the very heart of his 1985 proposal: 'The school must have as its central and innermost creed

141 S. Caplan, 'Immanuel College: The Beginnings of an Educational Project', *Studies in Education* 7 (1995), 56.

142 Goldstein drafted the key document, 'Ethos of the New School: A Discussion Document', 6 June 1987. CR C6 10.

143 Chaired by Worms, the committee also included, among others, Dennis Felsenstein (who ultimately became principal of the school), Philip Skelker (principal of Carmel College), and Clive Lawton. See Worms, *Life*, 241.

the fostering of a future leadership at every level of Jewish society'.[144] He criticized the organized community and existing Jewish secondary schools for having failed to nurture future communal leaders, arguing that the brightest and most dynamic of Britain's young Jews were little involved in communal affairs.[145] Caplan wanted to create an environment that inculcated responsibility for the community and wider society, on the model of the Haberdashers' and City of London independent schools, which were known for leadership development. Caplan and Goldstein envisaged graduates as continuing their studies at Jews' College or the Institute of Education, University of London, and then assuming lay and professional leadership roles. Indeed, they hoped to inspire other schools to emulate Immanuel in this regard, and ultimately engender change throughout the day-school system.

Though the professionals saw the school as an impetus to revitalizing Anglo-Jewish life, the parents' expectations were more modest; their sole goal was academic achievement, and mainly in secular studies. While parents saw the curriculum as clearly divided into two domains, secular and religious, the educators sought to integrate Jewish learning with general subjects. For example, Goldstein suggested that 15 per cent of the curriculum be devoted to Jewish studies, 5 per cent to Hebrew literature, and 7 per cent to integration of Jewish values with the core curriculum.[146] Divergence was also evident over the question of single-gender classes. Whereas the parents did not want separate-gender learning, the educators did. Aware of the sensitivity of the issue, they couched their preference for single-gender classes in the rhetoric of research that 'proved' better academic results were attained in single-gender classes.[147]

Jonathan Sacks described the school's objectives as follows:

144 S. Caplan, 'The Case for a New Jewish Grammar School in North West London' [undated but presumably 1984/5]. CR C6 10.
145 See Chapter 2 on Kopul Rosen's expectations for the development of a leadership cadre at Carmel College. Black's history of the JFS mentions only two rabbis, Rabbis Tann and Myers, who were Old Boys, see Black, *JFS*, 220.
146 Goldstein, 'Ethos', n 142 above, 5.
147 Caplan, 'Immanuel', 63.

The proposed school will aim ... at producing students who are thoroughly at home in both contemporary society and the full range of Jewish heritage. [The school] will unashamedly aim at creating leaders in all spheres of contemporary life, individuals whose sense of Jewish responsibility is deep and broad, encompassing an identification with the Jewish people in its totality, with Jewish history in its diversity, and with the State of Israel in its centrality. It will promote the traditions of principle and tolerance, intellectual depth and social concern, loyalty and generosity, academic rigour and ethical example. It will take as its task the projection of an Orthodox way of life and thought that earns the admiration of others of whatever faith. It will aim at creating in its pupils an integrated personality whose Jewish identity is knowledgeable, secure and proud, a spur to achievement and responsibility, and a challenge to exemplary citizenship in an ethically and religiously plural society.[148]

Sacks's credo for the new school was not merely an updated version of the Hirschian '*Torah im Derekh Eretz*' philosophy. Whereas Hirsch's dictum asserted that Torah was to be lived *alongside* the ways of the world, Sacks, writing of multicultural Britain in the late twentieth century, proposed a holistic, integrated approach.[149] Sacks was, in essence, redefining modern Orthodoxy for the contemporary British context. He rejected Anglo-Orthodoxy's traditional compartmentalization, and sought to replace it with an organic synthesis of Englishness and Jewishness.

Most parents of prospective pupils had no real interest in this new synthesis. They cared little about the Jewish studies curriculum and were against adoption of overly-rigid Orthodoxy. Their expectations for the school were better defined by Sacks's description of the ideal graduate's attributes:

A commitment to hard work, intellectual achievement, honesty and integrity. A mature Jewish identity together with an understanding of the depth of knowledge an intelligent Jewish identity requires. A sense of Jewish responsibility. A mature sense of the necessary interaction between Jew and non-Jew and between religious Jew and non-religious Jew.[150]

---

148   J. Sacks, 'The Profile of an Educated Jew – Outline of an Educational Philosophy for a New Jewish Secondary School', submitted to JEDT November 1988. CR C6 10.
149   J. Sacks, 'Britain in the 1980's: A Jewish Response', *L'Eylah* 1, 1978, 10–15.
150   Quoted in Caplan, 'Immanuel', 65.

Sacks's ideal graduate is meaningfully engaged with the broader society. The notion of barriers between the broader society and the Jewish community is absent, as is the notion that the non-Orthodox streams must be rejected. Of course, Sacks was interested in building a coalition of parents, professionals, and religious leaders, hence his profile of the ideal graduate had a pragmatic motivation, allowing all those engaged in building the school to believe their visions would be realized. The profile had to appeal to disparate constituencies:

> To the average trustee of the JEDT, they ... identified the school as an equivalent of the local non-Jewish independents – a Jewish version of Haberdashers'. To the 'Young Israel' modern-Orthodox parent or Jewish educator, they were beacons lighting up a path towards an integrative modern-Orthodox approach. To some readers, the distinguishing feature of the list was to connect the best elements of British education, whereas to others, the distinguishing feature was to disconnect the school from the worst features of Anglo-Jewish education.[151]

Opposition to opening the new school in Bushey, near Haberdashers' Aske's, was not ideological. Initially, there was little public hostility to the plan, though some felt its ambitious nature would tie up funds that could be put to better use stabilizing the finances of existing education institutions. Privately, the Hasmonean School worried that the new educational endeavour would skim off some of its pupils, a fear shared by the JFS.[152] The very idea of a new secondary school in North West London intimated that the existing institutions were failing.

For the United Synagogue, the building of an exceptionally expensive Orthodox school, a school with explicitly ideological pretensions, was disconcerting. It created the impression that its own educational endeavours were faltering, and others were leading the modern-Orthodox educational effort. In an attempt to rectify this perception, the United Synagogue scrapped the LBJRE, in which it had always been the dominant partner, replacing it with its own Board of Education.[153] Sidney Frosh, president of the United Synagogue, would have preferred that the money directed to

---

151   Ibid., 65–6.
152   Frankel to Kramer 21 October 1985; 11 November 1985. CZA A434 Box 33.
153   *JC* 19 December 1986, 5; 13 March 1987, 6. CR C3 10.

the Bushey School be used to open a state-aided comprehensive school in Redbridge. A school in Ilford could have been purchased at a third of the cost and would have served the same number of pupils. Bermant observed that in supporting the new school, the Chief Rabbi was 'acting on the principle that unto him that hath shall be given.'[154] But a school for the elite was not contrary to the ethos of North West London Jewry.

The Immanuel School had been intended by its founders to correct the JFS's 'lax Orthodoxy' and the Hasmonean's circumspect Zionism. These deficiencies had indeed been addressed, but the school's fee-paying nature and stress on superior academic achievement reflected the middle-class values of the growing North West London modern-Orthodox community.

Closing thoughts

What was the impact of multicultural Britain on Anglo-Jewry and Jewish education in England? The arrival of more-visible minorities was generally interpreted by Anglo-Jewry as affording the community some relief from xenophobia: racist groups would focus their opposition on the more recent arrivals and leave the Jews alone, at least for the time being.[155] While recognizing that the new immigrants were subject to discrimination, Anglo-Jewry's leadership was not prepared to risk its successful integration into British life by allying with the ethnic minorities or fighting for their interests. Anglo-Jewry preferred to model itself on the white upper middle class, whose values and manners it had adopted. Yet this was not mere selfishness: the ethnic minorities were perceived as hostile to Jews and Zionism.

154 Bermant, *Lord Jakobovits*, 201.
155 Hackney Jews surveyed by Ginsberg saw the National Front as first picking on the Blacks, 'but the moment they finish with the colored, they'll start with the Jews', see Ginsberg, 'Jewish', 213. This view was also voiced by Anglo-Jewry's leaders, see, e.g., the statement by Greville Janner MP, President of the Board of Deputies, in 'Voice of Jewry' [pamphlet], London, 1980. Board of Deputies archives, LMA.

Multi-ethnic Britain was nonetheless liberating in another sense. The ethnic minorities generated a more cosmopolitan atmosphere, especially in London, and the public expression of difference became more acceptable. It has been claimed that wearing skullcaps in public followed in the wake of pride in Israel's achievements during the Six-Day War, but it can be argued that the presence of ethnic minorities speaking a variety of languages and wearing saris, dishdashas, and turbans, signalled that public expressions of Jewish identity would also be tolerated.

Britain's changing social attitudes and adoption of multicultural policies imparted a new political assertiveness to certain segments of the Jewish community, particularly the ultra-Orthodox. This was manifested in the public and unabashed efforts of the Yesodey Hatorah and Lubavitch foundations to attain state-aided status for their primary schools. Though unsuccessful, they ultimately secured funding for leisure and nursery facilities by embracing the 'ethnic minority' designation, thereby becoming eligible for affirmative action grants distributed by the GLC's Ethnic Minorities Unit. And in addition to direct financial benefits, the new haredi assertiveness also had political advantages in areas where the haredi community was large enough to influence council affairs. The Board of Deputies, however, rejected the 'ethnic minority' rubric, preferring the traditional denominational self-definition.

The modern-Orthodox were also impacted by multiculturalism. They too became more confident about their identity and assertive of their needs. Together with the ultra-Orthodox, they sought to put up an *eruv* (Sabbath boundary marker) in the Golders Green area. Although the ensuing debate divided the Jewish population, the readiness of the Orthodox communities to assert their religious requirements stood in marked contrast to earlier expressions of communal lobbying, which tended to emphasize universal values, as in the campaign for Soviet Jewry, which invoked the language of human rights.

The new self-confidence was also expressed in the demand for voluntary-aided denominational education. However, unlike the ultra-Orthodox, the modern-Orthodox followed the prescribed processes, while seeking out quiet alliances with ministers, MPs, and the other denominations. The modern-Orthodox educational agencies also nurtured relationships with their Anglican and Roman Catholic counterparts, coordinating efforts regarding legislation and council decisions.

Anglo-Jewry was divided over multiculturalism-related issues that arose in the late 1970s and 1980s. Adoption of the multi-faith syllabus for religious education in state schools met with a mixed response. Some parents and teachers expressed satisfaction with the academic and neutral position on religion, other parents and rabbis regretted the decision to terminate withdrawal classes, which they viewed as an opportunity to provide a modicum of Jewish education to children who would otherwise receive none. The community was also divided over the issue of separate education for ethnic minorities. Though no formal position on this subject was adopted, most Jews concurred with the prevailing sentiment that separate ethnic schools were likely to inculcate a separatist attitude to British society, and thus objectionable. This position was in line with Swann Commission's majority view, which embraced diversity, provided it was experienced under a common roof.

Yet by this time, the community had warmed to the idea of Jewish day schools, coming to see them as both enhancing integration into British society, and facilitating a healthy synthesis of Jewish and English identity. Although dissatisfaction with the perceived academic level and student culture in the large comprehensive schools of the state system remained the key impetus for choosing Jewish day-school education, in the 1980s the multi-ethnic nature of British society encouraged Jewish parents to consider denominational schools for their children. The expression of religious and ethnic identity in the public sphere had gained legitimacy. Despite mainstream Anglo-Jewry's discomfort with 'ethnic minority' rubric, it was an accurate characterization of the community. While the core expression of this ethnicity was religious practice, its 'Jewish self-identification' was based more on a feeling of belonging than on religious belief. Behind the community's formal self-presentation as a religious denomination lay more powerful ethnic bonds between its members. Rejection of the 'ethnic minority' label was a strategic move motivated by the conviction that Anglo-Jewry should distance itself from the ethnic minorities, who were suspected of separatist inclinations. Despite Anglo-Jewry's successful integration into virtually every realm of British life, its leadership continued to harbour fears as to its relationship with the wider society.

Other forces also affected Anglo-Jewry's attitude to schooling. In particular, Anglo-Jewry's continued upward mobility produced an alignment with the value system of the upper middle class, and its preference for independent schools. A record number of Jewish children now attended these selective schools, whose Jewish quotas had been rescinded following the financial crisis of the 1970s.

These factors, taken together, led to a breakthrough: in 1987, more Jewish children received their Jewish education in day schools than in any other framework. Moreover, this expansion did not appear to be a temporary trend. Several new primary schools had opened in the 1980s, and a large new secondary school was being established in London. Opposition to Jewish day schools had not dissipated,[156] but communal forums were not inclined to be swayed by this view; day-school education now dominated the Jewish educational scene. With respect to improving the curriculum, two major advances were made in the 1980s: the *Ivrit b'Ivrit* method was successfully adopted in a number of primary schools, and efforts to integrate Jewish studies into the secular curriculum were in progress. Prospects for teacher recruitment and training were looking up, as Jews' College and the University of London's Institute of Education achieved unprecedented enrolment in their respective programmes.[157] The JEDT's success in providing funding and organizational aid to Jewish day schools suggests that after fundraising for Israel, Jewish education had become one of Anglo-Jewry's main priorities. The contrast with the situation in 1944 could not have been more stark.

---

156   Research undertaken by the United Synagogue in 1991 revealed considerable opposition to Jewish day schools. Of those interviewed, 41 per cent supported Jewish primary schooling, but only 26 per cent supported secondary schooling, see Kalms, Time for Change, n 97 above, 256.

157   In May 1993, 150 students were enrolled in programmes at Jews' College, compared to 20 in 1982. During this period, connections to the Institute of Education were established, and about 20 students annually enrolled in post-graduate teaching training or Masters degree programmes in education. See S. Caplan, Community and Education, Project Paper submitted to Jerusalem Fellows Programme, 1992/93, 16.

CHAPTER 7

Conclusion

Overview

The period from 1965 to 1979 was a watershed in the history of Anglo-Jewish education. Within a relatively short interval, loss of faith in the state system, following the demise of the grammar schools and their replacement with non-selective comprehensives, generated unprecedented parental enthusiasm for Jewish day schools. Attendance at Jewish day schools soared, and many had long waiting lists. There was also much interest in 'public' schools, but this was not surprising, since a 'public' school education had long been acknowledged as the best route to academic success and upward social mobility.

Some have invoked an Anglo-Jewish religious and spiritual revival associated with the Six-Day War and the campaign for Soviet Jewry to account for the increased willingness, beginning in the mid-1960s, of Anglo-Jewish parents to send their children to Jewish day schools. As we have seen, however, the explanation for the change in parental enthusiasm for day schools is far more prosaic. For Jewish parents, state-aided Jewish day schools were appealing primarily due to their academic excellence, as well as the fact that, like the other state schools, they were free. The Jewish studies component was, overall, of little concern to most parents. More attractive was the perception that Jewish schools embraced traditional values and provided a more disciplined and secure environment than did the state schools, which were considered impersonal, overly permissive, even dangerous. Jewish parents were often worried by the high proportion of immigrant children and ethnic minorities in comprehensive schools, a phenomenon they associated with lower academic achievement. While

Jewish day schools were attended by children with a broader range of academic abilities than the traditional grammar schools, there was nonetheless a feeling among parents that compared to the comprehensive schools, Jewish schools were less affected by rebelliousness and objectionable street culture. More generally, they were perceived as shelters from the turbulence of British society as it found its way through dramatic social, demographic, and cultural change.

On British Jewry's traditional self-understanding, one's religious affiliation was relevant in the home and synagogue, but ought not be manifest in the public sphere. Anglo-Jewry's embrace of Jewish day-school education attests to a certain rethinking of this conception. Nevertheless, Anglo-Jewry was for the most part not comfortable employing the language of ethnicity, and preferred to conceive the day schools as institutions for the teaching of religion, rather than for the transmission of a national or ethnic culture. The curriculum, staff, and extra-curricular activities, to a very large extent, exemplified this approach. While, beginning in the late 1960s, events in Israel and the campaign for Soviet Jewry were high on the communal agenda, the curricula of Jewish day schools did not reflect this new focus of Jewish identity, and continued to teach the traditional syllabus of prayers, Bible, religious precepts, festivals and so on. With the exception of the ZFET day schools and the JFS, which were committed to integrating the Israeli experience into the curriculum, the impact of Israeli culture on the day schools was limited. Although the pressure to integrate into British society had lessened, and the terms of that integration were more pluralistic, the basic premise of Anglo-Jewish education remained constant: Jewish education is religious education in the traditional sense, and not education premised on the notion of the Jewish people, a shared cultural heritage, or a connection to Israel.

Changing parental attitudes to Jewish schooling

As we have seen, parental views on the preferred education for their children changed dramatically in the 1960s and 1970s. In 1944, only one in sixteen Jewish children attended a Jewish day school, whereas the corresponding figure for 1987 was one in two. There was a corresponding increase in the number of Jewish day schools, from twenty-three in the early 1950s, virtually all of them small, to seventy in 1989, many with hundreds of pupils.[1] Moreover, the increase in the number of day schools occurred at a time of demographic decline!

Jewish day schools had existed in the first half of the century, but attendance had been declining even before World War II. Most parents felt that the goal for which Jewish schools had been established, namely, protecting immigrant and second-generation children from proselytizers while they acquired essential schooling and became acculturated, i.e., Anglicized, had been reached. Accordingly, in the postwar period, the main objective of schooling shifted to academic achievement and upward mobility. Anglo-Jewry, motivated to extricate itself from inner city slums and working-class neighbourhoods, had chosen the British middle class as its reference group, energetically adopting its values and emulating its mores. A good education at a local primary school and then a selective grammar school was seen as the route not only to academic achievement, but to socialization into the middle class. And Jewish children were very successful in securing grammar school places.

Anglo-Jewry perceived the British middle class as confining religion to the private sphere of home and church, and as disapproving of denominational schooling and separate ethnic identification generally. It was aware that most middle-class children received their religious education at Sunday school, and that beyond that, religion did not appear to be a major force in middle-class life. The Jewish community adopted this part-time, low-intensity model of religious education.

---

1   Valins et al., *Future*, 9.

At the end of the 1940s, the Jews remained uncertain as to their status in England. Antisemitism had resurfaced, not just among Mosley's Fascists, but in the opinions of much of the population, as Mass Observation Polls attested. The Jewish community was apologetic, believing that by adopting the mores of the wider population, and downplaying their culture uniqueness, they would remove the reasons for antagonism. Jewish participation in the maintained non-denominational schools and, where affordable, independent schools, was a statement of willingness to conform to Gentile cultural norms.

During the 1950s and early 1960s, Jewish day-school education was preferred by three small sectors of Anglo-Jewry. One was Rabbi Solomon Schonfeld's strictly Orthodox community, associated with the UOHC. Schonfeld's JSSM was the largest of the Jewish day-school systems during this period. This community was committed to economic interaction but limited social integration with the wider society, and its schools endorsed the middle-class values upheld by most of Anglo-Jewry.

Naturally, the haredi community also rejected state schools for their children. The Yesodey Hatorah schools provided education for most of the haredi community until the late 1950s, when various hasidic and misnagdic groups started their own schools The fervently Orthodox had little interest in integrating into British society or the middle class. Immersed in punctiliously observing Jewish law, they were willing to forgo upward mobility. Parental educational goals for their children included knowledge of the Talmud and law codes with a view to preserving strict levels of religious observance.

The third group that sent their children to day schools were working-class London Jews who preferred the schools that had been established by the 'Cousinhood', and later came under the aegis of the LBJRE, to local state schools. Such parents, though themselves working class, were leery of their children's interaction with schoolmates who might not aspire to a grammar school education. After 1953, when the Zionist movement entered the field of day-school education, it harnessed these parental reservations about the educational aspirations of the English working class, and later, those of the New Commonwealth immigrants. As a result, the ZF schools, several of which were situated in working-class districts, were often oversubscribed.

Most Anglo-Jewish children, however, did not attend day schools, but Sunday or after-school Hebrew classes. Though these classes provided only a minimal Jewish education, this was deemed acceptable by most parents, whose priority was ensuring that their children received the best possible secular education.

By 1965, when the Labour government decided to end selective education by dismantling the grammar schools, much of Anglo-Jewry had successfully integrated into the middle class. Jewish parents were worried that non-selective comprehensive schools would jeopardize their children's chances of sustaining this achievement. They feared that an inadequate secondary education would put their children at a competitive disadvantage vis-à-vis university entrance, relative to 'public' school graduates. This concern led to the withdrawal of Jewish children from the state non-denominational schools.

For those who could afford it, private education was the preferred alternative, as the independent schools were perceived as the best means of ensuring academic achievement. And the timing was fortuitous: over the next decade, increasing numbers of Jewish pupils were able to gain entry to private schools. This was due to the ongoing financial crisis, which made it harder for the schools to restrict their intake by applying 'non-conformist' quotas to local non-Anglicans, yet still fill their available places. When faced with the choice between accepting foreign students and abandoning the quotas, they chose the latter. By the early 1980s, Jews comprised 40 per cent of the enrolment at certain independent schools in London and Hertfordshire, e.g., Haberdashers' Aske's.

For parents unable or unwilling to pay for private education, Jewish voluntary-aided schools offered a means of circumventing the comprehensive system. The demand for Jewish day-school education expanded.

The concerns about comprehensive education in general, we saw, were accompanied by parental concerns that the presence of a growing number of ethnic minority children in these schools would lead to lowered academic standards. These fears were compounded by apprehensiveness that their children might be influenced by the rebelliousness, promiscuity and radicalism associated with the 'permissive society' ethos. Jewish schools were naively perceived as untouched by these social trends, and hence capable of ensuring disciplined pursuit of academic achievement.

Yet Britain's transformation from a monolithic to a multicultural and multi-faith society also spurred the rise of the day schools in a more positive sense. New Commonwealth immigration began in the 1950s, and increased significantly in the following decade. The presence of these immigrants broadened Britons' exposure to new cultures, languages and religions. Although multiculturalism was consciously fostered as a general and educational policy only in the late 1970s, well before this it had created growing tolerance for and appreciation of diversity. Many Jews became more comfortable expressing their Jewish identity in public, but others maintained the community's traditional reserve, confining their Judaism to the private realm. The former were amenable to sending their children to Jewish day schools, the latter tended to disapprove of denominational schooling.

Most of the community, and certainly, its major agencies, preferred its traditional profile as one of Britain's religious denominations and did not view themselves as a self-avowed ethnic community. In keeping with this approach, Jewish educational organizations continued to co-operate with the mainstream ecclesiastical authorities and generally refrained from joint efforts with other ethnic minorities. This position was well illustrated by Anglo-Jewry's response to the establishment in 1979 of the Rampton (Swann) Commission. The Jewish community took no part in its proceedings. Alliances with the ethnic minorities were perceived as undermining Anglo-Jewry's integration into British society. Similarly, in the mid-1970s campaign against racism, the Board of Deputies opposed the Anti-Nazi League, believing it to be dominated by stridently anti-Israel ethnic minorities. Anglo-Jewry's response to the suggestion that Jews be classed under the 'ethnic minorities' rubric in the national census provides yet another example of its unease at being associated with ethnic minorities. The Board of Deputies opposed the suggested classification with unusual assertiveness.[2]

This attitude was manifest even in the day schools themselves. Attending such schools was viewed primarily as an expression of religious identity,

2   Englander, 'Integrated', 127–8.

and the curriculum and extra-curricular activities, to a very large extent, reflected this premise.[3] Although the pressure to conduct themselves in line with traditional British norms had lessened, Anglo-Jews remained wary of self-identification in the new language of ethnicity and multiculturalism.

Until the mid-1960s, Jews generally distanced themselves from the Conservative Party. But the period in which the shift away from Hebrew classes to day schools gained momentum also saw increasing Anglo-Jewish support for the Conservatives. By this time, most Anglo-Jews had climbed to the middle class, and Margaret Thatcher's personal story – the child of a grocer, she was educated at a local grammar school and went on to Oxford – resonated with them. Thatcher's friendliness to Israel and Jews – at one time her Cabinet had five Jewish members – was obvious, but the more important factor that generated Jewish support for the Conservatives was the party's defence of grammar and direct-grant schools. As we saw, Jews were enthusiastic supporters of grammar-school education. The efforts of Conservative MPs on behalf of Jewish day schools in their constituencies were also much appreciated.

Communal politics of Anglo-Jewish education

Jewish education in England over the past fifty years has been provided by various organizations espousing diverse conceptions of the relationship between Judaism, the Jewish people and British society. These organizations competed to extend their influence while preserving their autonomy, and their willingness to cooperate with each other was often limited.

In 1941, Chief Rabbi Hertz successfully thwarted an attempt by lay leaders of the United Synagogue and the Reform and Liberal movements to establish a community-wide framework that would be responsible for

3   See B. Chazan, 'Models of Ethnic Education: The Case of Jewish Education in Great Britain', *British Journal of Educational Studies* 26 (1978), 70.

Jewish education during the wartime emergency. Hertz feared that the integration of these streams would confer legitimacy on them, undermine central Orthodoxy's hegemony, and damage his relations with the ultra-Orthodox. An alliance with the separatist Schonfeld faction enabled him to become president of the Joint Emergency Committee for Jewish Religious Education (JEC), with the right to appoint teachers and vet curricula for Hebrew classes. Exclusion of the Reform and Liberal movements continued in 1946 with the establishment of the LBJRE. Yet cooperation with them on matters of common concern, such as withdrawal classes in state schools, would surely have been beneficial.

Hertz's hand was strengthened by the state authorities' tradition of relating to Anglo-Jewry as they did to the Anglicans and Roman Catholics. Just as they consulted with the ecclesiastical authorities on educational matters, so too the Chief Rabbi, rather than a communal body such as the Board of Deputies, or the Consistoire in France, was taken to be the address for such consultations. Hertz sought to prevent the Board of Deputies from playing a major role in the educational sphere, and to limit its jurisdiction to issues such as lobbying the government over school examinations scheduled on Jewish holidays, objecting to the textbooks deemed antisemitic, and challenging alleged Jewish quotas in independent schools. His objection to the Board of Deputies' involvement in educational affairs stemmed from his belief that Jewish education was coextensive with religious education, and hence outside the purview of lay bodies.

The Chief Rabbi's position as head of the LBJRE meant that he was a central figure in any controversy over Jewish education. In 1952, the trustees of the former voluntary-aided schools chose the LBJRE as the body to be charged with re-establishing the JFS. Rabbi Schonfeld objected, claiming that his JSSM was the major provider of day-school education in London, and the LBJRE had no day-school experience at all. As we saw in Chapter 2, Schonfeld's opposition impeded the process of securing government approval for transfer of the dormant trust funds and rebuilding the JFS. At the centre of the trust funds controversy was the question of which stream of Orthodoxy should lead the day-school effort, centrist Orthodoxy, associated with the LBJRE and the United Synagogue, or the stricter Orthodoxy of the Schonfeld camp.

The ZF entered the day-school field in 1953, generating controversy over the content of Anglo-Jewish education. Ought it remain, as the Chief Rabbi argued, solely religious in nature, or should it be broader, encompassing Jewish culture more generally? The latter rubric included contemporary Jewish history, modern Hebrew literature and study of Israel. Orthodox groups viewed the entry of the Zionists into Jewish day-school education with trepidation, fearing that the Zionists, having 'captured' the LBJRE, would, with the assistance of the Jewish Agency and local philanthropists, establish a network of schools where the traditional religious curriculum was replaced by a secular, nationalist approach. The *kulturkampf* then taking place in Israel over such issues as Sabbath observance, conscription of women, and the sale of pork, compounded Orthodox concerns. These fears were unwarranted, for Zionist leaders in England were well aware of Anglo-Jewry's consensus as to the religious nature of Jewish identity, and fully intended their day schools to be consonant with nominal Orthodoxy. They were successful, over time, in introducing study of modern Hebrew (with Sefardic pronunciation), Israeli culture and Jewish history, as well as short school trips to Israel or even a full term of study there. But none of the schools under the ZF aegis adopted a secular Zionist approach to Jewish identity. The Zionist curriculum remained merely a supplement to traditional Jewish education. More generally, although events in Israel and the campaign for Soviet Jewry were high on the communal agenda, the curricula of Britain's Jewish day schools did not, in the main, reflect this focus of Jewish solidarity.

Attempts by the Chief Rabbi and the United Synagogue to create a coordinating body for Anglo-Jewry's educational effort failed, principally due to antagonism between Schonfeld's JSSM and the ZF. Such a centralized body might have prevented further embarrassment over internal communal divisions, but would have had only a minimal impact on government policy. Compared to the Anglican and Catholic systems, the Jewish day schools were marginal, and any concessions won by the former would in any event be extended to the latter. Yet cooperation between the various Jewish educational organizations would have been beneficial at the local level, for example, in coordinating applications for voluntary-aided status, and in choosing sites for new schools. Cooperation could have rationalized allocation of scarce resources, avoiding duplication and waste, but once again, as had happened during the war, polarization within the community and the resolve of each agency to safeguard its autonomy prevented collaboration. Even where a clear mutual interest existed, as in the establishment of a Hebrew department at the JFS jointly administered by the ZF and the LBJRE, the joint enterprise soon became an arena for clashes between the organizations.

In 1969, Chief Rabbi Jakobovits hoped that deepening communal concern over assimilation and out-marriage would encourage philanthropists to fund a large-scale, community-wide day-school campaign. This was no easy task because, as we saw, following the Six-Day War the community's charitable efforts were focused almost entirely on Israel's needs. Key philanthropists continued to express reservations about the desirability of day-school education, and existing educational agencies, such as the ZFET, were anxious lest the Chief Rabbi's initiative undermine their own fundraising needs. It took five years of negotiations to secure an agreement between the Chief Rabbi and the JIA, whereby its top 200 donors would earmark an extra 10 per cent of their annual contribution for Jewish education. Nevertheless, the endeavour's ultimate success attests to the emergence of a new communal commitment to domestic needs, as well as a new generation of philanthropists who did not defer to the argument that Israel needed their donations more than did local Jewish education. This made possible the building of several large new schools, which were later awarded state-aided status.

Jewish education in England: From separation to integration

We have explored the provision of Jewish education in England in the decades following World War II. In the first two post-war decades, most secular, traditional, and nominally Orthodox British Jews were content to have their children receive a minimal Jewish education at a synagogue afternoon school (*cheder*, Hebrew classes, religion classes). A minority sent their children to day schools: a few still-functioning Cousinhood schools (e.g., Solomon Wolfson and Stepney Jewish), day schools run by the ZF through its ZFET, or after 1958, the JFS. Families affiliated with the strictly Orthodox community sent their children to the state-aided Jewish day schools run by the JSSM, while the fervently Orthodox sent their children to small independent Jewish day schools. The dominant form of Jewish education was, then, supplementary classes. A smaller segment of Anglo-Jewry sent its children to Jewish day schools of three main types: centrist; strictly Orthodox schools; and haredi schools.

Jacob Braude, a lay statistician, fleshed out this tripartite classification.[4] Torah-oriented day schools (i.e., haredi schools), emphasizing intensive study of religious texts, included the Yesodey Hatorah, Lubavitch, Pardes House and Satmar schools. At these schools, 20 to 25 hours per week, i.e., 50 per cent of the timetable, was devoted to Jewish studies. '*Torah im Derekh Eretz*' schools, i.e., the JSSM schools, allocated 25 per cent of the timetable, or 8 to 12 hours a week, to Jewish subjects. Schools whose ethos was based on Israel and the unity of the Jewish people offered five to six hours of Jewish study a week, and emphasized modern Hebrew rather than classic religious texts.

But the tripartite classification does not provide a full picture of Anglo-Jewish education. It covers only day schools, yet most Anglo-Jewish children did not attend day schools, but supplementary schools – Hebrew classes, religion school, etc. – and withdrawal classes. Moreover, it encompasses only Orthodox (at least nominally) day schools, not contemplating schools such as the Reform movement's Akiva School. And it is too categorical to accurately reflect the full spectrum of the day schools' ideological orientations. Within the second category, for instance, it does not distinguish Zionist from non-Zionist schools. In 1977, the JSSM was ambivalent about Zionism, but by the 1980s, there were several day schools that fit the '*Torah im Derekh Eretz*' profile, yet were unambiguously Zionist in outlook (e.g., Independent Jewish Day School). The third category, too, lacks nuance: the curriculum of the ZFET schools was, as we have seen, still traditional, and centred on precepts, religious texts, and festivals.

---

4   Braude, 'Jewish Education', 123.

A more comprehensive classification of the institutions that provided Anglo-Jewish education can, however, be constructed on the basis of their stances on integration into British society. These stances fall on a continuum between total integration with, and total separation from, the broader society.

Schools catering to parents who chose haredi schooling for their children are clustered near the 'separation' pole. These parents belong to communities that set clear boundaries limiting interaction with non-Jewish and non-ultra-Orthodox society. Haredi schools generally teach secular subjects in reluctant deference to local and national educational authorities, but often consider them a threat to Torah values. When the boys reach school-leaving age, they usually transfer to yeshivas.

Jewish education that endorses full integration with the broader society would be situated at the other end of the spectrum. Strictly speaking, this concept is oxymoronic: how can a provider of parochial denominational education endorse full integration into the wider society? That is, we would expect to find an empty set at the 'integration' pole of the continuum, and indeed we do. Moving in the direction of separation, however, it is clear that historically, there were indeed day schools that had as their objective anglicization of immigrant Jews, albeit while maintaining observance of religious precepts. After the period of mass immigration, when children spoke English from birth and such intensive acculturation was no longer deemed necessary, parents still sought to foster their children's integration into British society. Fearing that separate Jewish schools would hinder this by undermining academic achievement and limiting social contact, they rejected separate schools, and opted instead to send their children to state non-denominational schools. Often, they aspired to send them to independent non-church foundation schools such as Haberdashers' Aske's.

Typically, such parents considered religious observance a private matter, and took instruction therein to be of secondary importance. Some parents gave their children no Jewish education at all; others enrolled them in part-time Jewish education. These parents clearly valued quality Jewish education less than they valued social mobility. Moving inward from the integration pole, then, we find synagogue Sunday schools, religion schools, and Hebrew classes – generally sponsored by the LBJRE – as well as withdrawal classes in state non-denominational schools. The population of supplementary class students overlapped, to a considerable extent, that of withdrawal class attendees, as it was rare for pupils to participate in withdrawal classes if they had not had some type of supplementary Jewish education up to Bar/Bat-Mitzvah age. It should be noted that some parents who evinced little interest in seeing that their children acquired a good grounding in the tenets and practices of their faith nonetheless encouraged their children to be active in youth groups and youth movements that provided informal Jewish education.

Moving toward the centre of the spectrum, we find the centrist schools such as the JFS and ZFET schools, which were sponsored by top-down educational agencies. Many of their pupils came from homes that did not reflect the religious Orthodoxy of the sponsoring organization. For most parents, the appeal of these schools was not the Jewish education they provided, but their pupils' academic achievements, which generally surpassed those of pupils at the local state non-denominational schools. Many would just as soon have sent their children to independent schools or maintained non-denominational schools, and been satisfied with Hebrew classes and the withdrawal classes available in these schools.

Another cluster, situated further toward the centre of the spectrum – with some very close to the centre – represents bottom-up or community-based modern-Orthodox day schools. These schools, which became popular beginning in the late 1970s (e.g. the Independent Jewish Day School), fostered tolerance and open-mindedness toward both the non-Orthodox and the broader society. The pupils' homes were generally in religious and ideological harmony with the school's ethos, and the Jewish studies programme was not merely acquiesced in, but the school's very raison d'être. Yet these schools ascribed great importance to general studies and high academic achievement. 1981 saw the opening of the Akiva School, a Reform-movement variant of this type of day school; other such schools have opened since. The latter schools differed from their modern-Orthodox counterparts not only in the orientation of their Jewish studies, but also in that they did not scrutinize home ritual observance, and their acceptance policies – for pupils and Jewish teaching staff – did not invoke the halakhic definition of Jewishness. Both types of community-based schools saw no contradiction between separate schooling and full engagement in British society. Parents who chose these schools were comfortable with public expression of Jewish identity.

Passing the centre of the spectrum, and moving toward the 'separation' pole, we come to the JSSM schools. Here too, although Jewish studies were held to be fundamental to the school's ethos, general studies and high academic achievement were deemed important. But there was less openness to the non-Orthodox and the outside world. Professional and civic integration was encouraged, social and cultural integration was not. These schools, like the modern-Orthodox schools, but in contrast to the ZFET, JFS, and LBJRE schools, were by definition religiously selective, carefully scrutinizing the applicant's level of observance.

Independent haredi schools, as we said, were located at the 'separation' pole.

Overall, for parents affiliated with centrist-Orthodox, Reform, and Liberal synagogues, the dominant concern throughout this period was academic excellence, not Jewish literacy. From the end of World War II to the early 1960s, the working-class status of Anglo-Jewry meant that independent schools were beyond its means, and hence state grammar schools were the ideal choice for secondary education. When the grammar schools were transformed into comprehensive schools, parents sought alternatives. For some Anglo-Jews, upward mobility meant that independent non-denominational schools were now within reach. But for a growing number of parents, Jewish voluntary-aided and fee-paying schools were perceived as the only way to ensure academic achievement. Thanks to Britain's burgeoning multicultural ethos, such parents no longer saw any contradiction between 'Englishness' and their public expression of Jewish identity, or any conflict between desiring integration and sending their children to separate Jewish schools. Over the period covered by this book, Anglo-Jewry – apart from the haredi communities – had gained a more nuanced understanding of 'integration' and 'separation', an understanding that made space for a new model of Jewish education. No longer was the Anglican Sunday school the paradigm of acceptable religious education, and Jews, like Roman Catholics, could seek state financial support for separate day schools that would allow for provision of comprehensive, high-quality Jewish education.

The role of state support for denominational schools

The state has, we have seen, been generous to denominational schooling, especially in comparison with the United States, where the church – state separation principle entails that denominational schools must be privately funded. However, economic and political considerations have impacted government funding of these schools.[5]

The 1944 Butler Education Act was crucial for determining the status of denominational schools, including Jewish day schools. Despite proposals by senior civil servants during the preparatory stages of that legislation to end state support for denominational schools, the government decided to avoid a collision with the ecclesiastical authorities. Schools that opted for 'voluntary-aided status' had half their building and maintenance costs covered by the state, provided their premises, syllabus, pedagogy, teaching staff and administration met government-set criteria. In 1959, at the behest of the denominations, the government raised its subsidy from 50 to 75 per cent; by 1975, the subsidy was 85 per cent.

Financial constraints limited the expansion of the state-aided denominational schools. The denominational authorities had to prove that within the locale of their proposed school there was a need for additional school places. During the 1950s, because of the post war baby boom, there was little difficulty in proving a shortfall in existing school places, but Anglo-Jewish parents had little interest in denominational education, and did not take advantage of the government's largesse. By the time Jewish attitudes changed, aided status was more difficult to secure, as a significant decline in the birth-rate reduced the overall need for new school places. After 1973, the inflationary spiral caused by the Arab oil embargo led to drastic cuts in governmental spending on education. This forced the community to fund its own school building projects in the hope that subsequently, applications for the coveted voluntary-aided status would be accepted.

---

5   See David Mendelsson, 'Issues in Anglo-Jewish Education: Day Schools, State Funding, and Religious Education in State Schools', in H. Miller, L. Grant, and A. Pomson (eds), *International Handbook of Jewish Education* (New York: Springer, 2011), 2:1105–23.

Later, when multiculturalism became a key issue on the political agenda, ideological opposition also hindered expansion of the aided sector. The Labour party was popularly perceived as more sensitive to the needs of ethnic minorities, and Labour-controlled London councils adopted a policy of affirmative action. But Labour disapproved of separate ethnic and religious schooling, believing it fostered racism and was harmful to the professional advancement of ethnic minorities. It preferred multicultural schools where diversity would be embraced, for example, by classes on world religions and the celebration of a spectrum of religious festivals. Given this policy, the LEAs rejected haredi and Muslim applications for voluntary-aided status, though couching this rejection in the rubric of 'failure to meet national and local criteria'.

The Conservatives saw the existing denominational aided schools – Anglican, Roman Catholic and Jewish – as upholding an ethos that was broadly in line with Tory thinking. Indeed, denominational schools were often held up as examples of academic achievement, in contrast to the alleged failings of the comprehensive schools. Moreover, the party's commitment to guaranteeing parental choice entailed support for denominational schools. Though the Tories shared Labour's fears that ethnic minority schools would promote separatism, when minority groups such as Muslims and Sikhs demanded state-aided status for their schools, the Conservatives could not deny to one religious group what they endorsed for others.

Final remarks

Neither the communal agenda, the objectives set by the state authorities, nor the wider socio-cultural context determined the prevailing mode of Jewish education in post-World War II England. Rather, it was the parental agenda that determined what form the delivery of Jewish education would take. Until the mid-1960s, neither generous governmental subsidies for denominational schools, nor the poor quality of supplementary Jewish education, sufficed to persuade many Anglo-Jewish parents to send their children to day schools. Most parents simply did not consider Jewish education a priority, and were eager for their children to attend state grammar schools. In the 1970s and 1980s, however, neither the availability of withdrawal classes and de-confessionalized nature of religious instruction in the state schools, nor the fact that Jewish day schools allocated a significant portion of the timetable to instruction in traditional religious texts and precepts, sufficed to deter them from doing so. Jewish parents were now almost as eager to send their children to Jewish day schools as they had been averse to doing so in the 1950s. But this eagerness arose from concerns about the academic level and quality of education in the comprehensive schools, and did not reflect a desire to give their children a thorough grounding in their faith and heritage.

What determined parental choice of an educational framework was not, then, the Jewish rabbinical – communal agenda, which endorsed maximal Jewish education to preserve religious observance and communal continuity, nor the governmental agenda, which sought to create a non-tiered educational system to equalize opportunity for all, but rather, the parents' own agenda. Initially, parents sought to ensure their children's integration into British society and the middle class, and later, when this was taken for granted, into the professional classes. Also important, though not to the same degree, was ensuring that their children's affiliation with the Jewish community was maintained, at least to the minimal level of having a Bar/Bat-Mitzvah, familiarity with basic rituals and religious holidays, and socializing within the community. When comprehensive education was introduced, Jewish parents were wary, and sought ways to preserve selective education, even if that meant embracing denominational education, or paying for independent schools. The unintended side effect was that, for the many parents who chose Jewish day schools, this entailed giving their children greater exposure to Jewish education – the very outcome sought by the communal leadership, but previously ignored by parents. The Jewish parental agenda persisted despite changes in the funding and organization of the broader educational system. Though the state system endeavoured to provide a modicum of religious education, the same parents who were satisfied by minimal Jewish education in the pre-comprehensive era, nonetheless – when they feared their goal of facilitating high academic achievement for their children was in jeopardy – abandoned non-denominational state education and embraced the Jewish day schools.

Bibliography

Archives

ACC   London Metropolitan Archives (LMA) [formerly Greater London Records Office]

CR   Chief Rabbi's Office, now housed at LMA

CZA   Central Zionist Archives, Jerusalem

ISA   Israel State Archives, Jerusalem

JNUL   Jewish National and University Library, Jerusalem

M-O   Mass Observation Archive, University of Sussex

MS   University of Southampton, Anglo-Jewish Archives

PRO ED   National Archives [created between 2003 and 2006 from four government bodies, including the PRO (Public Record Office)], Kew, Richmond, Surrey

Mocatta Library, University College, London
Oral History Division, Harman Institute of Contemporary Jewry, Hebrew University of Jerusalem
United Synagogue archives, LMA

Periodicals

The Jewish Chronicle (JC) (available at the British Library Newspaper Reading Room in Colindale, North London, and the *JC* website, http://www.thejc.com/)

Jewish Year Book (available at Mocatta Library, University College, London)

The following periodicals are housed at the Central Zionist Archives, Jerusalem:
Gates of Zion
Jewish Monthly
Jewish Observer
Jewish Observer and Middle East Review
Jewish Review
Jewish Tribune
L'Eylah
News and Views [Agudas Israel Organization of Great Britain]

Reports

JEC [Joint Emergency Committee for Jewish Religious Education], First Report, 1941. JNUL.
JEC Report, 'Jewish Education Today and Tomorrow, 1943.' London, 1944. JNUL.
JEC Report, 'Jewish Education, 1944 and After.' London, 1944. JNUL.
JEC Report, 'Jewish Education, 1945,' London, 1945. JNUL.
Kalms, S. A Time for Change: United Synagogue Review, London, 1992.
Kosmin, B. The Structure and Demography of British Jewry in 1976, mimeograph, WZO, 1976, 6–7. JNUL; LMA.
LBJRE Annual and Biennial Reports. LMA [United Synagogue archives].
Questions and Answers: Facts and Figures of Jewish Economic Life and History', pamphlet issued by TAC, London, 1945, 18–19. LMA [Board of Deputies archives].

Secondary Sources

Akenson, D. 'Patterns of English Educational Change: The Fisher and Butler Acts,' *History of Education Quarterly* 11 (1971).

Alderman, G. 'British Jews or Britons of the Jewish Persuasion?', in *National Variations in Jewish Identity: Implications for Jewish Education*, ed. S. Cohen and G. Horenczyk (New York: SUNY Press, 1999), 125–36.

—— *The History of Hackney Downs School* (London: Clove Club, 1972).

—— *The Jewish Community in British Politics* (Oxford: 1983).

—— *London Jewry and London Politics 1889–1986* (London: Routledge, 1989).

—— *Modern British Jewry* (Oxford: Clarendon, 1992).

Aldrich, R. 'Educational Legislation of the 1980s in England: An Historical Analysis,' *History of Education* 21 (1992), 57.

Bardi, B. 'New Dimensions in Religious Education,' *Living Judaism* (Summer 1968).

Barou, N. *The Jews in Work and Trade* (London: Trades Advisory Council, 1945).

Barwell, B. 'Facets of Anglo-Jewish Education: Review and Evaluation,' in D. Noy and I. Ben-Ami (eds), *Studies in the Cultural Life of the Jews in England*, Folklore Research Center Studies 5 (Jerusalem: Magnes, 1975).

Bedarida, F. *A Social History of England* (London: Routledge, 1990).

Ben-Bassat, N. 'The Jewish School and the Community – a Look at their Interrelationship in Great Britain,' *Journal of Jewish Education* 55 (1987), 24–9.

Bermant, C. *The Cousinhood* (London: Eyre & Spottiswoode, 1971).

—— *Lord Jakobovits* (London: Weidenfeld and Nicolson, 1990).

—— *Troubled Eden* (London: Vallentine Mitchell, 1969).

Black, E. *The Social Politics of Anglo-Jewry 1880–1920* (Oxford: Basil Blackwell, 1988).

Black, G. 'The Jews of Hackney Downs School,' in S. Massil (ed.), *The Jewish Yearbook 2001* (London: Vallentine Mitchell, 2001), 53–60.

—— *JFS: A History of the Jews' Free School, London, since 1732* (London: Tymsder, 1998).

Braude, J. 'Jewish Education in Britain Today', in Lipman and Lipman (eds), *Jewish Life*, 119–29.

Brook, S. *The Club* (London: Constable, 1989).

Brotz, H. 'The Outlines of Jewish Society in London,' in M. Freedman (ed.), *A Minority in Britain* (London: Vallentine Mitchell, 1955), 137–97.

Caplan, S. 'Immanuel College: The Beginnings of an Educational Project,' in W. Ackerman (ed.), *Studies in Education* 7 (Jerusalem: Magnes, 1995), 54–80.

Cesarani, D. 'A Funny Thing Happened on the Way to the Suburbs: Social Change in Anglo-Jewry between the Wars, 1914–1945', *Jewish Culture and History* 1 (1998), 5–26.

—— *The Jewish Chronicle and Anglo-Jewry 1841–1991* (Cambridge: CUP, 1994).

—— 'The Transformation of Communal Authority in Anglo-Jewry, 1914–1940,' in idem (ed.), *The Making of Modern Anglo-Jewry* (Oxford: Basil Blackwell, 1990), 115–40.

Chadwick, P. *Shifting Alliances: Church and State in English Education* (London: Cassell, 1997).

Chazan, B. 'Models of Ethnic Education: The Case of Jewish Education in Great Britain,' *British Journal of Educational Studies* 26 (1978), 54–72.

Chitty, C. *The Education System Transformed: A Guide to the School Reforms* (Manchester: Baseline, 1992), 63–6.

Cohen, Norman. 'Trends in Anglo-Jewish Religious Life,' in Gould and Esh, *Jewish Life*, 44–61, and Esh's comments, 88–9.

Cook, C. and J. Stevenson, *British History from 1945* (London: Longman, 1996).

Cromer, G. 'An Intergenerational Comparison of Educational and Occupational Aspirations in the Jewish and non-Jewish Family', *Research in Education* 15 (1976), 55–67.

—— 'Intermarriage and Communal Survival in a London Suburb', *Jewish Journal of Sociology* 16 (1974), 155–69.

Cruikshank, M. *Church and State in English Education: 1870 to the Present Day* (London: Macmillan, 1963).

Davis, R. *The Grammar School* (Harmondsworth: Penguin, 1967).

Dent, H. C. *Education in Transition* (London: Kegan Paul, 1944).

Domb, C. *Memories of Kopul Rosen* (London: Carmel College, 1970).

Englander, D. 'Integrated but Insecure: A Portrait of Anglo-Jewry at the Close of the Twentieth Century,' in Parsons, *Growth*, 1:106.

Fishman, I. and H. Levy. 'Jewish Education in Great Britain,' in Gould and Esh (eds), *Jewish Life*, 67–74.

Freedman, M. (ed.). *A Minority in Britain* (London: Vallentine Mitchell, 1955).

Gartner, L. *The Jewish Immigrant in England 1870–1914* (London: Allen and Unwin, 1960).

Ginsberg, Y. 'Jewish Attitudes toward Black Neighbors in Boston and London,' *Ethnicity* 8 (1981), 206–18.

Glanville, B. *The Bankrupts* (London: Secker and Warburg, 1958).

Goodman, M. 'A Research Note on Jewish Education on Merseyside, 1962,' *Jewish Journal of Sociology* 7 (1965), 43–4.

Gordon, P. *Selection for Secondary Education* (London: Routledge, 1980).

Gordon, P. et al. *Education and Policy in England in the Twentieth Century* (London: Woburn, 1991).

Gould, J. *Jewish Commitment: A Study in London* (London: Institute of Jewish Affairs, 1984).

Gould, J., and S. Esh (eds). *Jewish Life in Modern Britain* (London: Routledge and Kegan Paul, 1964).

Grunfeld, J. *Shefford: The Story of a Jewish School Community in Evacuation 1939–45* (London: Soncino, 1980).

Howard, A. *Rab: The Life of R. A. Butler* (London: Jonathan Cape, 1987).

Jackson, B., and D. Marsden. *Education and the Working Class* (London: Routledge & Kegan Paul, 1962).

Jacobs, L. *We Have Reason to Believe* (London: Vallentine Mitchell, 1962).

Jacobs, F., and V. Prais. 'Development in the law on state-aided schools for religious minorities', in Lipman and Lipman, *Jewish Life in Britain*, 130–41.

Jakobovits, I. *The Attitude to Zionism of Britain's Chief Rabbis as Reflected in their Writings* (London: Jewish Historical Society of England, 1981).

Janner, G. 'Black-Jewish Controversies in Britain,' *Patterns of Prejudice* 20 (1986), 4–11.

Jeffereys, K. 'R. A. Butler, The Board of Education and the 1944 Education Act,' *History* 69 (1984).

Jewish Year Book 1894; 1905/6; 1939. See above, Archives and archival materials.

Khan-Cheema, M. 'British Muslims and the Maintained Schools,' in S. Ali Ashraf and P. Hirst (eds), *Religion and Education: Islamic and Christian Perspectives* (Cambridge: Islamic Academy, 1986).

Kosmin, B. *The Structure and Demography of British Jewry in 1976*. See above, Archives and archival materials.

Kosmin, B., and N. Grizzard. *Jews in an Inner London Borough* (London: Board of Deputies, 1975).

Kosmin, B., and C. Levy. *Jewish Identity in an Anglo-Jewish Community: The Findings of the 1978 Redbridge Survey* (London: Board of Deputies, 1983).

Kosmin, B. et al. *The Social Demography of Redbridge Jewry* (London: Board of Deputies, 1979).

Kosmin, B. et al. *Steel City Jews* (London: Board of Deputies, 1976).

Kranzler, D., and G. Hirschler (eds). *Solomon Schonfeld: His Page in History* (New York: Judaica Press, 1982).

Krausz, E. 'The Economic and Social Structure of Anglo-Jewry,' in Gould and Esh, *Jewish Life*, 27–40.

—— 'The Edgware Survey; Demographic Results,' *Jewish Journal of Sociology* 10 (1968), 83–100.

—— 'The Edgware Survey: Occupation and Social Class', *Jewish Journal of Sociology* 11 (1969), 75–95.

—— *Leeds Jewry* (Cambridge: W. Heffer, 1964).

—— 'A Sociological Field Study of Jewish Suburban Life in Edgware 1962–3 with special reference to Minority Identification', PhD thesis, University of London, 1965, 93, 103.

Kushner, T. 'Jews and Non-Jews in the East End of London: Towards an Anthropology of "Everyday" Relations', in G. Alderman and C. Holmes (eds), *Outsiders and Outcasts* (London: Duckworth & Co., 1993), 32–52.

—— *The Persistence of Prejudice: Antisemitism in British Society during the Second World War* (Manchester: Manchester University Press, 1989).

Lawson, J., and H. Silver. *A Social History of Education in England* (London: Methuen, 1973).

Lederhendler, E. *The Six Day War and World Jewry* (Bethesda: University Press of Maryland, 2000).

Let My People Know (London: Office of the Chief Rabbi, 1971).

Levin, S. 'Changing Patterns of Jewish Education', in idem (ed.), *A Century of Anglo-Jewish Life 1870–1970* (London: 1970).

Lipman, Sonia L., and Vivian D. Lipman (eds). *Jewish Life in Britain 1962–1977* (New York: K. G. Saur, 1981).

Lipman, V. D. *A Century of Social Service, 1859–1959: The Jewish Board of Guardians* (London: Routledge and Kegan Paul, 1959).

—— *A History of the Jews in Britain since 1858* (Leicester: Leicester University Press, 1990).

—— *Social History of the Jews in England 1850–1950* (London: Watts, 1954).

Lowe, R. *The Welfare State in Britain since 1945*, 2nd edn (London: Macmillan, 1999).

Marmur, D. *Beyond Survival* (London: Darton, Longman and Todd, 1982).

—— *Reform Judaism: Essays on Reform Judaism in Britain* (London: Reform Synagogues of Great Britain, 1973).

Marwick, A. *Britain in the Century of Total War* (Harmondsworth: Penguin, 1968).

—— *British Society Since 1945* (London: Penguin, 1996).

Mason, D. *Race and Ethnicity in Modern Britain* (Oxford: Oxford University Press, 1995).

Mendelsson, D. 'Between Integration and Separation: The History of Jewish Education in England 1944–1988' (PhD diss., Hebrew University of Jerusalem, 2002).

—— 'Embracing Jewish Day School Education in England 1965–79', *History of Education* 38 (2009), 545–63.

——'Issues in Anglo-Jewish Education: Day Schools, State Funding, and Religious Education in State Schools', in H. Miller, L. Grant, and A. Pomson (eds), *International Handbook of Jewish Education* (New York: Springer, 2011), 2: 1105–23.

Miller, H. 'Meeting the Challenge: The Jewish Schooling Phenomenon in the UK', *Oxford Review of Education* 27 (2001), 501–13.

Miller, S. 'The Impact of Jewish Education on the Religious Behaviour and Attitudes of British Secondary School Pupils', in J. Aviad (ed.), *Studies in Education* 3 (Jerusalem: Magnes, 1988), 150–65.

Moonman, J. *Anglo-Jewry: An Analysis* (London: Institute of Jewish Affairs, 1980).

Morris, N. 'Jewish Education in Time of Total War', in *Jewish Education in Great Britain; Two Talks* (London: JEC, 1946).

Murphy, J. *Church, State, and Schools in Britain, 1800–1970* (London: Routledge & Kegan Paul, 1971).

Neustatter, H. 'Demographic and Other Statistical Aspects of Anglo-Jewry', in Freedman, *Minority*, 55–133.

Newman, A. *The United Synagogue* (London: Routledge & Kegan Paul, 1977).

Nielsen, J. 'Islamic Communities in Britain', in P. Badham (ed.), *Religion, State and Society in Modern Britain* (Lampeter, UK: Edwin Mellen, 1989), 225–41.

Parkes, J. 'History of the Anglo-Jewish Community', in Freedman, *Minority*, 3–51.

Parsons, G. 'There and Back Again? Religion and the 1944 and 1988 Education Acts', in Parsons, *Growth*, 2: 161–98.

Parsons, G. (ed.). *The Growth of Religious Diversity: Britain from 1945*. Vol.1: Traditions (London: Routledge, 1993); Vol. 2: Issues (London: Routledge, 1994).

Patterson, S. *Immigration and Race Relations* (London: Oxford University Press, 1969).

Paxman, J. *The English: A Portrait of a People* (London: Penguin, 1999).

Pedley, R. *The Comprehensive School* (London: Penguin, 1969), 10–13.

Pollins, H. *Economic History of the Jews in England* (London: Associated University Presses, 1982).

Prais, S. J. 'Polarization or Decline?', in Lipman and Lipman, *Jewish Life*, 3–16.

——'A Sample Survey on Jewish Education in London, 1972–73', *Jewish Journal of Sociology* 16 (1974).

Prais, S. J., and M. Schmool. 'The Size and Structure of the Anglo-Jewish Population 1960–1965', *Jewish Journal of Sociology* 10 (1968), 5–34.

——'The Social Class Structure of Anglo-Jewry 1961', *Jewish Journal of Sociology* 17 (1975), 5–15.

Rae, J. *The Public School Revolution* (London: Faber and Faber, 1981).

Romain, J. (ed.), *150 Years of Progressive Judaism in Britain 1840–1990* (London: London Museum of Jewish Life, 1990).

Romain, J., and A. J. Kershen. *Tradition and Change: A History of Reform Judaism in Britain 1840–1995* (London: Vallentine Mitchell, 1995).

Roth, S. *The Impact of the Six Day War* (London: Macmillan, 1988).

Sacks, J. 'Religious and National Identity: British Jewry and the State of Israel', in *Israel and Diaspora Jewry: Ideological and Political Perspectives*, ed. E. Don-Yehiya (Ramat-Gan, Israel: Bar Ilan University Press, 1991), 5–34.

Schaefer, R. 'The Dynamics of British Racial Prejudice', *Patterns of Prejudice* 8 (1974), 3.

Schmool, M. and S. Miller, 'Jewish Education and Identity among London Synagogue Members', in S. DellaPergola and J. Even (eds), *Papers in Jewish Demography 1993* (Jerusalem: Institute of Contemporary Jewry, 1997), 349–58.

Schonfeld, S. *Jewish Religious Education* (London: National Council for Jewish Religious Education, 1943).

——*Message to Jewry* (London: JSSM, 1959).

Securing Our Future (London: JEDT, 1992).

Sherman, A. *Island Refuge* (London: Elek, 1973).

Shimoni, G. 'Selig Brodetsky and the Ascendancy of Zionism in Anglo-Jewry', *Jewish Journal of Sociology* 22 (1980), 125–61.

Simon, B. *Education and the Social Order* (London: Lawrence & Wishart, 1991).

——'The 1944 Education Act: A Conservative Measure?' *History of Education* 15 (1986), 31–43.

——*The State and Educational Policy* (London: Lawrence & Wishart, 1994).

Steinberg, B. 'Anglo-Jewry and the 1944 Education Act', *Jewish Journal of Sociology* 31 (1989), 81–108.

——'Jewish Education in Great Britain during World War II', *Jewish Social Studies* 29 (1967), 27–60.

Tomlinson, S. *Home and School in Multicultural Britain* (London: Batsford Academic and Educational, 1984).

Troyna, B. *Racism and Education: Research Perspectives* (Buckingham, UK: Open University Press, 1993).

Valins, O. et al., *The Future of Jewish Schooling in the United Kingdom* (London: Institute for Jewish Policy Research, 2001).

Waterman, S. and B. Kosmin, *British Jewry in the Eighties* (London: Board of Deputies, 1986).

Worms, F. *A Life in Three Cities* (London: Halban, 1996).

Ziderman, A. 'Jewish Education in Great Britain', in H. Himmelfarb and S. DellaPergola (eds), *Jewish Education Worldwide: Cross-Cultural Perspectives* (Lanham, MD: University Press of America, 1989), 267–300.

Index